strategies for

Differentiating Instruction

third edition

strategies for Differentiating Instruction

best practices for the classroom

Julia L. **Roberts, Ed.D.,**
& Tracy F. **Inman, Ed.D.**

Prufrock Press Inc.
Waco, Texas

Library of Congress Cataloging-in-Publication Data

Roberts, Julia L. (Julia Link)
Strategies for differentiating instruction : best practices for the classroom / by Julia L. Roberts & Tracy F. Inman. -- Third Edition.
pages cm
Includes bibliographical references.
ISBN 978-1-61821-279-5 (Paperback)
1. Individualized instruction. 2. Mixed ability grouping in education. I. Inman, Tracy F. (Tracy Ford), 1963- II. Title.
LB1031.R57 2014
371.2'52--dc23
2014024355

Edited by Rachel Taliaferro

Cover and layout design by Raquel Trevino

ISBN-13: 978-1-61821-279-5

Prufrock Press Inc.
P.O. Box 8813
Waco, TX 76714-8813
Phone: (800) 998-2208
Fax: (800) 240-0333
http://www.prufrock.com

CONTENTS

CHAPTER
1

One-Size-Fits-All? You've Got to Be Kidding!

> The key to school success is to be found in identifying or creating engaging schoolwork for students. —Phillip Schlechty

Imagine a one-dish dinner, the cook's favorite, lovingly prepared with the freshest ingredients. Great attention is put into not only the choice of the meal itself, but also into shopping for its perfect ingredients. Every part of the dish is prepared according to the recipe with special consideration to the cooking verbs involved (we don't want to fry instead of sauté!) and the sequence of preparation (the sauce must come last). Even the table itself undergoes scrutiny as the cook decides whether the white china or the dark green pottery will make a better presentation of the dish and if the centerpiece calls for fresh daisies or the more formal roses. At last, with everyone seated, the cook dances out of the kitchen with the dish in hand—ready to satisfy the appetites of all!

Now imagine the vegetarian who inwardly winces at the smell of chicken emanating from the table, and the lactose-intolerant person evaluating the amount of cream in the sauce. Think of the guest with food allergies who tries to quietly discern whether the green is the palatable spinach or the hive-inducing kale. Note the diner with the gluten allergy steering clear of the noodles. Look at the diabetic mentally calculating the amount of insulin to take after the meal. Consider the reaction of the diner who had the exact same meal 2 days earlier and its warmed leftovers the day before! And, what about the child who whines, "Eww, it's all mixed together. I don't like it, and you can't make me eat it!" Granted, several people around the table eagerly spoon helpings on their plates, devouring the food, admiring the presentation (although one sneezes from the roses), and complimenting the cook. The cook, pleased with herself, notices the second helpings of some—but she doesn't notice the chicken cut up but left on the plate, the scraped-off cream sauce, the spinach (kale?) spread around the china to give the impression that some of it is gone, or the barely-touched plate. As for the child, she dismisses the reaction, rationalizing that the child will eat it when he's good and hungry or he can just starve! When the guests are gone, she puts away the leftovers and congratulates herself on a job well done. She then pulls out the recipe book for the next dinner party.

Because the focus of this book is on learning, this dinner party really isn't a dinner party at all—it's a metaphor for teaching. The teacher (cook) has a specialty area (favorite dish) and thoroughly enjoys sharing that passion with others (hosting the dinner party). She consults the standards (recipe book) and follows their guidance carefully. She gathers her teaching materials carefully (ingredients), and then considers how best to present the material (flowers and china). She really wants to do her best because she genuinely cares about her students (invited special guests), and she loves her content (her favorite dish). The intent is honorable. Because there is only one person obviously displeased (the "Eww" child)—"there's one in every crowd"—she mistakenly believes that everyone learned something (the plates looked as if they'd been eaten from). The silent sufferers (from food and gluten allergies or lactose intolerance) take what they can from the lesson without complaint. They may very well need additional learning on the topic later (just as some guests may swing by a fast-food restaurant on the way home). The student who already knew the material (the diner who had leftovers the day before) groans about the repetition and tires of not learning new material. If she feels compliant, she may participate in the lesson (eat the food again); however, if she's not compliant, then she just might not participate or the lesson may be rejected (and the plate may be broken on the floor or left untouched—plus she'll probably refuse a repeat invitation to dinner). The complaining student may well have learned the content if it had been presented in pieces instead of the whole (perhaps if the chicken were to the side of the green vegetable).

Think how much more successful the lesson would have been for everyone if the teacher had questioned herself about the learners. Who already knows the material (the one eating the dish for the third day in a row), and what can be done to continue the learning (perhaps serve a dish that's new to her)? How does each student learn best? (The "Eww" child needs food—i.e., concepts—separated into parts.) What learning differences do the students have? (The vegetarian may have enjoyed the meal if the meat had not been included, and the diabetic could have come prepared with her insulin if she had been notified of what was being served beforehand.) How can the teacher best address the different needs of her students? (Just because a person is allergic or lactose intolerant doesn't mean he can't eat and enjoy new foods, as long as some accommodations are made.) Yes, learning went on, but think how many more children and young people could have been a part of that learning if the students' interests, strengths, and levels of readiness were taken into consideration. (Kids would have been so hungry for more that leftovers would not have been possible!)

The focus of this book is on *differentiating* for students so that learning occurs. More specifically, the book will help teachers implement strategies that allow all students to learn on an ongoing basis—in other words, strategies that remove the learning ceiling and allow each student to make continuous progress. You'll see the phrase *continuous progress* several more times, because that's what learning is all about—students learning each day they are in school.

Who should read this book? The target audiences are teachers who want to differentiate but really don't know where to start and preservice teachers who are learning their craft. This book describes the basics of differentiation—the essentials that make differentiation defensible. Chapters will explore strategies teachers can use to tier learning experiences to address students' varying levels of knowledge and readiness to learn so that all students are learning new things every day (i.e., continuous progress). Strategies will address the interests students have in the topic being studied and strengths of students in order to motivate them to produce their best work. We also provide convenient electronic access to a selection of forms included in this book at the following URL: http://www.prufrock.com/Assets/ClientPages/strategies_for_differentiating.aspx. Notice that we haven't mentioned writing new curriculum. We believe that basic differentiation is concentrated on *making modifications* to the curriculum rather than writing curriculum that differentiates. For experienced teachers, that means taking a unit you've already designed and "tweaking it" (via one of the strategies presented in the book) so that it becomes a differentiated unit intentionally designed to address the interests, strengths, or readiness levels of your students. This book will prepare you to tier learning experiences to provide challenge and give you the confidence you need so that you can move on to one or more of the numerous books that examine differentiation at more sophisticated levels and from other perspectives. This book, however, is designed for those just beginning the differentiation adventure.

The easiest way to prepare to teach a class is to make one plan that will work for all students (remember that one-dish marvel). The problem is that the one-dish-pleases-all or the one-size-fits-all theory doesn't work with all students in a classroom. In order for *all* students to make continuous progress, differentiation strategies must be used. Students who are the least likely to make continuous progress when one plan is used are those who need more time to learn and modifications of the content, as well as the ones who already know the content (or know most of it) and those who benefit from learning it in greater depth or complexity.

Consider a class that includes Antoine, Maria, Jamie, Jimmy, Clarissa, and Walker.

Antoine is very interested in science. He and his father spend time outside of school pursuing scientific interests and questions. Antoine is an excellent reader, one who is fascinated with factual books. He loves long-term projects that allow him to explore a problem in depth.

Maria is uncertain about school. At home, her mother and grandmother speak Spanish, so Maria is learning English at the same time she is learning social studies, science, mathematics, and language arts. Sometimes she is very frustrated and wonders if she isn't very smart.

Jamie is a very good reader and loves to write. She is especially interested in dance and drama. She spends most of her time after school taking ballet lessons, playing with neighborhood friends, and reading and writing plays.

Jimmy likes to come to school even though reading continues to be a challenge for him. Resources that are too difficult are frustrating to him. He thoroughly enjoys time involved in playing team sports. When involved in sports, Jimmy is at his happiest.

Clarissa has many interests—writing, piano, math, and art. She becomes very engaged in learning experiences when they include one of her passions. Clarissa works hard when she finds the learning experience interesting; otherwise, it is difficult for her to be motivated. When motivated, she does her best work.

Walker would prefer to stay home rather than come to school. There, he can watch television most of the time. His favorite times at school are lunch and recess. Occasionally he is intrigued by a project in art.

Classrooms everywhere are filled with students like Antoine, Maria, Jamie, Jimmy, Clarissa, and Walker, plus many other students who also differ in their experiences. Their varied backgrounds impact their interests, strengths, and levels of readiness in relation to the content to be learned. A single, daily lesson plan cannot address the various reading levels and interests of these six students, much less 18 or more others in the classroom. Learning experiences must be differentiated if Antoine, Maria, Jamie, Jimmy, Clarissa, and Walker are to learn what each needs to know in order to advance. Antoine cannot learn what he already knows. Jimmy cannot read resources beyond his ability to read. The lesson that is stimulating and challenging for one will be a disaster for another. A plan with differentiated experiences could accommodate the wide range of learner needs.

And, needs come in all shapes and sizes—from reading three grade levels behind, to reading three grade levels ahead, from not speaking English at home, to being limited by learning opportunities prior to starting school. Most of us consider needs to stem from our weaknesses or inabilities. Please remember that needs for students who are gifted and talented are created by strengths rather than deficiencies. They really don't look needy, but their needs are real—just as real as other learning needs.

DIFFERENTIATION: WHAT IS IT?

Differentiation is a popular term in education today, and it is a term with multiple meanings. Roberts and Inman (2013) define differentiation as being the match of the curriculum and learning experiences to learners. A teacher who differentiates effectively matches the content (basic to complex), the level of the cognitive (thinking) processes, the sophistication and choice of the product, and/or the assessment to the student or cluster of students. The purpose for differentiation is to facilitate ongoing continuous progress for all students. The long-term goal for differentiation is to develop lifelong learners. Differentiation is the key focus, so it will be developed and elaborated upon in all of the chapters in this book. Each chapter will add information and examples to help you plan and implement differentiated instruction in your classroom.

TO DIFFERENTIATE OR NOT: THE BIG QUESTION

To differentiate or not is a huge question that needs to be answered before a school year begins. Stop and ask two questions: What are all the reasons teachers don't differentiate and what are all the reasons teachers should differentiate? Those two questions will lead to the realization that all of the reasons not to differentiate are about *teachers* and all of the reasons teachers should differentiate are about *students*. Now that realization should provide the motivation to read on.

Whether we're preservice teachers or veteran teachers, we all know we need to differentiate. So, why don't teachers differentiate their lessons? A study of differentiation practices (Westberg, Archambault, Dobyns, & Salvin, 1993) showed that teachers do not use strategies that differentiate very often; in fact, they hardly do at all. Ten years later Westberg and Daoust (2003) repeated the study with similar results. Teachers reported that they didn't differentiate often, if at all. Why is that?

REASONS TEACHERS DON'T DIFFERENTIATE

Several responses seem to appear frequently when teachers describe factors that work against differentiating. Do one or more of these reasons resonate with you as you reflect on your school or your classroom?

TIME

The number one reason teachers don't differentiate is time. No doubt it takes more time to plan learning experiences that will take into account students' interests, strengths, and levels of readiness than to plan one set of experiences for the entire class. It takes time to find resources, time to modify the curriculum, and time in class to make it happen. You may think that you don't have time to preassess, but Chapter 4 will highlight that preassessing actually saves you time because students don't spend time on concepts and skills they have already mastered.

RESOURCES

The second reason relates to resources. Varied resources (rather than one text) support a differentiated classroom. Often it takes time to gather the resources that will allow all students to be learning. You may have a range of reading levels that could stretch from three to four levels below grade level to three to four levels above grade level. That huge range of reading levels calls for having varied resources available to learn in your content area as well as books, journals, and online resources to allow learning on specific topics of interest to students who are studying in your content area.

LIMITED PREPARATION

The third frequently cited response is that teachers have had little or no instruction about how to differentiate or even why differentiation is important. Little attention is given to this topic during preservice classes or during professional development, especially as to how it relates to advanced students.

FEW ROLE MODELS

The fourth reason is that there are few role models for differentiating. It is so useful to watch differentiation in action. Visiting classrooms in which teachers are differentiating instruction is a great way to learn about doing so. Visitors can often learn about what works and what doesn't work by interviewing (discussing the topic and process of differentiating) the teacher.

CONCERNS WITH CLASSROOM MANAGEMENT

The fifth reason involves classroom management. A classroom in which every student is doing the same thing will likely seem easier to manage. Chapter 9 discusses management issues to make differentiation doable for both the teacher and the students.

"ADVANCED STUDENTS WILL BE FINE" MYTH

The sixth reason relates to the mantra that gifted students will "make it on their own," so there is no need to make extra effort for students who have already learned most of the grade-level curriculum. This statement is truly a myth, because students who do not learn how to study and to meet (and hopefully enjoy) an academic challenge are unprepared to tackle rigorous coursework whenever they may encounter a challenge. Teachers often expect to modify instruction for students who need more time and more basic instruction to reach class learning goals but often don't have the same expectation for planning modifications for students who need a faster pace and more complex content.

LACK OF ADMINISTRATORS' KNOWLEDGE OF OR SUPPORT FOR DIFFERENTIATING

The seventh reason that mitigates against differentiation is an administration that places emphasis on grade-level learning as opposed to students learning what they are ready to learn. Administrators may want to support differentiation but lack preparation for doing so—just like many teachers do.

The list of reasons why teachers don't differentiate is long and convincing, but not for educators who know and invest in the reasons why they must differentiate.

REASONS TO DIFFERENTIATE

CONTINUOUS PROGRESS

Of course, the primary reason to differentiate instruction is to enhance learning. Remember, students go to school to learn, and all students making continuous progress is the chief reason to differentiate. Effective differentiation allows each student to learn on an ongoing basis. Let's repeat that for emphasis' sake: Allowing each student to learn on an ongoing basis is the reason to differentiate. Let's even rephrase it for greater emphasis: *Differentiation allows continuous progress for all students!* Student needs provide the motivation for teachers to differentiate instruction.

All reasons to differentiate support that primary reason—facilitating continuous progress. Differentiation makes perfect sense as educators know that students differ in multiple ways, including the wide range of experiences they bring to their studies. They differ in their levels of reading, their knowledge of scientific concepts, their writing skills, and in numerous other dimensions. Differentiated learning experiences motivate students when they are matched to their interests, strengths, and levels of readiness for any topic or concept being studied. A mismatch of learning experiences to readiness levels results in frustration that the expectations are too difficult or too easy.

PRODUCTIVE USE OF STUDENT TIME

Student time is more productively used when differentiated experiences are built into the curriculum. Time allotted for learning experiences is the greatest problem for children at the extremes—those students who need a fraction of the time to learn a new concept and those who need more time than others to learn what they are expected to learn.

STIMULATING TO THE BRAIN

Brain research is a popular topic among educators these days. Students learn more quickly when the learning experience is made relevant to them. In fact, the brain changes physically and chemically when challenged (Clark, 2013). Without challenge, the brain doesn't increase in its capacity or speed of learning, and neurons don't fire. Clark (2013) states, "New neurons respond best to tasks that are challenging, engaging, and most fun to learn" (p. 34). Just think—you as the teacher make the difference in whether each student in your room has the opportunity to become a more effective learner. Some young people need additional time and/or modifications of the curriculum to learn the required content. Without modifications, both the students who need more time and those who need less time will be frustrated. Stress also relates to brain research; stress keeps the brain from working optimally, so the students think at the most basic level (Clark, 2013). (Consider what happens to you when you are put under extreme stress—that is hardly when you do your best thinking.) The level of challenge in a particular learning experience may be too difficult for some students but may not present any challenge to others in the class. When time is held as a constant in the classroom, some students are held back from learning. They become discouraged and may use their time for misbehavior. Other students may not be given enough time to learn a new concept and may become frustrated when they must move forward before they fully understand the material or have mastered the skills. That is why differentiation is a *must* if all children are to make continuous progress.

FAIRNESS AND EQUITY

Discussions about differentiation typically turn to the subject of fairness because not all students are doing the same thing at the same time. What is fair? Fair is when every student has the opportunity to participate in learning experiences that allow for continuous progress. Fairness does not mean that everyone does the same thing. It is no more fair to require every learner in one grade to wear the same size of shoe (think of the blisters!) than it is to provide one set of lesson plans for students who read at various levels (a single class may have students reading three grades below and others reading three or more grades above the grade level). Fairness is each student making continuous progress, and the one-size-fits-all approach doesn't allow for ongoing learning for all students.

A teacher usually will choose not to differentiate unless he believes that it will make a difference in learning in the classroom. Reasons offered for not differentiating are based on *teacher needs* and beliefs or the teacher's lack of preparation to differentiate. On the other hand, all of the reasons to differentiate relate to *student needs.* Which stands out as most important in your school—teacher considerations or student considerations? Which do you want to characterize your school?

NOT DIFFERENTIATING: MISSED OPPORTUNITIES

It is not possible to learn if the basic building blocks are missing. If Susan is reading at the second-grade level but the text is written for fifth graders, she will not comprehend what she is reading. Providing a different text or supplementary resources and modifications to the curriculum will be a basic way to ensure that she will learn what you have planned for all students in your class to know, understand, and be able to do at the conclusion of the unit.

Likewise, students can't learn what they already know, understand, or can do. Repeating learning experiences year after year (e.g., learning fractions in grades 5, 6, and 7) doesn't improve mastery for the student who learned the concept the first time it was presented or perhaps knew it before the concept was introduced in class. Tom learns concepts at mastery levels the first or second time they are taught, so repeating what he has mastered wastes his time and hinders his continuous progress. It may even lead to disruptive behavior and likely will create habits that create an underachiever. The joint policy statement of the National Middle School Association (NMSA, now the Association for Middle Level Education) and the National Association for Gifted Children (NAGC; 2004) highlights the need for academic challenge:

> Equity in the middle grades requires that all learners have an opportunity to participate in curriculum that is rich in meaning and focused on thought and application. Excellence requires support necessary to show continual growth in knowledge and opportunities to work at degrees of challenge somewhat beyond their particular readiness levels, with support necessary to achieve to new levels of proficiency. In addition, educators should address student interests and preferred modes of learning in planning curriculum and instruction that is appropriately challenging for individual learners. Educational resources should be of sufficient range of complexity to ensure challenge for advanced learners. Flexible pacing and flexible grouping arrangements are important instructional adjustments for many highly able middle level learners. Because of the inevitable variance among high-ability learners, they, like other middle school students, need curriculum and instruction proactively designed to accommodate their particular needs. (para. 7)

At the elementary, middle, and high school levels, it is important that all learners have academic challenge and that each student has ongoing opportunities to make continuous progress. Just remember that "opportunities to work at degrees of challenge somewhat beyond their particular readiness levels, with support necessary to achieve to new levels of proficiency" (NMSA & NAGC, 2004, para. 7) require differentiated learning experiences. What those learning experiences will look like will be determined by the information you gain through the preassessment (to be discussed in detail in Chapter 4). What you know for certain is that the one-size-fits-all-students unit will bypass a lot of children. They will miss opportunities to become the best learners they can be. They will miss opportunities to make continuous progress.

DIFFERENTIATION TIES TO ASSESSMENT

Differentiation and assessment are two of the hottest topics in education today. Educators who understand the link between the two concepts increase the opportunity to reach assessment goals and enhance the possibilities for all students to learn. Defensible differentiation depends on ongoing assessment (see Chapters 4 and 10). Assessment results allow you to make a match between what is expected and what is accomplished; the results allow you to determine at what levels your students and clusters of your students are in terms of meeting content standards that have been set by the school, district, state, or nation. Tiered questions, strategies, and learning experiences can be planned to match what students know and are able to do to with regard to the expected standard,

1. *Planning Question*—What do I want students to know, understand, and be able to do?
2. *Preassessing Question*—Who already knows, understands, and/or can use the content or demonstrate the skills? Who needs additional support in order to know, understand, and/or demonstrate the skills?
3. *Differentiation Question*—What can I do for him, her, or them so they can make continuous progress and extend their learning?

Figure 1.1. Three questions for effective differentiation.

allowing each to learn what he or she is ready to learn with an appropriate level of challenge. Differentiation and assessment should go hand in hand to lead student learning. When all students are learning, assessment results will show gains. Everyone, teachers and students alike, will be winners.

KEY QUESTIONS LEADING TO DIFFERENTIATION

This book will provide a roadmap to differentiation. In fact, three directional questions guide you to the road of continuous progress for your students (see Figure 1.1).

All three questions prove critical on your differentiation journey. If the strategies are to be defensible, planning and preassessment must precede differentiated learning experiences. Without the first two steps, differentiation is whimsical: Why are you changing the content for Emilio and not for Suzy? Why does Dakota get to learn in a group, but DeShayne is working on her own? Why does Zoe's group use computers in their research and Josh's group work with texts? Effective differentiation is *intentional.* Let's repeat that because it is perhaps the most critical point we make. You make modifications based on information, not whimsy. Because you have planned the instructional unit and found out who already knows the information and/or can do what the unit is planned to teach and who is not yet ready to master the learner outcomes, you can defend your instructional decisions. Students can engage in learning using various differentiated strategies: You make learning meaningful for all students, including those who need less time and more complex content, as well as those who need modifications that include more time and basic content. As a professional, your educated intent dictates your practice.

In *Alice's Adventures in Wonderland* (Carroll, 1865/2000), Alice asks the Cheshire Cat to tell her the right way to go. When the cat inquires as to where she is going, Alice responds that she doesn't know. The Cheshire Cat then answers that it doesn't matter which route she chooses to go, as any road would get her there because she hasn't specified a destination. This excerpt from *Alice's Adventures in Wonderland* is analogous to planning for differentiating learning experiences. Unless you plan the unit and know what you want the students to know, understand, and be able to do, preassessment to determine who already knows, understands, or can do the work at the desired level is impossible. You simply must plan so that you know where you are going. Only when you plan the destination (i.e., learner outcomes) will you recognize when your students have arrived or when you need to make adjustments in your route to get students where you have planned for them to go. Planning your learning outcomes allows you to know how far along the way students are if they haven't reached the destination and when each of them has reached the end-point on the journey—or can demonstrate the learner outcome(s) for the lesson or unit of study.

WHAT DIFFERENTIATION ADDS TO THE CLASSROOM

Patrice McCrary (2002) described the motivation to differentiate quite well. A kindergarten teacher and the 2003 Kentucky Teacher of the Year, McCrary explained the importance of differentiating learning experiences:

> The pretest is the map for instruction. The formative tests are the detours. The posttesting is the determination of how successful we are in finding the final destination. I tell my children that I don't want them "running in one spot over and over" like a cartoon character may do [see Figure 1.2]. I want them to run and jump into new adventures all the time. (p. 3)

Differentiation involves planning the instructional unit, preassessing to determine the starting place for instruction for individuals or clusters of students, and providing differentiated learning experiences so that no child is "running in one spot over and over." Continuous progress on the road to knowledge—that's what it's all about.

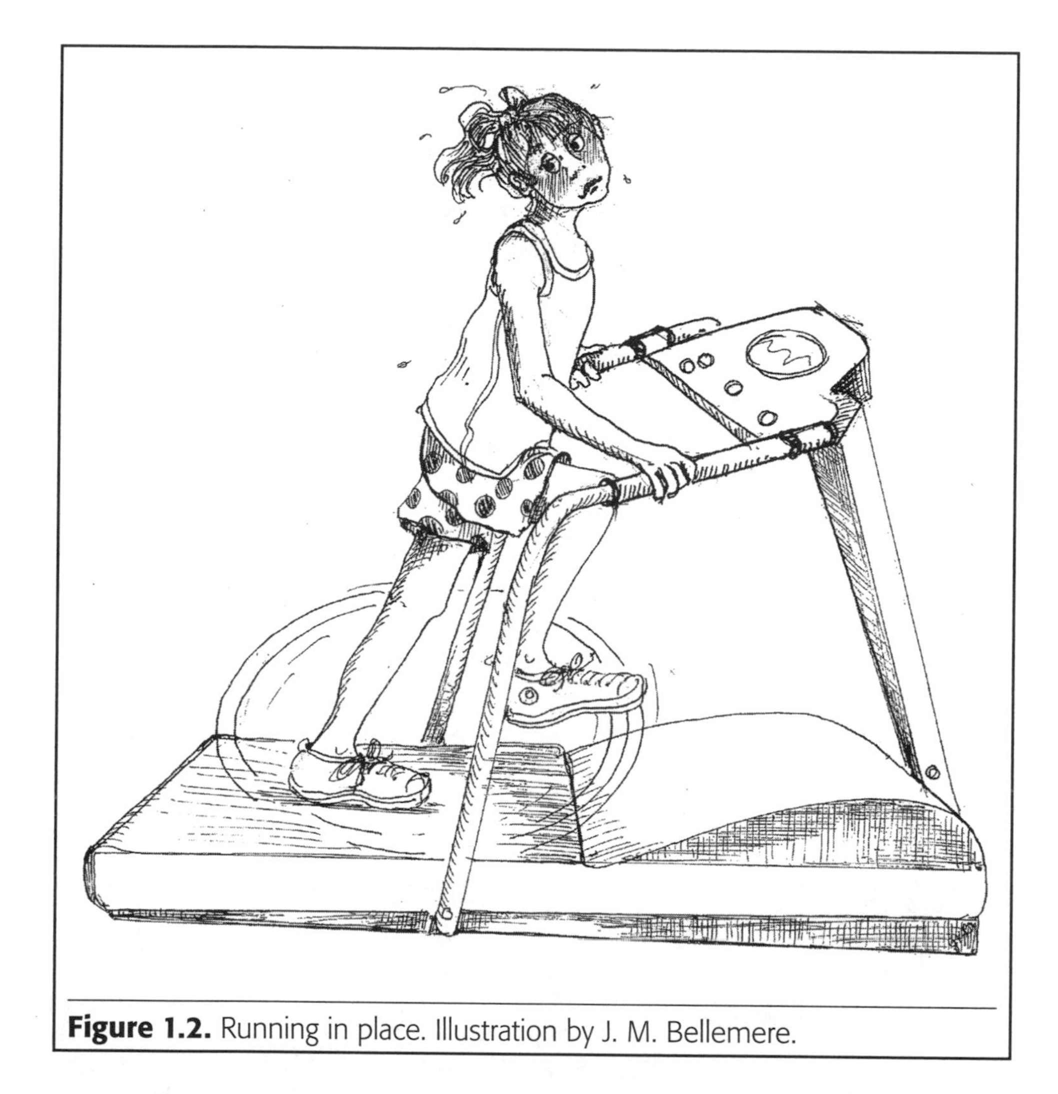

Figure 1.2. Running in place. Illustration by J. M. Bellemere.

WHO BENEFITS FROM DIFFERENTIATED LEARNING EXPERIENCES AND HOW?

All students benefit when they have opportunities to learn what they are ready and motivated to learn—especially those gifted and talented students who learn differently from the norm. *A Nation Deceived: How Schools Hold Back America's Brightest Students* (Colangelo, Assouline, & Gross, 2004) highlighted the 20 most important points from research about acceleration. The authors noted, "When bright students are presented with curriculum developed for age-peers, they can become bored and unhappy and get turned off from learning" (p. 2). Keeping all students engaged in learning—including those who are gifted and talented—is the key to successful teaching.

Differentiation does indeed benefit all students. Tomlinson (1999) provided the following description of a differentiated classroom:

> In differentiated classrooms, teachers provide specific ways for each individual to learn as deeply as possible and as quickly as possible, without assuming one student's road map for learning is identical to anyone else's. These teachers believe that students should be held to high standards. They work diligently to ensure that struggling, advanced, and in-between students think and work harder than they meant to; achieve more than they thought they could; and come to believe that learning involves effort, risk, and personal triumph. These teachers also work to ensure that each student consistently experiences the reality that success is likely to follow hard work. (p. 2)

When differentiated learning experiences are provided, all students win. Winning means that each student is learning at appropriately challenging levels and all students are making continuous progress. When this happens, motivation to learn is high, and disciplinary problems are few. This book is full of the essentials that you need to know in order to differentiate learning experiences in your classroom by matching them to what students know, understand, and can do.

IMPORTANT TAKE-AWAYS

- A one-size-fits-all curriculum misses many students.
- Reasons not to differentiate revolve around the teacher.
- The main reason to differentiate is to foster student learning.
- Fairness is doing what students need rather than doing the same thing for all students.
- Assessment is closely tied to effective differentiation.
- Three key questions guide effective differentiation: planning, preassessing, and differentiating questions.

CHAPTER
2

Multiple Ways to Define Academic Success

What Resonates With You?

> Success and failure. We think of them as opposites, but they're really not. They're companions—the hero and the sidekick. —Laurence Shames

Certainly most people would agree that a main goal of education is to have young people achieve academic success. Their definitions of academic success, however, vary considerably. Many parents would say their children have achieved academic success if they make good grades—without even considering how easy the content is. Others argue their children are successful only when those high grades come from learning challenging content. And, some would equate academic success with the love of learning. What the adults, both educators and parents, see as academic success usually shapes the young person's view. So, what you think about academic success really matters!

A strong visual for this concept is a ladder of academic success with the varying views creating its rungs (see Figure 2.1). Let's look at those levels. The first rung is getting high grades with little effort. This occurs when the student already knows most of the material and has previously acquired the skills, or the content is so easy that she learns it quickly. When proficiency is the goal in a classroom or school, it is actually no goal at all for children who are already at the proficient level or even beyond it. Remember that proficiency is grade-level learning. (This proficiency learning ceiling is discussed again in Chapter 3.) Yet this lowest stage of academic success may please the parent who doesn't see past the good grade to think about what the student doesn't learn when he isn't

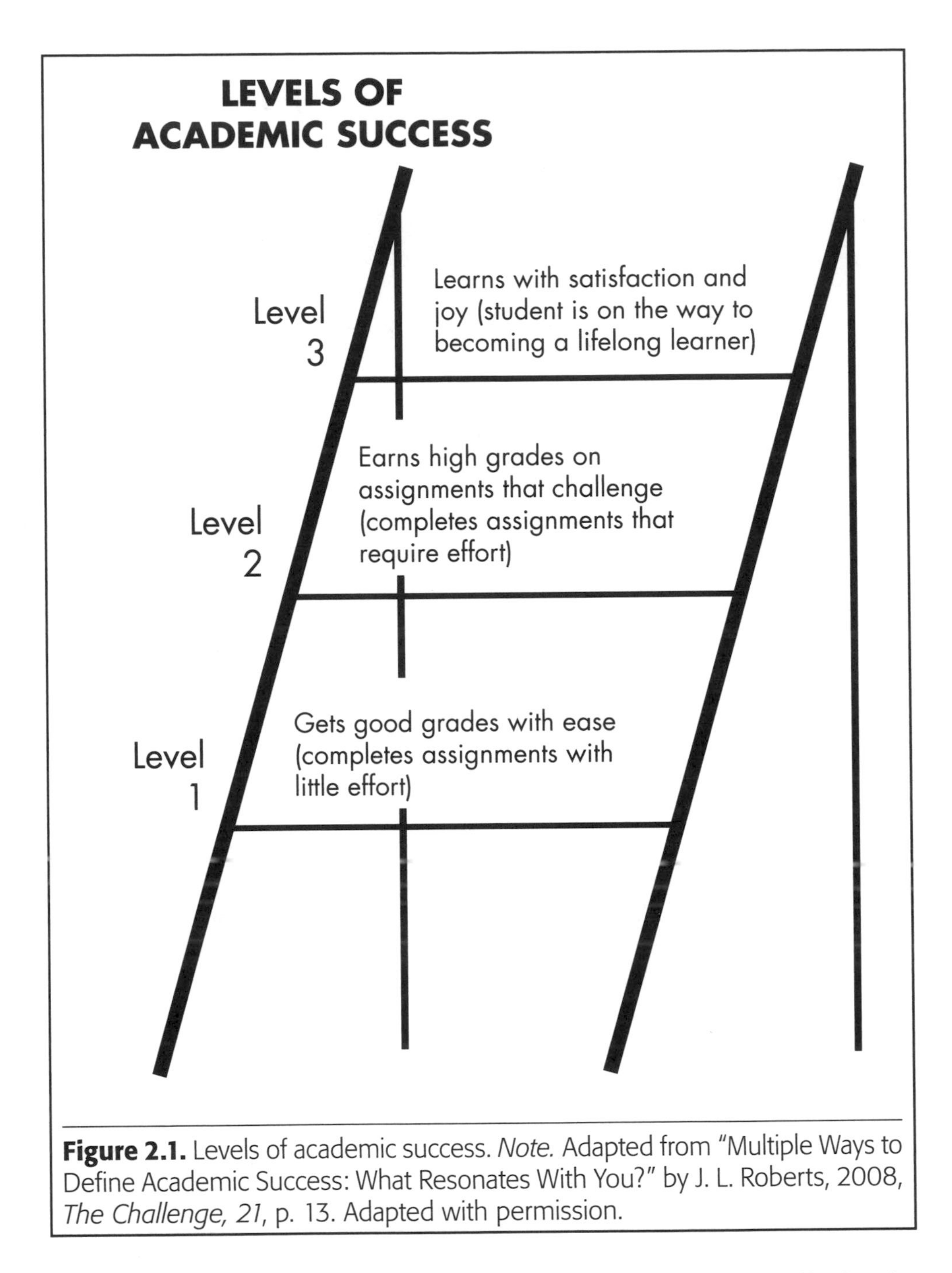

Figure 2.1. Levels of academic success. *Note.* Adapted from "Multiple Ways to Define Academic Success: What Resonates With You?" by J. L. Roberts, 2008, *The Challenge, 21*, p. 13. Adapted with permission.

challenged. High grades alone will not prepare a student to do well when he eventually meets an academic challenge; but perseverance, study skills, a strong work ethic, and problem-solving abilities will. A student only learns these skills and values when confronted with challenge, so the first rung of the ladder of academic success is a precarious place to stay. Grades alone do not guarantee success in future learning opportunities that require focus and hard work to succeed.

The second rung of the ladder of academic success features high grades that are earned when the student meets an academic challenge. Reasonable academic challenge is the key—not too difficult to achieve the goal but certainly not so easy that little or no effort is required. (Perhaps this reminds you of Baby Bear in the story—you want the challenge to be "just right.") The student takes the most rigorous classes available, acquiring study skills and developing a work ethic. You and the other adults play a significant role in reaching this rung when you encourage, even insist, that a student take the courses that will stretch his intellect and expand his experiences. This second level on the academic success ladder really can prepare a young person for future academic success. It is critical for students to reach this level if they are going to be ready for success in postsecondary opportunities. After all, elementary, middle, and high school are preparatory for postsecondary opportunities that, in turn, prepare young people to be successful in their careers.

The third rung on the ladder of academic success describes the lifelong learner: the young person who enjoys reading when a book has not been assigned, conducting an experiment when there is no science fair in the near future, or investigating a question just because she is interested. Remember that developing lifelong learners is one important goal for differentiating. This top level of the academic success ladder is reached when the focus is on learning rather than solely on grades. The parent asks his child, "What did you learn in school today?" and then takes the time to listen when she talks about what she found interesting at school that day. Another query that promotes curiosity is "Did you ask a good question today?" Barell (2008) highlights the importance of asking questions saying, "If we want our students to be curious about the world, we need to model our own curiosities within an invitational environment" (p. 106). Such modeling is best when it is a regular occurrence at home and at school. It is ideal to have the parent and child make learning an ongoing pattern in their everyday lives—the way that they approach life. Parents who enjoy learning make great role models for their children. Seeing parents read, solve problems, and engage in learning encourages children and young people to follow suit. Other ways to encourage learning are to make regular visits to the library; plan and take trips to museums, historical sites, and parks; and engage in problem solving on a regular basis. Discussing ideas and thinking through problems set the tone for young people to continue doing these things.

Educators also model lifelong learning when they share their interests in their content area—English teachers who write poetry, science teachers who have hobbies that relate to their teaching area, and art teachers who show their paintings at local galleries. Educators can model problem solving and questions they ponder about their content area.

STRATEGIES TO ENHANCE ACADEMIC SUCCESS

What can you and other adults do to facilitate students moving up the ladder of academic success? Important ways to facilitate this movement toward lifelong learning are highlighted in Figure 2.2 and included below.

The very important first step is to support the student if she finds that a rigorous class or an assignment takes both time and hard work. Often classwork has been exceptionally easy for some students; consequently, they are uncomfortable when they don't readily have the answers. Do not rescue a young person from the challenge or let anyone else do so, but rather support her in successfully reaching high academic standards. This is not the easy thing to do, but it is the right thing to do in the long run. Prepare the student by letting him know that not everything will be easy to learn, but that learning to meet the challenge is important for his long-term success. Parents and teachers, you won't be there at college or beyond when young people are faced with challenges. Ensuring that they develop problem-solving skills, resilience, and a strong work ethic will carry them through. Young people don't develop problem-solving skills, resilience, and a strong work ethic when they are rescued from challenging learning opportunities and are not allowed to struggle in order to achieve academic success.

Help a young person find interests in and outside of school, and then encourage the young person to develop those interests. Deep interests and passions motivate young learners and promote lifelong learning. Interests usually accentuate or build on strengths. A young person must have exposure to a topic, subject, or talent before developing an interest. It is unlikely that one will develop an interest in the hula hoop before trying one or in science before engaging in learning about a topic that piques his interest. Such interests could begin with parents walking in the woods with their child and talking about phenomena or by doing the same at the zoo or as they complete a project or garden in the backyard. Talking about what you are thinking about is the "minds-on" component of projects and learning experiences. Minds-on learning must accompany hands-on learning in order to maximize the opportunity to learn.

Help others realize that academic success must be defined by more than just good grades. Talk to young people, parents, colleagues, and decision makers. Advocate for continuous progress and excellence at various levels of decision making at both the school and district levels. Band together with others who share these interests in academic excellence. No one reaches excellence without hard work and persistence. That is true for advocates as well as learners.

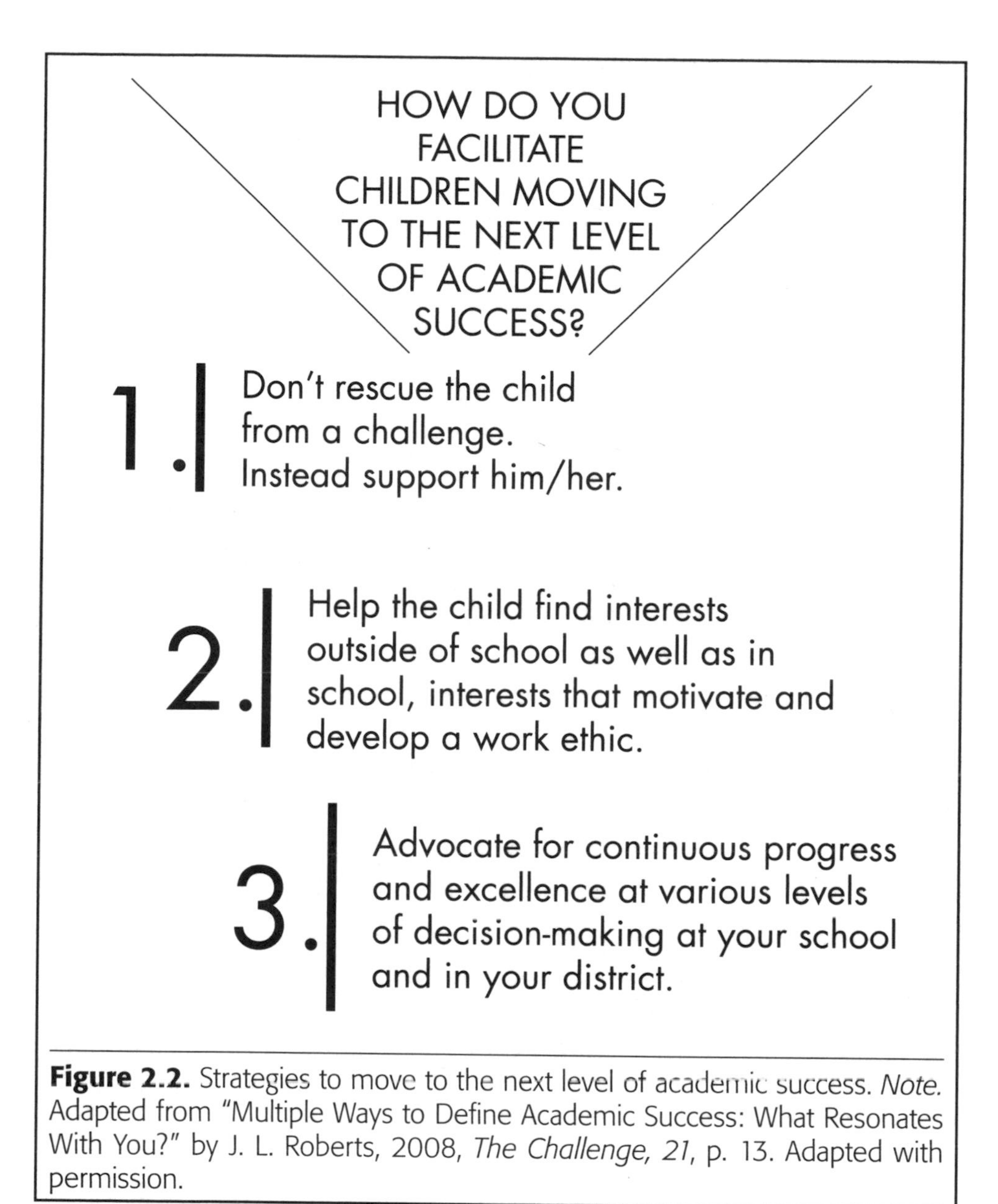

Figure 2.2. Strategies to move to the next level of academic success. *Note.* Adapted from "Multiple Ways to Define Academic Success: What Resonates With You?" by J. L. Roberts, 2008, *The Challenge, 21*, p. 13. Adapted with permission.

Educator Laureen Laumeyer described in a personal communication the pride and satisfaction that comes after working hard to reach a goal or to complete a challenging project:

> In order to be proud of an accomplishment, there must first be an accomplishment. Many times we "cheat" our students out of the feeling of pride and satisfaction by relieving them of the "hard work" it takes to get there. It is important to require the assignment, provide the learning

> opportunities, and give support as needed—but DO NOT let students "off the hook" in completing the assignment. As a teacher, it is my job to not rob them of this feeling of accomplishment. The "Thrill of Victory!"

Working through an assignment that initially seemed very difficult and successfully completing it create a backlog of experiences that prepares students for future success.

UNDERACHIEVEMENT: THE PROBLEM FROM LIMITED CHALLENGE

So, why should you and other adults be concerned as long as a student makes good grades even if challenge is absent from the picture? Underachievement sets in early when children are allowed to acquire high grades with little effort. To complicate the situation, underachievement is difficult to reverse. McCoach and Siegle (2013) summarized research on underachievement, stating "although some students are able to reverse their underachievement, many students who become underachievers in junior high school remain underachievers throughout high school, and the effects of this underachievement may persist into college and even into their adult occupations" (p. 695). The first rung of academic success is equated with "easy." In fact, one danger is that the child with a history of good grades for easy work will doubt his ability when schoolwork is not easy and effort is required. An individual's definition of academic success will influence what she does in school and the academic goals that she sets—likely transferring to many other aspects of her life. If a particular definition for academic success is "good enough now," will it be tomorrow? That is such an important question for educators and parents to think about. The end goal is for the young person to be successful in pursuits beyond school but for which the school or learning experience should prepare her.

Underachievement results from the one-size-fits-all curriculum. Winebrenner (2001) stated:

> When gifted students discover during elementary school that they can get high praise for tasks or projects they complete with little or no effort, they may conclude that being smart means doing things easily. The longer they are allowed to believe this, the harder it is to rise to the challenge when they finally encounter one. (p. 1)

Without appropriately challenging learning opportunities, underachievement sets in and becomes very difficult to reverse.

GROWTH MINDSET: BELIEVING YOU CAN DEVELOP YOUR TALENTS AND ABILITIES

An important concept to understand and encourage is a growth mindset. Dweck (2006) presents the concept of mindset and describes mindsets as growth or fixed in nature. A mindset is one's belief system about his abilities. A person with a fixed mindset believes he has talent and only needs to demonstrate his abilities. This outlook becomes precarious when the person encounters a challenge that is not easy to address. He often doubts what he had perceived as his ability, rather than rallying his effort and working hard to address the challenge. The person with the growth mindset, on the other hand, believes that talents are developed through effort—hard work. When faced with a challenge, she employs strategies and exerts effort in order to work through the challenging situation. Educators and parents support the growth mindset by providing feedback that acknowledges effort as the reason students are successful and lack of effort as the reason students fall short in reaching a goal. If schoolwork is easy (your students make A's with little effort), they don't have opportunities to develop a growth mindset.

Important to know about mindset is that one can change one's mindset. That is most likely to happen when parents and/or teachers support the young person during the change. It is vital that their future students learn to attribute their success or lack of success to their own efforts rather than to luck or other external factors.

AN IMPORTANT QUESTION FOR EDUCATORS AND PARENTS

Oftentimes, teachers, administrators, counselors, and parents don't understand the almost irreparable damage that can be done to students when little is expected of them. This thought-provoking question examines just that: "If during the first 5 or 6 years of school, a child earns good grades and high praise without having to make much effort, what are all the things he doesn't learn that most children learn by third grade?" Whether this question is presented to superintendents, teachers, parents, or students themselves, the answers are the same. These answers are the building blocks to a successful future: the importance of hard work, responsibility, time management, study skills, how to face disappointment and failure, perseverance, and so forth. When a child is earning A's and the parent doesn't see effort at home, the parent should be worried. Appropriately high expectations develop the skills that are needed for lifelong learning. (See

Appendix A for an article "What a Child Doesn't Learn . . . " It's an article that can be shared with a variety of audiences.)

CONCLUDING COMMENTS

So how do the levels of academic success and the concepts of underachievement and mindsets relate to differentiation? The lowest level of academic success or making good grades with little effort often leads to underachievement. Differentiation is an essential step to move students up to making A's or good grades that require effort. Differentiation is also required for students who become lifelong learners. Differentiation allows students to engage in learning that is appropriately challenging and that taps their interests and builds on their strengths. Mindsets come into the picture because the growth mindset is basic to students working hard to build their skills and learn at high levels.

IMPORTANT TAKE-AWAYS

- Academic success for all students depends upon effective differentiation.
- Good grades may not signal student success unless the classwork is appropriately challenging.
- Lifelong learners enjoy learning even when no one gives them assignments to complete.
- Underachievement is difficult to reverse, so working to avoid students becoming underachievers is very important, and appropriately challenging differentiation can prevent underachievement.
- A growth mindset prepares young people to encounter disappointment and/or failure and develop their abilities and talents in school and over a lifetime.
- Parents and educators need to support rather than rescue learners when they encounter work that isn't easy for them.

CHAPTER
3

Climate
Creating a Comfort Zone

> It is certainly the case that teachers who lead effectively for differentiation operate from a clear sense that classrooms should model a world in which learning is rewarding and in which mutual respect, persistent effort, and shared responsibility make everyone stronger.
> —Carol Tomlinson and Marcia Imbeau

An April evening in San Francisco calls for a light jacket, warm long underwear is a must when traveling Down Under in August, and don't forget to take along an umbrella if you're adventuring in Hawaii during the rainy months of October and November. Seasoned travelers know to check the climate of a location before making travel plans or else they may be paying top dollar (or yen or euro) for that must-have article needed for comfort. Now, of course, weather updates are critical for day-to-day travel wear—that selection of "What do I wear today?" as you sift through the suitcase. We all know that weather can change daily (and sometimes hourly), but it typically stays within the climate parameters. It's the climate that is predictable: the average rainfall, temperature, and the like. We plan for the typical.

So, when we discuss the climate of a classroom, we're looking for the norm. We expect it. We plan for it. Just as we can predict how much rain we'll get in Toledo in June, we can predict how students who learn differently from the norm will be treated in Mrs. Differentiated's classroom (and in Mr. Teach-to-the-Middle's classroom). Due to climate, we know to pack extra sunscreen and sandals if we're traveling to Rome in June, and we know that all children (regardless of interests, strengths, or levels of readiness) will be studying the letter A for a week and then the letter B for a week in Mrs. I've-Always-Done-It-This-Way's kindergarten classroom. We can count on snow in northern Montana from November to May, just as we can count on a number of choices of ways to learn in Mr. Meet-Their-Needs' class from September through May. Climate is predictable. Moreover, classroom climate goes one step further—classroom climate is intentional, or at least it should be intentional. The climate plays an integral role in the academic success of our students.

As professionals, the climate we establish becomes the norm, the typical, the "this is what to expect here" for our students. They pack their semester- or year-long suitcases with the articles and accessories necessary for comfort and success. In order for students to be prepared and successful, the climate must be consistent, clearly established, and communicated from the start. It certainly shouldn't be an afterthought.

CLIMATE OF DIFFERENTIATION

When climatologists determine a region's climate, they carefully measure and average the temperature, precipitation, and wind over a long period of time. These are the principle components of climate. When an educator intentionally creates the classroom climate, he must carefully develop and support the principle components of an effectively differentiated classroom:

- a differentiated classroom respects diversity;
- a differentiated classroom maintains high expectations; and
- a differentiated classroom generates openness.

A DIFFERENTIATED CLASSROOM RESPECTS DIVERSITY

Doctoral dissertations, scholarly journals, and graduate classes have explored minute aspects of diversity in myriad ways. The bottom line, however, is that people differ—period. Now, most of us are very sensitive when it comes to issues that affect us personally. Perhaps we are females in a male-dominated field or bright, young Hispanics who do not speak English in an English-speaking elementary school. Maybe we are homeless families struggling to find food and work or teens stricken with cerebral palsy working toward graduation. Not only are we sensitive to our own issues, but we also empathize with those who share those same issues. But, oftentimes our vision is limited to just these issues. Problems arise when we encounter people with other issues. We often lose that sensitivity.

As educators, our classrooms come statistic-laden. For example, we may have 24 fifth graders (half are 10-year-olds, the other half are 11-year-olds). Of those, 30% may qualify for free and/or reduced lunch, 8% may have been identified with learning difficulties, 12% may need gifted services, 6% may come from homes where English in not the first language, 20% may be minorities, 50% may be on grade level in reading (but 30% are as many as three grade levels behind while the other 20% may be as much as four grade levels ahead!)—and we haven't even addressed learning profiles, gender, or interests. Yes, our classrooms are indeed diverse. Therefore, the educator must meet that challenge head-on in order to provide continuous progress for each learner.

That last thought merits reiteration: Teachers should strive toward the goal of continuous progress for *each* learner. This is the key to instilling a love of learning so that children and young people become lifelong learners. Isn't that a main goal of education? Isn't that the highest level of academic success?

Establishing and honoring a respect for diversity sets the stage for differentiation as it becomes the climate of the classroom. The Council for the Accreditation of Educator Preparation (2013) defines students as "children or youth attending P–12 schools including, but not limited to, students with disabilities or exceptionalities, students who are gifted, and students who represent diversity based on ethnicity, race, socioeconomic status, gender, language, religion, sexual identification, and/or geographic origin" (p. 3). From ethnicity to gender, socioeconomic status to interests, and ability to culture, American classrooms exemplify diversity. It falls on the educators' shoulders to deliberately and carefully respect and celebrate those differences. In fact, the Council of Chief State School Officers' Interstate Teacher Assessment and Support Consortium's (InTASC; 2011) *Model Core Teaching Standards: A Resource for State Dialogue* argues that understanding diversity is essential for teachers: "The teacher understands that learners bring assets for learning based on their individual experiences, abilities, talents, prior learning, and peer and social group interactions, as well as language, culture, family, and community values" (p. 11). The understanding of those differences, along with individual students' learning profiles, abilities, needs, and interests, can be capitalized on so that all students learn a variety of content on a variety of levels in a variety of ways.

This variety paradoxically calls for consistency. It is imperative that diversity is consistently honored. Although an isolated lesson that is differentiated based on diversity is better than no differentiation at all, that lesson could well be viewed with discomfort on the learner's part (e.g., "Why is my assignment different from hers? That's not fair!") or lack of support on the home front (e.g., "Susie had to write her assignment. Why didn't her friend have to?"). From day one, diversity must be acknowledged, embraced, and celebrated by all stakeholders. Although this is not an easy task, it most certainly can be accomplished.

The following sections describe how to create a classroom that respects and celebrates diversity.

Step 1: Begin at the beginning. From day one, highlight the differences among the students to the students themselves—and the importance of using those differences in the learning process. One excellent activity to begin the school year and to emphasize this message is the How Do You Learn It? Activity (explained below).

A scenario of what the activity may look like. Thirty-one seventh graders bustle, meander, or shuffle into your math (or language arts or science—you fill in the blank) classroom fully expecting 50 minutes of rules, procedures, and a syllabus on their first day of class. Instead, they take their seats while noticing four large white sheets of paper placed at different points around the room. After your welcome is issued and the necessary business is completed, you start talking about the game of tennis. It might sound similar to this: "I don't know how many of you play tennis, but it's a sport that has always challenged me. I've tried it a few times, and, if I'm lucky, the ball might go over the net occasionally." Or, it could be told like this: "All my life, tennis has been a passion of mine. I enjoy playing it, watching it, coaching it—I even enjoy just thinking about it!" You then encourage the students to think about tennis and their ability to play the game. Ask them to consider, given their ability to play, what specific things a teacher or coach would need to do in order for them to become better tennis players. Point out the papers on the wall, explaining each: "The sheet of paper marked 1 is for those of you who have never played tennis before. You may know about it; you may not. Sheet 2 would be for those of you who may have dabbled in the game. Perhaps you enjoy watching it. Perhaps you enjoy hitting the ball around. The third sheet is for those of you who play the game. You don't have to play on a team, but you enjoy the game. Finally, the fourth sheet would be for those of you who play competitively. Maybe you even give lessons. Now think of where you belong, go to that sheet, and then brainstorm answers to this question: 'What strategies, techniques, etc. would best help me improve my ability to play tennis?'"

Suddenly the whole room moves and talks. At Sheet 4 you hear Emil and Shelly debating which racquet is better: Prince or Head. At Sheet 3 comments and phrases bounce around the group: "one-on-one advice," "I need help with my backhand," and "playing against someone as good as me—no, maybe a bit better." As you move to Sheet 2 the conversation changes: "I think I know the rules," "I need somebody to show me how to serve—show me, watch me do it, then give me feedback," and "Please don't make me watch videos. I just can't watch it and then be expected to do it!" And, at Sheet 1 Anthony is trying hard to add more to the sheet besides "explanation of rules" and "cute instructor," but the others have broken into pairs and threesomes discussing classes, texting, the other gender, and the mall. The interest and motivation just aren't there.

After 5 minutes or so, you announce another topic: playing an instrument. Ask them to think about what would help them improve their ability to play an instrument. Groans mingle with excited chatter as band kids move to Sheets 3 and 4 while Emil laughingly goes from Sheet 4 to 1. They place a check mark by those strategies already written on the paper that would help them learn to play an instrument better (substituting musical concepts for the sports ones) and then add additional ones. After a few minutes, you introduce finding information on the Internet as the new topic, and people shift yet again. Later, baking cookies from scratch causes even more movement and laughter. You will probably announce more topics depending on what you've observed.

Once the kids are seated again, the most important component of the activity falls upon your shoulders. Debriefing is critically important as *you spend time discussing the different strategies needed to increase learning based on differing readiness and motivation levels.* You point out how difficult it was to pull Emil and Shelly away from the discussion of tennis to focus on instruments, because of their passion for tennis. You also debrief the reasons that the people at Sheet 1 had a tough time staying on topic (i.e., when there's little interest in a topic, there's little motivation to discuss it). Most importantly, though, is your emphasis on the fact that everyone moved. Everyone has areas of strength and interest—and those aren't the same as everyone else's in the class. But, these folks don't stay at the fourth sheet for every topic; just because you're talented in one area doesn't mean you're talented in all. If enough topics are introduced, everyone will be on the beginning level at some point. This does not indicate the inability to learn. It only means that we're different. We're interested in different things. We learn in different ways. We have different strengths, weaknesses, and needs. We have different experiences.

From there, you spend the last 10 minutes of class focusing on how you will honor and embrace those differences by looking at their interests, strengths, and readiness levels as you teach them math (or reading or whatever discipline you teach). Not everyone will be learning the same thing in the same way, but all students will learn. Continuous progress is what school's all about!

How you do the activity: The steps to make it happen. Place four sheets of chart paper and a marker for each sheet around the room, providing enough space for students to gather. Label each sheet of paper with a category that ranges from a beginning to an expert level. In Kentucky, for example, the headings could mirror the state assessment language: *novice, apprentice, proficient,* and *distinguished.* Louisiana students would relate to *unsatisfactory, approaching basic* (approaching the standard), *basic* (meeting the standard), *mastery* (exceeding the standard) and *advanced.* Teachers in New Jersey could use three sheets of paper to parallel their three-step scale: *partially proficient, proficient,* and *advanced proficient.* Maryland students would relate to three descriptors as well: *basic, proficient,* and *advanced.* One approach is to use the language that students know. On the other hand, however, you may want to deliberately steer clear of state assessment language. New descriptors may seem more inviting to the student or less intimidating.

Instruct students to think about the topic or activity (e.g., playing baseball, using the quadratic equation, rebuilding a motor, bargain shopping) and their ability in that topic. Mentally, they need to consider their mastery level and think about what strategies would best help them improve their tennis playing or whatever the topic may be. It's your job to ask questions to guide them especially with this first topic. (Remember that continuous progress is the goal for all students, regardless of ability level.) Explain the categories, and then have students move to the area that best describes their ability level (students will be using self-assessment). After moving to one of the sheets of paper, students should brainstorm what they would need in order to learn how to play baseball better, to understand the quadratic equation better, etc. The teacher visits the group, posing thoughtful questions or introducing additional strategies.

Introduce an additional topic (e.g., playing an instrument), and have the students move to the appropriate level that best describes their skill level for that topic. Once there, students will place a check mark by the strategies that were listed for that previous topic that also would work to improve their skills in the new topic. They can then brainstorm additional strategies.

This process continues with more topics (e.g., baking cookies, creating webpages, geometry, speed texting) until sufficient movement has occurred. It is critical that you see movement in all students. This may mean you have to be creative by introducing such topics as playing RPG video games, taking apart tractor engines, or drawing anime. Sometimes, too, it's very effective to bring up multiple areas just before they return to their seats. Mention a topic and have students raise their hands for each level instead of physically moving. Rapid-fire ideas (such as crocheting, jumping on a pogo stick, and mowing the lawn) greatly emphasize the variety of interests and abilities of the students.

Have the students go back to their seats for a debriefing period: What did you discover about yourself? How does your readiness level affect the strategies you need to learn something? (You may need to explain readiness level.) What role does motivation play? What role does intelligence play? What role does experience play? What role does hard work play? Use those answers to emphasize students' differences (i.e., interests, strengths, and levels of readiness) and how those differences will be honored in the classroom. At this step, students are reflecting on the activity, which is an important aspect of all learning experiences.

Step 2: Discover all you can. The second step to respecting diversity in the classroom is to collect as much information as you can about students. From their individual sets of interests to their preferred learning styles, these bits of information will help you adapt the classroom to meet each student's unique needs. The following tools and strategies are good places to start.

Inventories. Inventories not only provide important information for differentiation, but students typically enjoy discovering their learning profiles, strengths, interests, leadership styles, product preferences, and so forth. According to Tomlinson and Imbeau (2010), the learning profile encompasses four categories of influence on how students approach learning: gender, culture, intelligence preferences, and learning style (pp. 17–18). The concept relates to how young people take in and process information. Although research does not necessarily link learning style to achievement, it has shown that providing multiple avenues to access content improves learning (Hattie, 2014).

As you process the results of these instruments and inventories, explain that throughout the semester students will be doing different activities and having different assignments as a result of the measures. Examples of such differentiated assignments can be found throughout this book. If explained thoroughly, students will come to understand the benefits and take pleasure in the individual approach to their learning.

My Way . . . An Expression Style Inventory. Kettle, Renzulli, and Rizza (n.d.) developed an instrument that assists students in determining their preferences in creating products: "Teachers can use the instrument to remind young people that, like practicing professionals, they must select a product to communicate what they have learned to their audience" (pp. 1–2). The instrument (see Appendix B) is a simple survey of 50 questions that ultimately ranks a student's preference in 10 product categories: written, oral, artistic, computer, audio/visual, commercial, service, dramatization, manipulative, and musical. (This is part of a computer profiler that can be found at http://www.renzullilearning.com.) This tool can be used in a differentiated classroom, because it not only tells the learner more about him- or herself, but it also guides the teacher in product options. You'll learn how important that can be in Chapters 6 and 8.

Multiple Intelligences Checklist. Heacox (2002) adapted a Multiple Intelligences Checklist from Armstrong (2000), designed for parents about their children. It could easily be adapted for older students to complete themselves. To score, you simply look for check marks next to any of the 58 characteristics listed. These can be quickly linked to the multiple intelligence (MI) the characteristic indicates. Once determined, differentiated learning can be centered around the results. Remember that once the preferred learning style or multiple intelligence preference is determined, then product options can easily be designed.

Another MI inventory is TIMI—the Teele Inventory for Multiple Intelligences (Teele, 1997). This pictorial instrument offers a high reliability rate and has been used with all ages (as young as 2) in more than 25 countries. Online Multiple Intelligences assessments exist as well. For example, Birmingham Grid for Learning out of the United Kingdom developed a 40-item measure that quickly determines a student's Multiple Intelligence preference and even explains the results: http://www.bgfl.org/custom/resources_ftp/client_ftp/ks1/ict/multiple_int/what.cfm.

Learning styles. Part of a learner's profile, learning styles can be assessed through myriad inventories, including numerous online ones. A Google search showed over two million hits. VARK (Fleming, 2012), for example, has both print and online versions of their inventory, available at http://www.vark-learn.com/english/page.asp?p=questionnaire. VARK uses a 16-question format to determine if a learner is primarily a Visual, Aural, Read/Write, or Kinesthetic learner.

Please remember that no research directly links increased achievement to learning experiences that incorporate learning styles. Although some argue, via common sense, that students might be more motivated if their learning styles are incorporated into their learning, there is no quantifiable evidence.

Interest inventories. More generic interest inventories taken at the beginning of the year or even periodically through the semester can be beneficial. Winebrenner (2001) included an excellent survey in her book *Teaching Gifted Kids in the Regular Classroom*, as did Heacox (2002) in *Differentiating Instruction in the Regular Classroom*. Winebrenner, for example, included items such as "If you could talk to any one person from history, who would it be? Why? Think of three questions you would ask the person" and "Tell about your favorite games." A sampling of Heacox's questions shows the general information that can be gleaned from an inventory: "What subject makes you think and work the hardest? Why is it the most challenging?" and "Rate the following topics according to your interests. (1 = very interested, 2 = somewhat interested, 3 = not interested)," and then topics from dance, to computers, to business are listed. (See Appendix C for an interest inventory.)

Step 3: Communicate, communicate, communicate. Without strong communication, a differentiated classroom climate cannot be established. That communication takes place on several levels. First comes the administration. Ideally school leadership embraces and encourages a respect of diversity and the necessity of differentiation. At the very least, the leadership should be aware of your philosophy and support you in communicating with parents.

Next, of course, are the parents or guardians. Standard procedures of most classrooms dictate parents' knowledge of class rules and procedures. A teacher of a differentiated classroom must go beyond that. This teacher must go to great lengths to ensure that the parents understand differentiation and the importance of recognizing and accommodating diversity. A parent meeting is ideal. The How Do You Learn It? Activity works beautifully with parents. They internalize that they, too, have different interests, varying levels of ability depending on the content, and individual needs for instruction. Most importantly, perhaps, is their realization that just because they're unfamiliar with a topic (or uninterested) does not mean they are incapable of learning it or that they are low achievers. Of course, the teacher must process this so that the parents appreciate the correlation to what their own sons and daughters will be learning in this differentiated classroom.

Another strategy would be for parents to take one of the inventories—again, with appropriate processing. Many methods can get across the same idea: In this classroom, not all students will be studying the same content in the same way—the individual person's strengths, interests, and levels of readiness will come into play whenever possible. This message must be repeated throughout the year. Written communication (perhaps a one-page article describing instruction based on learning profiles, a snippet of research supporting differentiation, or sample student reactions to a differentiated lesson) will emphasize the importance of a classroom that respects diversity.

The last level of communication—and perhaps the most important—is with the students themselves. Tomlinson and Imbeau (2010) suggest discussing these questions near the beginning of the year:

- Who are you as learners? (Are you all alike or are there important differences?)
- Given the differences we see, how should I teach you?
- If our classroom is going to work for all of us, what will it be like? (How will it need to function? What roles will each of us play?)
- How can I learn more about your starting points, interests, and best ways of learning?
- If we have a differentiated classroom, can it be fair? (What will "fair" mean in this room?)
- What will success in this class mean? (How will I know if you're succeeding? How will you know?) (pp. 45–46)

The conversation stimulated by those questions helps establish an effectively differentiated classroom.

In spite of the strong initial introduction to diversity and teaching based on those differences, students will need reminders throughout the year. Sometimes a simple verbal reminder suffices: "Now remember that your assignment may look different from your neighbor's. Your assignment stems from the interest inventory you took." Or, you may choose to space out the inventories. Perhaps you administer one on general interests the first week of school, and then you wait until the end of the first quarter before giving them a learning modalities inventory. That opens up another discussion on how the students learn, how unique learning may be to each individual student, and how much they learn when their instruction is designed to accommodate their needs. Another form of communication could be students sharing their work in front of the class, followed by purposeful discussion of the variety of assignments/content for different learners. Whether the communication is written or verbal, the message is critical, and that message must be reiterated to administrators, parents, and students throughout the year.

A differentiated classroom respects diversity. Ethnicity, gender, learning profile, ability level, pace of learning, cultural background—the ways in which learners differ are almost endless. When a classroom's climate celebrates and builds upon those differences, continuous progress is possible for all learners.

A DIFFERENTIATED CLASSROOM MAINTAINS HIGH EXPECTATIONS

When intentionally establishing the climate of your differentiated classroom, not only must you ensure that diversity is respected, but you also must be sure to maintain high expectations. These high expectations must be threefold: One, teachers must have high expectations for their students; two, students must have high expectations for themselves; and three, teachers must have high expectations for themselves. Remember that young people become lifelong learners when learning takes place through challenging tasks.

High expectations for students. Just as one approach to teaching doesn't address the needs of the entire class, one set of high expectations doesn't either. A differentiated classroom calls for matching the content with the strengths, interests, and levels of readiness of the students. Coupled with that matching is pairing high expectations with individual students. For example, if Mr. Rodriguez expects all of his sixth-grade students to read on the sixth-grade level, he may have expectations appropriate for only 4 of his 31 students. For his students already reading beyond that level, his expectations are entirely too low and will result in underachievement, student boredom, and virtual stagnation (and perhaps even behavior problems). For his students reading at the third-grade level, his expectations set them up for total failure. For students near the sixth-grade level who are able to learn at a faster pace than their peers, expectations may be met in October—then what? In addition, consider the kindergartner who comes to school already reading. If the goal is to guarantee a horrible year for her, force her to do letter A for a week, then letter B for a week, and so on. Ideally, levels of expectation will vary based on the individual learner. Regardless of those varying levels, all expectations must be high.

Many educators of gifted young people raise this very issue of high expectations when discussing the federal No Child Left Behind Act (NCLB; 2001), which has been the driving force of education for well over a decade. Differentiation and gifted education expert Carol Ann Tomlinson (2002) argued:

> At present, the No Child Left Behind Act aims the nation's attention and resources at ensuring that nonproficient students move systematically toward proficiency. There is no incentive for schools to attend to the growth of students once they attain proficiency, or to spur students who are already proficient to greater achievement, and certainly not to inspire those who far exceed proficiency. . . . The No Child Left Behind Act, with its focus on proficiency rather than academic growth, enhances

> the likelihood that this broad swath of learners will be all but irrelevant in daily classroom planning. (p. 36)

Although numerous states have been granted waivers to NCLB, the premise of this argument remains: Proficiency is not a goal for someone who is already proficient. Varying expectations are necessary for growth. If NCLB sets the expectation at proficiency (albeit unintentionally), those expectations are too low for young people who are gifted and talented. Those expectations alone breed underachievement: "Once again we seem to forget that excellence and equity are required of a nation that wills itself to excel in the world" (Tomlinson, 2002, p. 36).

Consider a hypothetical class (see Figure 3.1) with various levels of knowledge of the subject. As Figure 3.1 depicts, students' levels of knowledge vary greatly within one classroom. To many, "equal" education means that all students are able to meet minimal standards, which are represented by a horizontal line in Figure 3.2. But, what about the students who are already above the line? In a classroom focusing on continuous progress, each student needs the opportunity to add equally to his or her knowledge, to make at least a year's gain in achievement (see Figure 3.3). Only when each student is making continuous progress can each one be academically successful.

Moreover, low expectations prohibit students who are gifted and talented from making continuous progress. According to Joseph Renzulli, former-Director of the National Research Center on the Gifted and Talented:

> Many of them will never, ever reach their potential without some type of advanced learning opportunities and resources. Equity goes both ways. It means we're going to accommodate the needs of students, whether they're struggling, average, or above average learners. (as cited in Schemo, 2004, p. A16)

For those above-average learners, that means removing the learning ceiling (i.e., the goal of proficiency). When educators or legislators set goals of achievement, they often inadvertently create limits to learning. So, if proficiency is the goal, then no one is really concerned with what lies beyond that—except, of course, those students who find themselves in that place or predicament.

The Fordham Institute released its report, *High-Achieving Students in the Era of NCLB* (Loveless, Farkas, & Duffett, 2008), examining the status of these students. The report explains that low achievers did indeed make gains, but the top achievers did not. So the achievement gap is lessening, but with a bottom moving up to the stagnant top. Fordham Institute president Chester R. Finn, Jr. remarked:

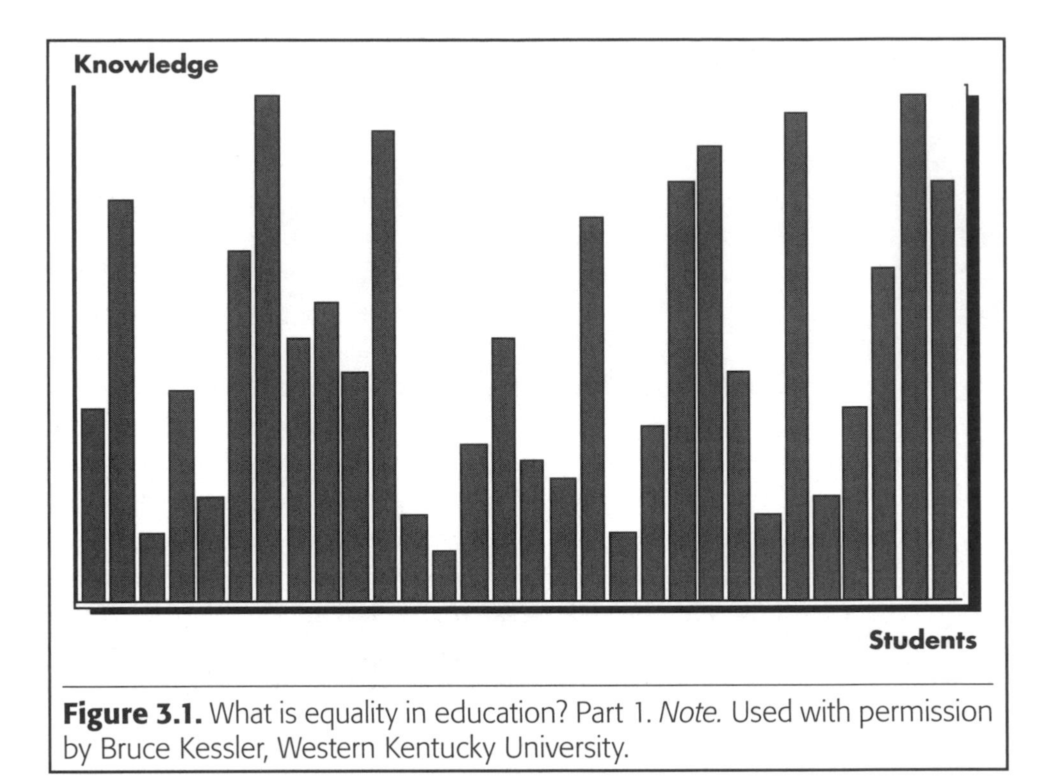

Figure 3.1. What is equality in education? Part 1. *Note.* Used with permission by Bruce Kessler, Western Kentucky University.

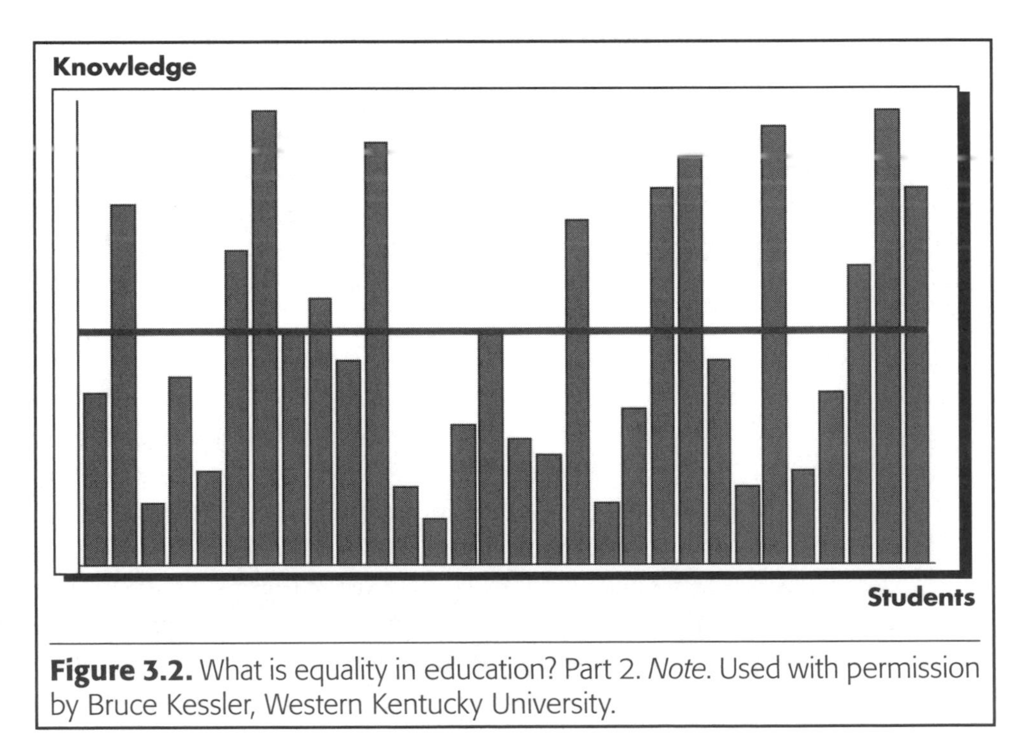

Figure 3.2. What is equality in education? Part 2. *Note.* Used with permission by Bruce Kessler, Western Kentucky University.

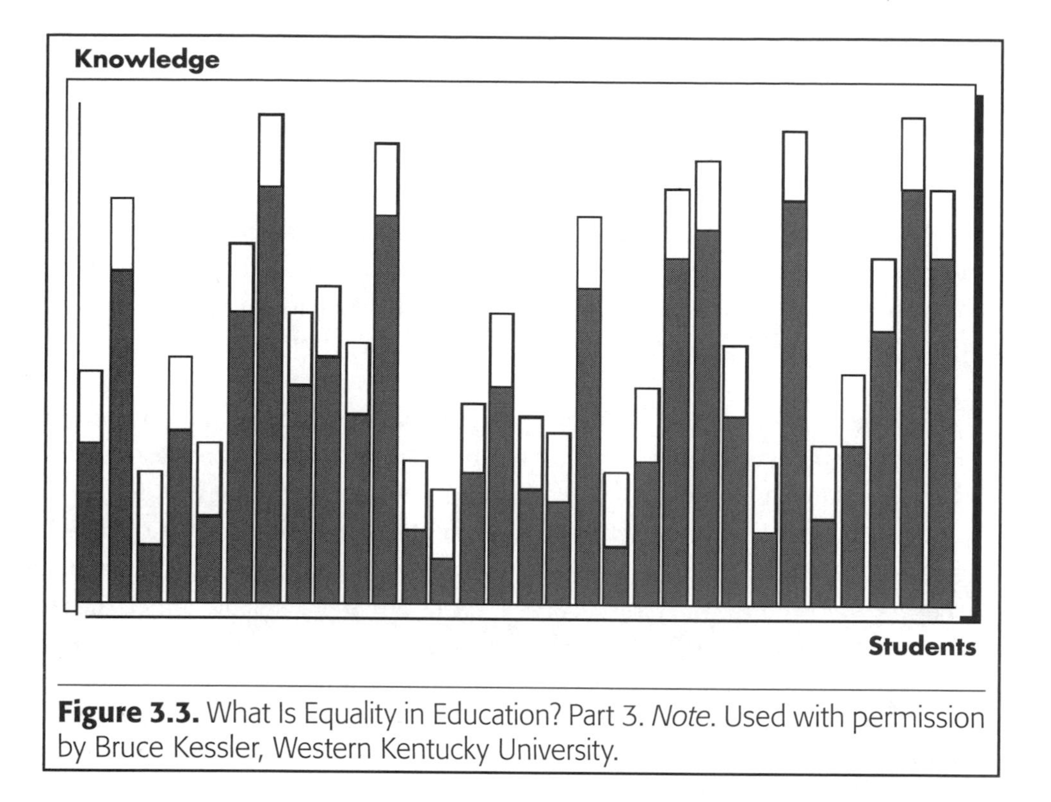

Figure 3.3. What Is Equality in Education? Part 3. *Note.* Used with permission by Bruce Kessler, Western Kentucky University.

> To its credit No Child Left Behind appears to be making progress toward its stated goal: narrowing achievement gaps from the bottom up. Let us celebrate the gains of our lowest achieving students. But in a time of fierce international competition, can we afford to let the strongest languish? As John Gardner once asked, "Can we be equal and excellent too?" Surely the answer must be yes. For America to maintain prosperity and strength on a shrinking, flattening planet, we need also to serve our ablest youngsters far better than we're doing today. (as cited in Kuhner, 2008, para. 2)

Equity and excellence should not be mutually exclusive. As the former president of NAGC, Tomlinson (2002) explained:

> How much more promising the No Child Left Behind Act would be it if it genuinely ensured that no child would be left behind in terms of developing his or her possibilities—if it unreservedly supported both equity and excellence. (p. 38)

Also damaging is the faulty understanding of *excellence*. When a school argues there is no need for gifted services because all classes are taught on that level, how does that school justify the level of teaching going on in the classroom? By what comparisons can that statement be made? When a teacher explains that his class is an honors class, and therefore it's taught at high levels, on what grounds can he make that assumption? The fact that a class has honors or Advanced Placement (AP) attached to its course title does not necessarily correlate to a challenging class taught on a high level. How many students take and pass the AP tests? How well do the school's achievement scores compare to others in the state or nation? As a nation we must be stringent on what excellence really means if we are to compete in a global economy. That preparation for competition begins with one student in one classroom.

However, the United States' perception of excellence pales in comparison to other developed countries'—at least as far as math scores are concerned. The Organisation for Economic Co-operation and Development's (OECD) Program for International Student Assessment (PISA) conducts an annual survey of knowledge and skills of 470,000 15-year-olds from the 65 countries that create 90% of the world economy. The latest scores (OECD, 2013) placed the United States 36th in math; this was significantly below the standard of readiness for college and careers. The U.S. fares no better on the *Trends in Mathematics and Science Study* (TIMSS) which has made international comparisons for students in grade 4 and 8 five times since 1995. There has been no measurable difference in the eighth-grade math average since 2007 (i.e., 507); in 2011 it was 509, nine points higher than the international average of 500. Moreover, we were behind 11 systems including Korea, Singapore, Chinese Taipei, Hong Kong, Japan, and the Russian Federation (Institute of Education Sciences, 2014).

The National Academies, in response to a Congressional charge, created the Committee on Prospering in the Global Economy of the 21st Century to propose the top 10 actions needed for America to prosper in this century. (Instead, they made four recommendations and 20 actions.) The Committee's (2005) report, *Rising Above the Gathering Storm: Energizing and Employing America for a Brighter Economic Future*, serves as a startling wake-up call to Americans:

> Having reviewed trends in the United States and abroad, the committee is deeply concerned that the scientific and technical building blocks of our economic leadership are eroding at a time when many other nations are gathering strength. . . . We are worried about the future prosperity of the United States. Although many people assume that United States will always be a world leader in science and technology, this may not be the case inasmuch as great minds and ideas exist throughout the world. We fear the abruptness with which a lead in science and technology can be lost—and the difficulty of recovering a lead once lost, if indeed it can be regained at all. This nation must prepare with great urgency to preserve its strength and economic security. (p. ES-2)

That wake-up call went unanswered as the follow-up report from the National Academy of Sciences, Institute of Medicine, and National Academy of Engineering (2010), *Rising Above the Gathering Storm, Revisited: Rapidly Approaching Category 5*, argued. The lack of action has actually worsened the situation. For the sake of our children and young people and for the nation, we must aim for excellence.

What, then, is excellence? Excellence is meeting the state and national standards at the very highest levels, given that there are levels beyond proficiency. The Commonwealth of Kentucky incorporated this notion of excellence in its assessment language when it added the *distinguished* category (see the How to Create a Classroom That Respects Diversity section). Moreover, they developed an exemplary level of development and implementation in their *School Level Performance Descriptors and Glossary for Kentucky's Standards and Indicators for School Improvement* (Kentucky Department of Education, 2000), the basis of their Scholastic Audit system for individual schools. For example, a Level 3 assessment statement reads: "Assessments provide a variety of opportunities for teachers and students to measure learning and make adjustments to ensure continuous progress" (Kentucky Department of Education, 2000, p. 8). But, the Level 4, or exemplary level, reads: "Continuous assessments provide a variety of opportunities for teachers and students to measure learning and offer a wide range of choice in the assessment type to ensure success in all content areas" (Kentucky Department of Education, 2000, p. 8). Excellence for this academic performance standard far exceeds the expectations for a school doing sufficiently well. Yes, of course, we want all Americans to read proficiently, but don't we also want as many Americans as possible to read beyond the acceptable level? (See Chapter 9 for our incorporation of this belief in an assessment tool.)

National standards agree. To illustrate, the *National Standards for Arts Education* (Consortium of National Arts Education Associations, 1994) provided two achievement standards for each content standard in grades 9–12: proficient and advanced. Excellence, then, goes beyond the proficient expectations.

If we are to compete in a global economy, then excellence is required for all learners from all populations. If our students are to accomplish this, they must understand clearly what defines excellence in any subject area—and be encouraged to reach for that, beyond simple proficiency.

High expectations for teachers. By far the most important component of an effectively differentiated classroom is the community leader, the teacher. It is critical that teachers expect excellence from themselves, and they must actively pursue avenues that lead to excellence. Gentry, Steenbergen-Hu, and Choi (2011) looked at characteristics, practices, and qualities of teachers deemed excellent, in part, by high student ratings. Four themes emerged:

- Theme 1. These teachers know and take a personal interest in their students.
- Theme 2. These teachers set high expectations for themselves and their students.
- Theme 3. These teachers make content and learning meaningful and relevant to the future and respect students' choices.
- Theme 4. These teachers have a clear passion for their students, teaching, and for their content. (p. 116)

Effective teachers believe they make a real difference in the lives of their students, and they are willing to do whatever it takes to make that difference.

Effective teachers must also be honest with themselves. They need to have an understanding of their strengths and weaknesses, including their ability to establish a culture that is conducive to addressing individuals' strengths, interests, and readiness levels. If their goal is continuous progress for all students, then they must take stock of their ability to make that happen. Heacox's (2009) Teacher Inventory on Differentiation Practices and Strategies (see pages 13–14 of her book, *Making Differentiation a Habit: How to Ensure Success in Academically Diverse Classrooms*) is an excellent tool to use for educators who want to self-assess their usage of differentiation strategies such as preassessment and flexible grouping. Heacox has also created a Continuum of Levels of Teacher Development in Differentiation (see pages 15–18 of the same book, in which she encourages educators to assess evidence of "active, planful differentiation"). These are helpful tools, that when used honestly, can shape professional growth. An effective teacher must be open to introspection.

Risk taking: An important expectation for both students and teachers. Risk taking is another critical component of a differentiated classroom. Many young people are afraid to take intellectual risks. Who wants to give a wrong answer in class? Who wants to be viewed by others as unintelligent? Who chooses an easy A rather than risk a B in a more challenging class? Students often choose the easier assignment when given choices just for this reason. Risk taking is a healthy part of a differentiated classroom, one where all students are learning in their Zone of Proximal Development (Vygotsky, 1978), wherein students are appropriately challenged so they must reach to learn.

One of the issues behind the lack of risk taking is the idea of a fixed mindset (Dweck, 2006), as discussed in Chapter 2. Dweck (2006), the cognitive psychologist behind the mindset concept, explained: "Success is about being your best self, not about being better than others; failure is an opportunity, not a condemnation; effort is the key to success" (p. 44). Educators must be very intentional about developing a growth mindset in their students, one that encourages taking academic risks. Ricci (2013) said:

> An educator's mindset directly influences how a child feels about him- or herself and how he or she views him- or herself as a learner. A child's mindset directly affects how he or she faces academic challenges. A child with a growth mindset perseveres even in the face of barriers. A child with a fixed mindset may give up easily and not engage in the learning process. (p. 4)

An effectively differentiated classroom must support risk taking and maintain high expectations for all stakeholders.

The responsibility for addressing learners' needs falls primarily on the classroom teacher. That teacher must maintain high expectations tailored to individual students in order to remove the learning ceiling for all students, including those who are gifted and talented. They must provide challenge to all. They must also encourage intellectual risk taking. These combine powerfully to help establish an optimum classroom climate for learning, especially when the teacher has high expectations for herself.

A DIFFERENTIATED CLASSROOM GENERATES OPENNESS

An excellent teacher must also be open to other things. The term *open* sounds vague, but it is meant to be all encompassing. For example, an excellent educator must be open to a differentiated classroom—one wherein students may be learning different concepts in different ways at different times. To what else does an excellent teacher need to be open?

New ideas. Even though Mrs. Revich has been in a primary classroom for more than 20 years, her enthusiasm for new ideas has never waned. If she wants her students to embrace new thoughts, experiences, and ideas, she knows how critical it is for her to lead the way. So, she volunteers to lead a book study group with other teachers who want to learn about differentiation of thinking and learning in today's world (Cash, 2011). She eagerly awaits her turn to attend conferences specializing in technology or reading strategies. Mrs. Revich carefully selects her professional development opportunities so that she is challenged with fresh approaches to teaching her content or recent research that will assist her in helping her students have continuous learning. She fully embraces the concept of being open to new curricular ideas, strategies, tools, resources, and research.

This openness impacts the learning that goes on in multiple ways—from what is being learned to how it is being learned. But, perhaps the most important impact is that students learn to be open to new ideas as well.

The idea that assessment drives instruction. Assessment is the cornerstone of instruction. In fact, it is so critical to a differentiated classroom that two chapters are devoted to it (Chapter 4 for preassessment and Chapter 10 for product assessment). Preassessment, when individual and written, prescribes the differentiation for the students. For example, if the preassessment contains content knowledge and understanding of concepts, the teacher can then provide differentiation for those students who aren't yet ready to learn the content, the students who are ready to learn at that level, and the students who have already mastered the content. Preassessment informs instruction. Formative assessment provides checkpoints throughout the unit or lesson. It encourages the educator to rethink the learning experiences and teaching processes in order to best address student needs. It is continuous. Summative assessment examines achievement—were the learning goals met and to what extent? It is often the grade that goes in the gradebook—the assessment *of* learning (Chappius, Stiggins, Arter, & Chappius, 2005). Assessment *for* learning occurs when "teachers use the classroom assessment process and the continuous flow of information about student achievement that it provides in order to advance, not merely check on, student learning" (Stiggins, 2002, p. 5). Bottom line: Effective differentiation is impossible in a classroom that does not base instruction on assessment.

Physical settings. When a teacher is accustomed to whole-group learning or direct instruction, sometimes the physical changes of a differentiated classroom can be overwhelming. Students may be clustered around tables, or desks may be abandoned as students scatter on the floor. The classroom may very well be a hub of activity and purposeful discussion. A corner of the room may be overflowing with supplies. In fact, the classroom may be noisier or filled with more movement than a traditional classroom would be. Instead of having all students sitting at their desks taking notes, teachers can expect a variety of activities: one group could be researching on the computer, while perhaps another group debates, and yet another builds a project.

Teachers' strengths. As educators, we all have our areas of passion, our niches. Ideally, if we are middle school and secondary educators (and even some intermediate teachers who departmentalize), we teach in this area. Primary and elementary educators may spend a portion of each day in a subject of intense interest, but other parts of the day are devoted to subjects that may not fall into their specialty areas. Likewise, a secondary English teacher who earned a master's degree in British literature may find himself teaching an American literature class, while the World War II expert spends her day in economics and geography classes. In short, regardless of the reason, we sometimes find ourselves just one step ahead of our students—and at times, we find ourselves one or two steps behind a student. This is where openness comes into play in the classroom climate.

Teachers must be open to the fact that we all have areas of strengths and weaknesses, and that *all* includes teachers. So, take advantage of that freshman who knows Greco-Roman myths thoroughly. Her source of knowledge can greatly enrich the class if allowed. Encourage the third-grade scholar of Native

Americans to share his experiences, even if that means a contradiction of what you thought you knew. It can be such a positive experience for a student to share her knowledge with others; it is not bragging or an attempt to make the teacher look bad when it's genuine enthusiasm for a subject. When you as the instructional leader are open to others and their knowledge, then you are modeling that openness for your students. You may be the guide on the side as you learn with students rather than the sage on the stage. It's a win-win situation.

Move beyond what they already know. An integral part of any European History AP class is World War II. Mr. McCoy carefully studies both state and national standards, plus the recommended materials for the AP Exam. (Remember those questions leading to differentiation from Chapter 1: Planning Question—What do I want all students to know, understand, and be able to do?) He creates an interesting, informative unit that should prove challenging to his students. He then preassesses. (Preassessing Question—Who already knows, understands, and/or can use the content or demonstrate the skill? Who needs additional support in order to know, understand, and/or demonstrate the skills?) He discovers that not only does Tabitha possess in-depth knowledge of all of the essential elements of the unit, but that she also burns with an intense passion for the subject matter. After talking with her, he realizes that she has a keen interest in aviation during the war but has not yet found time to explore it. (Differentiating Question—What can I do for him, her, or them so they make continuous progress and extend their learning?) Mr. McCoy and Tabitha decide upon an independent study focusing on aviation in World War II. Tabitha researches her topic while the others learn the causes for the war and who was fighting whom. She develops a Prezi using video clips and animation (new tools for her) while the rest of the class studies the battles. She then presents her project, emphasizing the critical role of warfare in the sky. By the end of the unit, everyone has learned something, including Tabitha.

Remember that the goal is continuous progress. It's impossible to have continuous progress if the material has already been mastered. Once we're open to the idea that students might already know the material, we move forward in our thinking. That allows learners to move forward as well.

Pace of instruction. Mrs. Hack quickly realizes that three of her seven fourth graders grouped on grade level in math are able to move at a much faster pace (the remaining 21 students in the class are being taught on third- or fifth-grade math levels). In fact, she discovers that these three only need a limited introduction to a new concept before they are able to work problems on their own. She also determines that working four challenging problems is more effective than working all the odd problems on the page. She considers moving them to the fifth-grade group, but Mrs. Hack realizes they aren't ready. Her solution? She groups these three students together, and they are ready to begin fifth-grade math by winter break. Because she is open to the idea that students learn at different paces, these young people are able to learn at their own speed.

Some young people only need to hear an idea once before they understand it. Others need three or even 10 repetitions. Being open to that difference encourages us to make accommodations for it. What happens to the student who understands it with the first explanation but is required to sit through eight more explanations with the rest of the class?

Student choice. Motivation increases dramatically when students are allowed to make choices. Choices include content, activities, assessment, products, or even working situations. When those options have been carefully prescribed and intentionally developed according to needs, interests, or abilities, then continuous learning occurs. Differentiating with Bloom's taxonomy (see Chapter 6) and the Think-Tac-Toe tool (see Chapter 8) helps incorporate student choice. If you as an instructor are open to student choice, then your students' motivation and achievement are sure to increase. Allowing students to make choices within limits often improves student behavior, too.

Teaching With Love and Logic, a work by Fay and Funk (1995), explores that concept. In fact, one of their key principles in their pedagogy is *shared control*:

> [It] meets a basic need we all seem to have for feeling some power and autonomy. Teachers who recognize this can learn to give kids what they need in ways that do not violate the teaching process. Classrooms with shared control are more than just happier places when compared to classrooms that involve daily power struggles. They provide an environment in which learning can more readily take place and teachers have less stress. (p. 155)

One way to promote this shared control is through choices. Fay and Funk (1995) devoted an entire section of their book to the idea of choice within limits. One of our favorite passages describes part of Fay's idea of self-concept:

> I would give kids lots of opportunities to use their individual abilities, interests, and learning styles in their academic learning. This would require planning a number of ways for them to demonstrate their skill mastery, devising as many ways for them to learn as I could think of, and letting the kids decide for themselves what ways would be best for them. *There is no question of academic integrity. The goal would be to demonstrate that they could learn a particular concept. How they demonstrated this would be their decision. Kids fly on their strengths* [italics added]. (Fay & Funk, 1995, pp. 209, 211)

Those last sentences are emphasized because that's student choice in a nutshell. Intentional student choices don't simply motivate kids and give them ownership in their learning; such choices also develop positive self-concepts for the students and prevent discipline issues. After all, Fay and Funk's (1995) work centers around classroom management. Sounds like an all-around winner, doesn't it?

Student input. As a writing teacher, Mrs. Wang knows the critical role that spelling plays in a piece of communication. Therefore, each week she compiles vocabulary words that students will work with throughout the week. In fact, on Mondays students define the words for homework. On Tuesdays they write the words five times each, on Wednesdays they use the words in sentences, and on Thursdays they create puzzles. All students take the vocabulary test on Fridays. She feels this structured approach provides optimal learning for all. After 2 weeks of this, third grader Stacy begins having problems with her homework at home. Each evening becomes a battle of wills as her mother and father encourage (and then force) her to complete her work. Often they spend more than an hour at the kitchen table—and Stacy is not the only one ending up in tears. The problem: Stacy already knows most of the words. It frustrates her to write words five times each—words she can already spell on Monday. "This is stupid!" and "But, I already know this!" are combated with short lectures on work ethic and responsibility. Finally, exasperated, Stacy goes to Mrs. Wang and explains the situation and her frustration. Mrs. Wang, instead of being defensive, listens to Stacy. That evening she looks at her resources and stumbles across Susan Winebrenner's (2001) work that offers ideas on just this topic. Her solution is simple. On Monday, Mrs. Wang gives out the words orally. She then uncovers the written list on the board, and students check their own work. The children who already know the words are able to select words they do not know. On Mondays, while most of the class defines Mrs. Wang's words, Stacy (and others) define the words they don't know. On Tuesdays they write their own words five times each and so on. Friday is test day. Stacy pairs with another student who also found his own words to give each other the spelling test. Frustration lessens and learning increases—all because Mrs. Wang really listened to her students. Sometimes we turn deaf ears to students, especially if we are expecting complaints. But, when we respect students enough to really listen to them, positive changes happen.

Unconventional ways to learn. Not all learners need 30 drills to learn a math concept. Some students may learn it after only five, while others may need 50 repetitions. In that same math class, there may be some gifted children and young people who cannot show their work—it's all done in their heads. To be forced to artificially create a structure could be frustrating and even detrimental. Not every student must take copious notes in U.S. history class in order to do well on the test. Some may listen, sketch random notes, and set the curve on the test. Others may not only need to take notes, but also may need to borrow someone else's in order to have all the necessary material to learn. Moreover, some students will learn about the elements of matter in a more lasting way if they can learn through discovery, not through teacher-led lessons. The point here is that you as the instructional leader must be open to unconventional ways of learning, and you must not only celebrate that, but provide opportunities for it to occur.

Routines and procedures simplify instruction. One of the most intimidating components of a differentiated classroom is the management of it. Teachers often question themselves: How do I get students started on different learning experiences at the same time? How do I keep people on task? What if one group finishes early or late? How do I keep track of who's doing what? How can I organize materials? The questions abound, but so do the answers. In fact, Chapter 9 explores the management of a differentiated classroom.

Well-developed lesson plans do not necessarily equate with effectively differentiated learning experiences. It is vitally important to design procedures and routines for dealing with issues such as multiple groups and grading; it is just as important for students to understand these expectations. And the earlier they embrace these, the better. Practicing desk or chair placement for various groupings, for example, allows for smooth transitions and ease in differentiating. Tips and strategies in Chapter 9 will assist educators in establishing routines and procedures.

When routines and procedures are established and practiced, when instruction is based on assessment, when appropriately high expectations and risk taking are encouraged, and when diversity is celebrated and supported, a foundation is created that develops two very important components of a differentiated classroom: a community of learners and excellence in teaching. Excellence in teaching was explored in the earlier discussion of high expectations, but the concept of a community of learners warrants further thought.

The idea of community. When students readily acknowledge diversity in their class and realize that learning experiences will tap into that diversity to enhance learning, they become more than a class of individual learners. They become a learning community. This sense of community provides the foundation for differentiated learning. Not only do students realize that each of them is an individual with different interests, strengths, experiences, and levels of readiness, but they also understand that together, they and their fellow classmates create an environment that values and supports its members as they work toward the common goal of continuous progress for all. They feel a responsibility toward each other.

This concept of community is acknowledged to be an integral part of the differentiated classroom. Beasley (2009) included the concept of community in her definition of differentiated instruction: It "is a proactively planned, interdependent system marked by a positive community of learners, focused high-quality curriculum, ongoing assessment, flexible instructional arrangements, [and] respectful tasks" (slide 2).

CONCLUDING THOUGHTS

Once teachers are able to establish classrooms that generate openness, maintain high expectations, and respect diversity, real differentiation can begin. In order for students to feel safe in this environment (because it is so atypical for them), this climate must be intentionally consistent. When presented with a choice of product to show what they have learned, students are able to trust that they can incorporate their individuality and creativity in that product. It is a safe environment for self-expression and thought. Because they are prepared for this climate from the beginning of the school year, they know what to expect, and they know what to count on.

This predictable climate allows students to pack their learning suitcases for the year. Just as surely as we take along a rain jacket for a springtime weekend in Seattle because we are aware of the wet climate, students pack risk taking and high expectations to prepare for their year-long adventure in a differentiated classroom.

IMPORTANT TAKE-AWAYS

- Establishing a climate for effective differentiation must be intentional and deliberate.
- A differentiated classroom develops and supports diversity, high expectations, and openness.
- A differentiated classroom develops and supports challenge, appropriately high expectations, and risk taking for all students, including those with gifts and talents.
- A differentiated classroom develops and supports instruction through assessment. Assessment guides learning experiences for students.
- A differentiated classroom develops and supports instruction through procedures and routines. Be sure to establish procedures and routines, then practice them early in the school year.
- A differentiated classroom develops and supports a community of learners.
- A differentiated classroom develops and supports excellence in teaching.

CHAPTER 4

Preassessment

Who Already Understands It or Can Do It?

> Diagnostic assessment (preassessment) is as important to teaching as a physical exam is to prescribing appropriate medical regimens.
> —Carol A. Tomlinson and Jay McTighe

In order for differentiation to be effective, assessment must be an ongoing part of teaching and learning. It is so important to ask students what they already know, understand, and can do, as this question provides the starting point for learning. Students can't learn what they already know and can do, so answering that question is essential if students want to avoid spinning their wheels. Preassessment, the second of the three key questions introduced in Chapter 1, is sandwiched between planning and differentiation. It is especially critical for you to preassess so that you can determine your students' levels of readiness to proceed with the new unit of study. Julian Stanley (2000) summed up the goal of education in the title of his article "Helping Students Learn Only What They Don't Already Know." This title highlights the purpose of continuous progress: teaching students content and skills that they need to master but haven't yet done so.

PLANNING: THE NECESSARY STEP BEFORE PREASSESSMENT

The first key question to think about before differentiating is "What do I want students to know, understand, and be able to do?"

Educators following best practices must plan their instructional objectives and student outcomes carefully. These objectives reflect the state and national standards, core content, and program of studies (these items may be referred to by different names in your state). If a teacher has not planned what she is teaching in a unit, then she certainly cannot guide her students to the desired outcomes, nor can she assess who already knows most or all of the material or has mastered the objectives/student outcomes, nor can she determine who will need additional support to reach the outcomes established for the class. She soon becomes more of a disciplinarian than a teacher.

Once objectives are created, you, the professional educator, must then ascertain who already knows the information or can perform the skill. You need to match the preassessment with your content, your students, and your own teaching style. Preassessment will tell you where to start with students in your class, and the starting point may differ for students and/or clusters of students.

PREASSESSMENT

The second key question leading to differentiation focuses on preassessment: "Who already knows, understands, and/or can use the content or demonstrate the skills? Who needs additional support in order to know, understand, and/or demonstrate the skills?"

Preassessment makes differentiation strategies defensible. That bears repeating: *Preassessment makes differentiation strategies defensible.* How can we possibly differentiate to match curricula to individual levels of readiness, interests, and strengths if we have no idea what those levels of readiness, interests, and strengths are? Without information to document the starting place for students, it is impossible to inform parents as to why their children are engaged in different learning experiences. Without preassessment information, how do we justify to learners why Stefano's group is doing something different from Kelly's group? But, with preassessment data, instructional strategies can be matched to individual levels of readiness, interests, and strengths; moreover, the reasoning for doing so is evident. Preassessment is a necessary step if instruction is to be meaningful and motivating to students; it establishes the starting point for learning experiences, so students can make continuous progress. And, remember, that's what teaching is all about—kids learning continuously.

Students can't learn something they already know, and that's one reason preassessment plays such a critical role in teaching. *Meeting the Needs of High-Ability and High-Potential Learners in the Middle Grades*, the joint position statement of the National Middle School Association and the National Association for Gifted Children (2004), included a section on assessment:

> Ongoing assessment is critical to informing classroom practice. Pre-assessment, in-process assessment, and post assessment should give learners consistent opportunity to demonstrate their knowledge, understanding, and skills related to topics of study. Assessments related to student readiness, interests, perspectives, and learning preferences provide educators with a consistently emerging understanding of each learner's needs in the classroom. Middle level educators should use data from such assessments to modify teaching and learning plans to ensure that each student—including those who already perform well beyond expectations—have consistent opportunities to extend their abilities. (para. 6)

What this statement indicates as crucial for middle school students is equally important for students in elementary and high schools. Assessment must inform instructional decisions. It is that professional judgment that guides instruction and forms the intent of why you're teaching what to whom and in what ways. Differentiated learning experiences are essential if *all* of your students, including those who need more time and more basic content and those who need less time and more complex content, are going to make continuous progress. Ongoing assessment will document that all students are making continuous progress and that they are learning on a day-to-day basis.

RECORD KEEPING: A MUST!

The purpose of preassessment is to *document* the need for differentiated learning experiences. It's evidence; it's proof that you have not made learning decisions based on whimsy. Preassessment can be done in myriad ways, from open discussion to pen-and-paper tests. However, preassessment methods shown in this chapter will be ones that individual students complete. Defensible differentiation requires the teacher to have a record of what the students know and are able to do before the unit begins. In short, the techniques we share all require something on paper (to be kept and filed for future reference) so that you are accountable for your decisions. It's not that you're paranoid and expect rioting parents or suspicious colleagues. It's simply because if you have students working on different content or learning in different ways, we need to ensure that the intent of our teaching isn't just making things different—it's providing the best match of content, process, and product to each student.

The examples presented in this chapter will provide evidence to make differentiated learning experiences defensible. Remember, the preassessment is kept in the student's file to document progress. Keeping a record of the preassessment facilitates communication of the learning progress between you and your students, as well as between you and parents. How exciting it is for students and parents to see the progress they make when you compare preassessments with final products, especially when you do this over time!

WHAT STUDENTS NEED TO KNOW BEFORE YOU PREASSESS

Two things that students should know provide the rationale for preassessing. The first of these important messages is that they are not expected to know all of the information or demonstrate all of the required skills. The preassessment takes a reading on where instruction should begin for students. The second message is that the preassessment gives students the opportunity to show what they know and indicate their interests in the topic to be studied as well as their strengths. Their strengths often indicate a student's preferred way of learning. Of course, no grades are attached to the preassessment.

PREASSESSMENT AS A TIME SAVER (NO, WE'RE NOT KIDDING)

Time is a precious commodity in a classroom. One reason many educators are hesitant to preassess is because they feel they can't lose those few minutes of instruction time to preassessment. But, what they don't see is that preassessment actually can save valuable learning time. The National Research Center on the Gifted and Talented conducted the Curriculum Compacting Study (Reis et al., 1993); the study title was "Why Not Let High Ability Students Start School in January?" because the researchers found that teachers could eliminate as much as 50% of the regular curriculum for the gifted students, and the students did equally well between the treatment and control groups on achievement tests. Students who already know, understand, and can do most or all of the unit objectives waste so much of their valuable learning time when forced to sit through a unit they've already mastered. Through preassessment, these students can buy time to continue learning the content at a more complex level and accelerated pace. If the students already can demonstrate mastery, they are still able to continue learning and are not held back because not everyone is ready to move on. Once again, preassessment paves the way for continuous progress, and that's what learning is all about. For students who need additional support to reach the objectives or outcomes, you will be prepared to provide that support if you know it is needed. Preassessment results will inform you of that need.

Is preassessment really worth my time? "YES!!!" was the response of a teacher who used preassessment information to differentiate instruction for her students. She saw that preassessment allowed for continuous progress, and it kept students from being "taught" things that they already knew.

The most important step is the first one—getting started. One must try preassessing and using the results in order to know the impact preassessment can have on learning.

PREASSESSMENT STRATEGIES

Various preassessment strategies provide you with information about what the student knows, understands, and is able to do prior to teaching the unit. Of the myriad ways to preassess, the ones described in this section include the following:

- end-of-the-previous-unit assessment,
- end-of-the-unit assessment,
- T-W-H and K-W-L Charts,
- mind map,
- the five most difficult questions,
- open-ended question(s),
- interest and experience inventory,
- Punnett Square Sheet, and
- the adapted Situational Leadership model.

Interest inventories (see Chapter 3) provide another means of preassessing—this time preassessing the interests of students.

END-OF-THE-PREVIOUS-UNIT ASSESSMENT

With learning material that builds on concepts and skills, the end-of-the-previous-unit test can provide the needed information about what your students know, understand, and are able to do. Of course, when the content and skills to be taught in the new unit depend upon the knowledge and skills that were assessed in the previous unit, you are a step ahead and can use information you already have. Such assessment data can inform you as you plan learning experiences that match the level of understanding and achievement of individual students and clusters of students. Using the information from the end-of-the-previous-unit assessment can direct your instructional decisions, but only if the new unit is built on the previous learning.

END-OF-THE-UNIT ASSESSMENT

End-of-the-unit tests are planned to measure learning. Is it really okay to use the assessment you have planned as the culminating experience of the unit as your preassessment? Won't that give students an advantage on that assessment? Well, if your objectives are clearly the learning focus throughout the entire unit, then the point is moot. There should be no great mystery as to what students are learning. Go ahead and use the final assessment as the preassessment. If a student already knows 80% of the material, there is no need for him to do it again. He's already mastered it. Let that sink in. A student does not need to participate in learning concepts she's already learned.

Using the assessment planned for the conclusion of the unit, you provide the opportunity for students to demonstrate what they know, understand, and can do in relation to the unit prior to even beginning it. Without the preassessment, you assume that how well the students do on the end-of-the-unit assessment is a result of your teaching the unit; on the other hand, students may be able to meet all or part of the unit goals before the unit begins, and you weren't even aware of it. All of those A's on the unit exam on the different states of matter could have been A's before you even taught the material. The time for those students (and you) has been irretrievably lost. What valuable information it is to know what students know, understand, or are able to do before beginning the unit.

T-W-H AND K-W-L CHARTS

The T-W-H Chart (see Figure 4.1) provides a terrific starting point for teaching a unit. It is a variation of the well-known K-W-L Chart—what the students know about the topic, what they want to know about the topic, and what they learned about the topic. The T-W-H Chart takes a different approach. The T prompts the student to write down what they *think* they know about the topic. Perhaps the T rather than the K will encourage more students to share information that they have or that they think is correct. The W asks students to tell what they *want* to learn about the topic, and the H permits them to say *how* they want to learn about the topic. The T-W-H Chart is an easy-to-use form to preassess individual students on whatever topic you are planning to teach. Information from the T-W-H Chart can guide instructional decisions that lead to highly motivated students learning new material and skills. What's more, you may pick up a great idea or two from their suggestions for what and how they want to learn. See Figure 4.2 for a completed T-W-H-Chart.

Figures 4.3 and 4.4 show two completed K-W-L Charts (in case you prefer the K-W-L Chart) that report what Sarah and Alex know about electricity, what they want to learn about the topic, and how they want to go about learning more about it. Each question provides information that will help the teacher plan the unit. For example, Sarah knows quite a bit about the basics of electricity and would prefer to work on group projects to learn more about the topic. Although Alex's information in the K column seems scant, his remarks in the W column indicate a high level of thought and knowledge of the basics. He would like to learn about electricity by doing experiments. Preferences can provide you with valuable information for grouping students. This preassessment also will tell you who has studied electricity before and who is experiencing it for the first time. Figure 4.5 explores a fifth grader's understanding of the Civil War.

T - W - H CHART

Topic/Unit______________________ Name______________________

What do you **T**hink about this topic?	What do you **W**ant to learn about this topic?	**H**ow do you want to learn about this topic?

Figure 4.1. T-W-H chart sample. From *Teacher's Survival Guide: Gifted Education* (p. 91) by J. L. Roberts and J. R. Boggess, 2011, Waco, TX: Prufrock Press. Copyright 2011 by Prufrock Press. Reprinted with permission.

T – W – H CHART

Topic/Unit 13 Colonies

Name Caroline

What do you **T**hink about this topic?	What do you **W**ant to learn about this topic?	**H**ow do you want to learn about this topic?
I think it would be a very intresting topic to learn more about. One thing I already know it is that it was like the 13 colonies were a new world for the colonist.	Two more things I would like to learn about are one, in what order were they formed? Two, what would the every day life be like for a girl my age?	Feild trips and renactments ☺

Figure 4.2. Completed T-W-H Chart

K – W – L CHART

Topic/Unit Electricity

Name Sarah

What do you **K**now about this topic?	What do you **W**ant to learn about this topic?	How do you want to **L**earn about this topic?
∘circuits ∘circuits need to be complete in order to work ∘Electricity is the transferring of energy ∘needs energy source ∘conductors of energy are metals except aluminum and another metal I can't remember	∘I want to know what that other metal is not a conductor ∘how to create a circuit ∘why a circuit has to be complete ∘what do the positives and negatives mean on a battery	I would like to learn about this topic w/ projects. Like making a circuit. I would preferr to do this in a group.

Figure 4.3. K-W-L: Electricity (Sarah).

K-W-L CHART

Topic/Unit Electricity

Name alex

What do you Know about this topic?	What do you Want to learn about this topic?	How do you want to Learn about this topic?
The circits Batteries	how it works why wire is made of copper whats inside a battery	by doing expiriments with wire and a battery

Figure 4.4. K-W-L: Electricity (Alex).

K-W-L CHART

Topic/Unit Civil war

Name Zach

What do you Know about this topic?	What do you Want to learn about this topic?	How do you want to Learn about this topic?
•North and south sides •main Generals: Robert E. lee, Ulyses S. Grant •North had factorys so more Machinery •South had Plantations, good Shooters. •clothing: Kepis, over coats, coats, pants, wool socks, boots •weapons: swords, revolvers, cannons, muskets.	•learn about weapontry •learn about different soldiers •learn about Generals lives •what did they eat? •where did they sleep? •How many men per Company?	•group Reenactments •projects •feild trips •going to Battlefeilds •Read Books about the civil war

Figure 4.5. K-W-L: Civil War (Zach).

MIND MAP

A mind map (Buzan, 1983) offers the opportunity for students to record what they know in a visual manner. A mind map is like an organic outline (see Figure 4.6). It allows you to add new ideas without starting over; it is organic in the sense that it can grow. This strategy is based on brain research and depends on techniques that enhance visual memory. Color, lines, capitalization, and connections all help encode the information in the brain.

The key concept—written in capital letters and a distinct color—forms the center of the visual presentation. Lines attach to the central concept, each representing an aspect of the concept or a category related to it. Students place one word on each line with all words written in color and in capital letters. No more than one word is placed on a line, and all lines connect to a central concept. Students who appreciate visual presentations and like to economize on words have a perfect strategy for showing you what they know and understand about a topic.

When Nick was asked to complete a mind map on the stages of child development, it became evident that he had quite an understanding even before the unit was taught—an indication that he would definitely need modifications (see Figure 4.7).

THE FIVE MOST DIFFICULT QUESTIONS

The Five Most Difficult Questions (Winebrenner, 1992) is a preassessment strategy that allows students who are ready to do so to move ahead with their learning. You simply determine the five most difficult questions that you want students to be able to answer by the conclusion of the unit (whether that be the most challenging improper fraction equations or the explication of theme, characterization, and author's style in a short story). You then provide the opportunity for all students who think they are ready to answer the questions before the unit starts to answer the five most difficult questions. This strategy works well with skills. In a math class, for example, ask the five hardest questions in the unit you will be teaching. If a student gets four out of five correct, then she doesn't need to study that material at the same level of complexity that the rest of the class will study it. The strategy also allows students to demonstrate what they understand and are able to explain, apply, or provide examples of the concept or topic.

All students would not engage in this form of preassessment; rather, those who want to demonstrate what they know, understand, and are able to do can earn the opportunity to continue learning at appropriately challenging levels. This allows the students who can demonstrate mastery the opportunity for continuous progress, which encourages lifelong learning. For example, the reward for demonstrating mastery of the material prior to beginning the unit is the opportunity to engage in independent study or some form of challenging, differentiated learning experience. Winebrenner (1992) recommended that the grade should be based

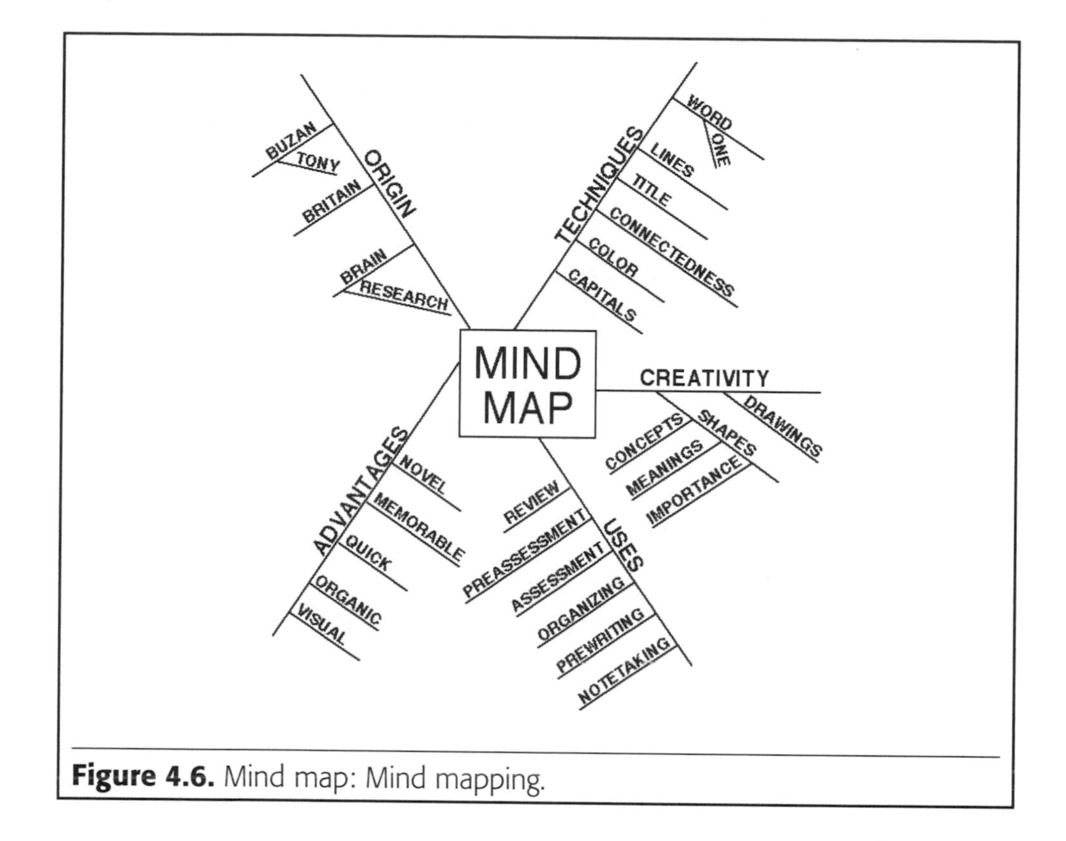

Figure 4.6. Mind map: Mind mapping.

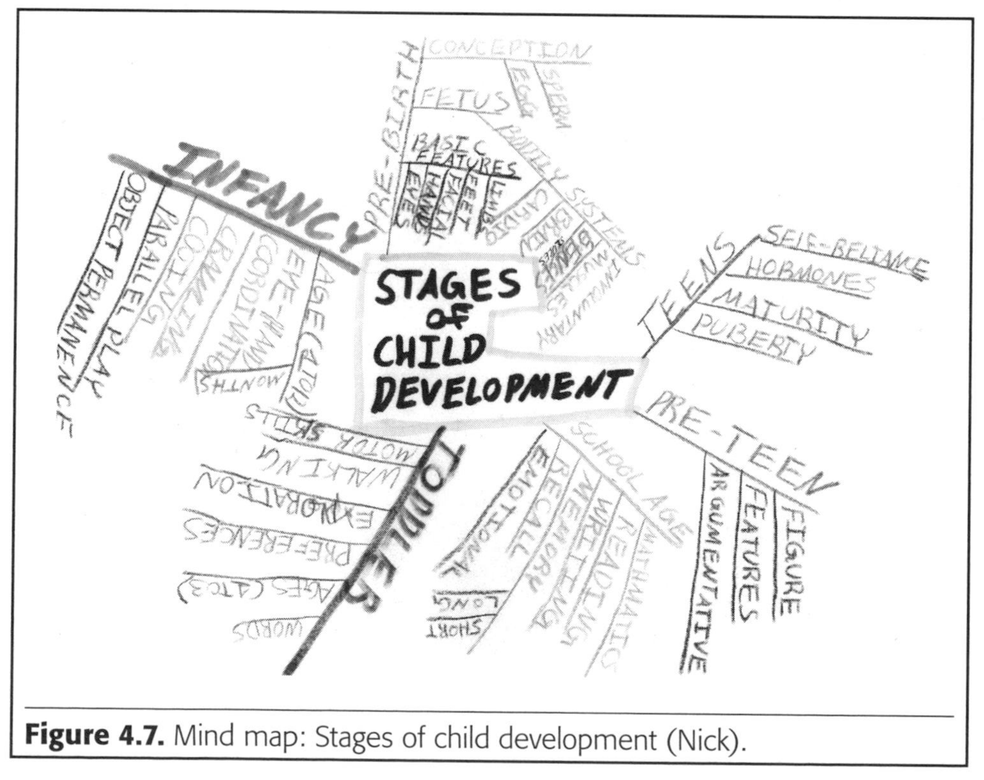

Figure 4.7. Mind map: Stages of child development (Nick).

on "testing out" of the unit; the goal for the student is to free her up to engage in an academically challenging learning experience on the same basic content but at a complex, in-depth level. No one wins when students are not challenged by new material to understand and apply. Everyone wins when each student makes continuous progress.

OPEN-ENDED QUESTION OR QUESTIONS

Even though our goal for preassessment is something written so that we can justify our instruction, it does not always have to be the printed preassessment in the teacher's manual (although those are handy to use and important to document the starting point). Before you begin a new unit on photosynthesis, for instance, you could instruct students to jot down what they know about the topic. A quick skim over the papers helps the teacher put them into three piles; those who write a page (complete with little drawings) go in one pile, while those saying "photo-what?" go in another, with the ones who are in between the two extremes placed in a third pile. You quickly have three groups who demonstrate very different levels of readiness to engage in a study of photosynthesis.

An open-ended question can provide the prompt for students to demonstrate what they know and understand about a topic. Open-endedness allows each student to respond at whatever level he understands the concept or topic. A student's response may range from no knowledge of the subject, to complex and in-depth knowledge and understanding. Obviously, these open-ended responses provide valuable information to you as you plan the learning experiences that will allow each student or cluster of students to make continuous progress.

The "what" is the concept or topic that you are teaching. It could be World War I in a U.S. history class, figurative language in an English class, or the structure of atoms in science. Just think about the difference it would make to you if a student or students already knew quite a bit about the concept or topic that you were preparing to teach. This presents an opportunity to allow him, her, or them to study the same concept or topic at a much more complex level. At the conclusion of the unit, the student can share what was learned with the class. Everyone is studying the same concept but just at different levels of complexity.

VENN DIAGRAM

A Venn diagram is familiar to educators, especially in its two-oval format. One use for the Venn diagram that may seem unusual is to use it as a means for preassessing students in a class. In its two-, three-, or four-oval format, the Venn provides a ready template for preassessing what students know about the concept/topic prior to teaching the unit of study. Figure 4.8. offers a filled-in example of a preassessment on weather.

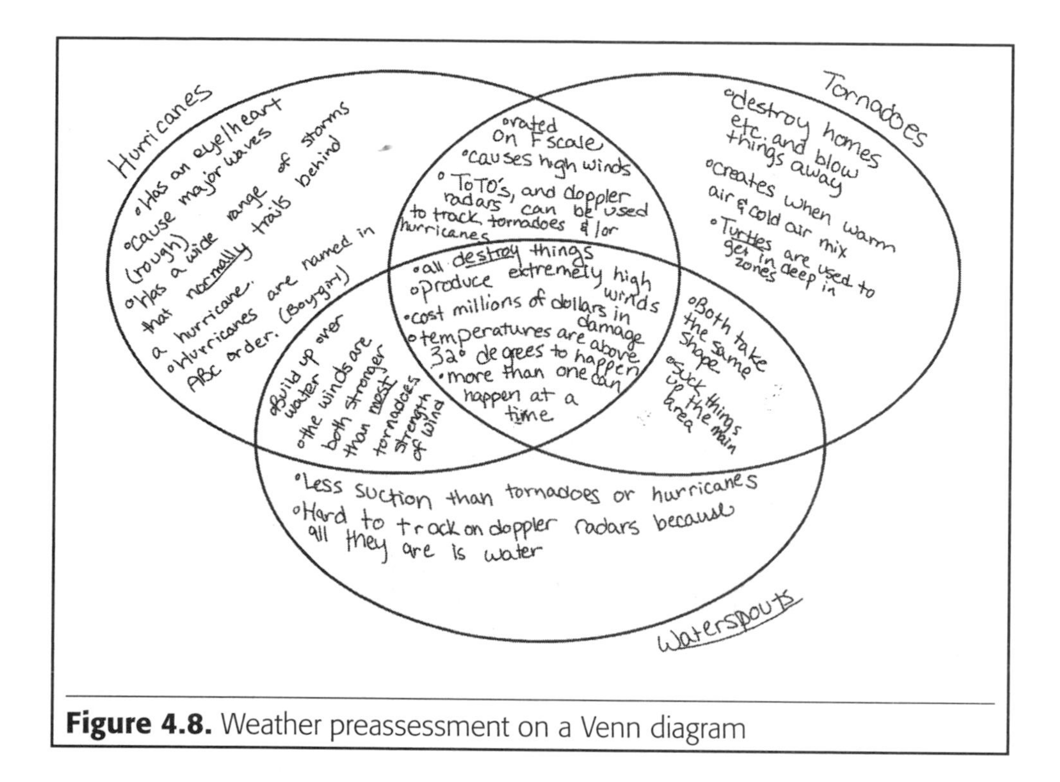

Figure 4.8. Weather preassessment on a Venn diagram

INTEREST AND EXPERIENCE INVENTORY

Finding out what students would choose to do and what experience they have had doing it can be instrumental in planning learning experiences that will be meaningful and motivating. This information can be obtained from an interest inventory. You decide what information would be most useful to you as you assign learning experiences to specific students. Take, for example, the inventory in Figure 4.9. Teacher Jennifer Chaplin designed this for a middle school unit on the Bill of Rights. Responses would let her provide the optimum opportunity for her students to learn about the Bill of Rights, with each student focusing on the freedom that is of greatest interest to him or her. Figure 4.10 provides another example of an interest and experience inventory on the Great Depression for a class project. This inventory provides valuable information for the teacher and makes possible a learning experience that capitalizes on each student's interest in the topic as well as his experience with skills required to complete the product.

PUNNETT SQUARE

If you are embarking on a study of a concept, a ready-to-use preassessment is the Punnett Square Sheet. The four boxes of the Punnett Square in Figure 4.11 provide the space for students to provide the definition of the concept, an example and a nonexample of the concept, and additional information they know

STAND UP, SPEAK OUT: A FREEDOM OF SPEECH UNIT

Interest Inventory

THE GREAT AMERICAN DOCUMENT

Please check one:

- o I have studied the United States Constitution thoroughly.
- o I have studied the Constitution and would like to study it again.
- o I have never studied the Constitution but would like to.
- o I have never studied the Constitution and am really not that interested in it.

GREAT SPEAKERS

Circle the speaker that you would most like to investigate during this unit of study. These multimedia explorations will include nonfiction books, articles, video clips, and other various print and nonprint sources. Your exploration will be shared with the rest of the class in a presentation.

Speakers:	John F. Kennedy	Martin Luther King, Jr.
	Inaugural Address, 1961 Famous Line: "And so, my fellow Americans: ask not what your country can do for you—ask what you can do for your country."	I Have a Dream, 1963 Famous Line: "I have a dream that my four children will one day live in a nation where they will not be judged by the color of their skin but by the content of their character."

FIRST AMENDMENT ISSUES

Study the pamphlets given to you today. Which topic would you most be interested in studying for this unit? Number 1 through 4 below to show your interest (with 1 being the most interested in). If you have had any personal experiences with a First Amendment right that you'd be willing to share, please place a star beside it.

______ Freedom of Speech
______ Freedom of Religion
______ Freedom of Press
______ Freedom of Assembly

STUDENT SPEECHES

Please check all that apply:

- ❑ I have researched First Amendment issues.
- ❑ I have studied how to write a speech.
- ❑ I have written a speech.
- ❑ I have presented a speech in front of my classmates before.
- ❑ I have presented a speech for a competition before.

Figure 4.9. Interest inventory: Bill of Rights. *Note.* Used with permission by Jennifer Chaplin, middle school teacher.

The Great Depression Preassessment

Circle all that apply.

- I have heard of the Great Depression.
- I have read some about the Great Depression.
- I have talked with relatives about the Great Depression.
- I have not yet been interested in the Great Depression.

Circle the response that best describes your experience interviewing people to get information.

- I enjoy interviewing to learn.
- I have no experience interviewing for a project but think I would like to give it a try.
- I have interviewed for a project but would prefer getting information another way.

Circle the aspect of the Great Depression that most interests you.

- Life in your town during the Great Depression.
- The life of a hobo during the Great Depression.
- The stock market crash of 1929.
- Other? You suggest a topic related to the Great Depression in the United States.

Circle the final product that you would prefer to complete to showcase what you have learned.

- A radio show
- A series of illustrations or graphs to accompany a report
- A monologue
- Other? Specify.

Figure 4.10. The Great Depression preassessment. From "Preassessment: The Linchpin for Defensible Differentiation," by J. L. Roberts, 2013, *The Challenge, 24*, p. 10. Copyright 2010 The Center for Gifted Studies, Western Kentucky University. Reprinted with permission.

about the concept. The graphic organizer is ready for you to print off and use as a preassessment, no matter what the concept is. Doing this preassessment a week or 10 days before you embark on the study will provide you plenty of time to assess the results and plan for clustering students so that all students have opportunities to make continuous progress in their learning about the concept, whether it is theme, plot, and character in language arts or fractions, decimals, and percentages in mathematics.

SITUATIONAL LEADERSHIP MODEL

Many teachers may not realize that a leadership model could provide an easy way to preassess students, but it can. The Situational Leadership Model (Hersey & Blanchard, 1978) provides an interesting way for teachers to determine which

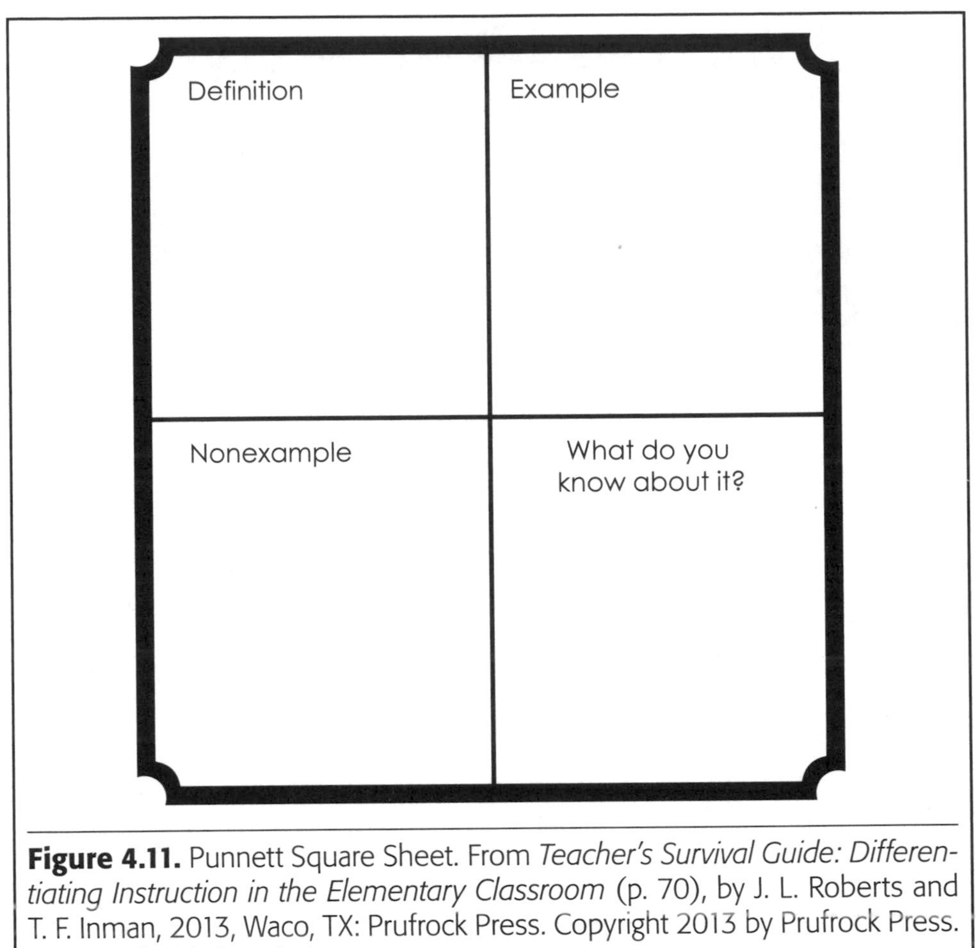

Figure 4.11. Punnett Square Sheet. From *Teacher's Survival Guide: Differentiating Instruction in the Elementary Classroom* (p. 70), by J. L. Roberts and T. F. Inman, 2013, Waco, TX: Prufrock Press. Copyright 2013 by Prufrock Press. Reprinted with Permission.

students have the experience and motivation to be treated in various ways in order to enhance learning. This model offers four leadership styles. These leadership styles (in this context they become teaching styles) can be matched to the student's level of experience with and willingness to learn about a particular topic or concept or the student's readiness for a learning experience.

The four teaching styles include:

- TS1 (Teaching Style 1)—The teacher is high in directive behavior and low in supportive behavior.
- TS2 (Teaching Style 2)—The teacher is high in both directive and supportive behavior.
- TS3 (Teaching Style 3)—The teacher is low in directive behavior and high in supportive behavior.
- TS4 (Teaching Style 4)—The teacher is low in both directive and supportive behavior.

The four teaching styles combine behaviors that are characterized as (1) directive or one-way communication (providing what to do, when to do it, and with whom to do it) and (2) supportive or two-way communication. Of course, two-way communication involves listening as well as talking. You can implement the four styles when you understand that each style is important for children who are at different levels of readiness to learn a specific topic. The four teaching styles are key to helping students take charge of their own learning. The goal of adapting situational leadership to teaching is to develop individuals who are responsible for their own learning; only then can they be lifelong learners.

Having the four teaching styles in your repertoire is key to developing young people into independent learners. If you are always needed to supply the direction for the task, when does the student who can provide the structure for the learning experience ever have a chance to develop independence as a learner? You are not mean or inconsiderate when you are low in supportive behavior or use one-way communication if that teaching style matches the student's readiness to reach the specific learning goal. What makes a teaching style appropriate is the match of the teaching style to the readiness of each student in order for her to take more responsibility for reaching the learning goal at the highest level. If you only use one or two of the styles, you will limit the development of students who need other styles to develop into independent learners. A teacher who has a repertoire of all four teaching styles in this model can use each teaching style when it is a match with the readiness of the student or students in order to enhance the opportunity for each to become lifelong learners.

Think of the missed opportunity when you tell students what to do and how to do it if they can supply that direction on their own. Or what happens to your students to whom you give directions and then leave alone to accomplish the task if they don't have the skills to do that successfully. Once again, you are the one who must be intentional. The results of preassessing your students can help you use the teaching styles that will develop your students into independent learners. Of course, that important step will not occur at one time in one way for all students in a class.

You can do a quick assessment of the students' readiness to complete the assignment or to learn the content. In the Situational Leadership Model, the readiness of a student is a combination of willingness and experience relevant to the student being able to complete the task. Readiness is task specific. Although the student may want to complete a PowerPoint presentation and has experience in creating one (which is a high level of readiness), he may have no experience with writing and performing a monologue. So, when the task or learning goal changes, the assessment of the readiness of the student will indicate a shift from Readiness Level 4 to Readiness Level 1, requiring a shift in teaching style if the student is to reach the goal at a high level of performance.

Readiness Level 1 (R1) describes the student who is new to the task. She has no experience with that task (learning objective) and may feel insecure. For example, the assignment is to do an independent study. She hasn't done an independent study before, so it is appropriate for the teacher to provide the structure for the learning experience or use the TS1 teaching style (high structure and low supportive behavior). As soon as the student develops confidence with the assignment, the teacher moves to TS2.

Readiness Level 2 (R2) describes the student who wants to do the task but has limited experience. The student needs the structure that the teacher provides for the learning experience, as well as two-way communication. With the independent study assignment, the teacher provides the necessary direction and answers any questions the student might have.

Readiness Level 3 (R3) describes the student who already knows how to do the task and who is able to supply the structure for it. The teacher can match R3 students with TS3, which is low in direction and high in supportive behaviors (two-way communication). R3 students also may know how to complete the task but just may not want to do it. In this case, the best chance of being successful is to open up two-way communication.

Readiness Level 4 (R4) describes the student who knows how to do the task and wants to do it. The TS4 style is the appropriate match for the R4 student on a particular task or learning experience. The teacher does not need to provide the structure for the independent study experience, for example, or high levels of two-way communication, because the student has the knowledge, experience, and the motivation to complete that particular assignment. Of course, TS4 doesn't mean abdicating responsibility for the student, but frequent two-way communication isn't necessary.

The Situational Leadership Model can help you as you move on to differentiating. You will have assessed for readiness levels using one of several preassessment measures in your repertoire. You will have assessed for willingness to learn as you have gleaned information about your students' interests and strengths and watched them as they get involved or are reluctant to get involved in learning tasks. Which ones do they do to the best of their abilities and which ones get surface attention or none at all? You will especially notice students who are unwilling to get involved. Opening up two-way communication with them is the secret to getting them motivated to engage in learning in your classroom.

READY FOR DIFFERENTIATION

Once you know what you want all students to know, understand, or be able to do, you must determine who already knows, understands, or can do it. The form of the preassessment isn't nearly as important as its utilization. Maybe your teaching style leans you toward a T-W-H Chart. Or, perhaps you are uncomfortable creating your own preassessment, so you use the end-of-unit test. One type of preassessment may fit one unit, whereas another works better with the next one. Perhaps you want to offer a variety of ways for students to show you what they know. For example, if you wanted to preassess your students on the responsibilities of the judicial branch before beginning a unit, you might offer students a choice of completing a mind map or answering an open-ended question. Either way, you would have the information you need to proceed. The preassessment itself—as long as it can be recorded—is totally secondary to what you do with it. Not only do you need to preassess, but you must also use those results in teaching the unit. That's where differentiation comes in.

The third key question leading to differentiation is "What can I do for him, her, or them so they can make continuous progress and extend their learning?" This focuses on your students who already have mastered what you have planned for the unit as well as students who will need extra support in order to master the learning outcome(s). Chapters 6–8 will describe basic differentiation strategies that will help you answer this important question.

IMPORTANT TAKE-AWAYS

- Preassessing students is the necessary step between planning and differentiating.
- You have numerous ways to preassess. Which one you use is up to you—the teacher and decision maker.
- The important consideration is that you use information from preassessment to differentiate.
- A written preassessment lets you document progress to communicate with the student and the parent.
- Preassessing what students know, understand, and can do actually saves time for you and for students.

CHAPTER 5

Tiering to Facilitate Continuous Progress

> In school, modifying or differentiating instruction for students of differing readiness and interests is also more comfortable, engaging, and inviting. One-size-fits-all instruction will inevitably sag or pinch—exactly as single-size clothing would—students who differ in need, even if they are chronologically the same age. —Carol A. Tomlinson

This book is about differentiating instruction with special emphasis on tiering learning experiences in order to facilitate students making continuous progress. Because the one-size-fits all approach to teaching a class of students misses students who are ready to move at a faster pace with more complex content as well as students who need additional time to learn the content, it is necessary for teachers to implement strategies that facilitate learning for students with a range of readiness levels, strengths, or interests in the topic being studied. Tiered assignments provide varying levels of difficulty, usually a minimum of three. The purpose of tiered assignments is to ensure that all students are learning about the topic being studied, no matter their starting points. Remember, continuous progress or learning on an ongoing basis is why students go to school.

So what does tiering mean when applied to classroom instruction? The Merriam-Webster's online dictionary (tier, n.d.) defines a *tier* as "a row, rank, or layer of articles; especially: one of two or more rows, levels, or ranks arranged one above another." When the term *tier* is applied to differentiating learning experiences, it refers to levels of learning experiences with increasing difficulty or complexity. The learning experiences are layered to match the levels of readiness, strengths, and interests of students. (Please note that we did not say with increasing amounts of work; differentiation and tiering do not mean more work—they mean different work.)

Kingore (2006) compares tiered instruction to a stairwell. Perhaps it works well to think of tiering as a stairway leading to ongoing learning.

> Tiered instruction is like a stairwell providing access within the large building called learning. The bottom story represents learning tasks for students with less readiness and fewer skills. The stairwell continues through enough levels to reach the appropriate challenge for advanced readiness students with very high skills and complex understanding. There isn't always a student working on every stairwell level as students progress through tiers of learning at different paces. Also, within each tier, there simultaneously can be multiple small-group activities presenting different ways to learn. Some floors in the stairwell even have multiple stairways as students access higher learning levels differently. (p. 5)

The analogy of tiering and the stairwell provides a visual to remember how tiering can enhance learning so that students studying the same concept are learning (reaching the top of the staircase) by different routes.

What does it mean to tier instruction? Adams and Pierce (2006) explain that tiered lessons "provide different paths toward understanding a particular concept. No matter which path the student takes, understanding the concept and the essential understanding (the big idea of a topic) should be the result" (p. 5). Heacox (2009) describes tiered assignments as having three levels: one that is on-target for students who are mastering grade-level standards, one for those who are more advanced in relation to this particular standard, and one for students who need additional support in order to master the standard. Heacox recommends starting with the learning experience designed for those mastering the standard and then modifying the learning experiences. Various specialists in education provide support for tiering instruction to ensure that all of the students are learning. The purpose of tiering is to ensure that all of the students are making continuous progress toward the learner outcomes.

Remember, a doctor doesn't prescribe a generic prescription that she gives to all patients regardless of their illness. She prescribes insulin for the diabetic but knows that is not the right match for the patient with strep throat. The diagnosis dictates the prescription. Neither should a teacher use the same assignment with all students who are in the third-grade math or the eighth-grade social studies class. Instead, teachers must differentiate learning experiences in order to facilitate all students making continuous progress. Tiering is one way to structure lessons to increase complexity and difficulty.

Tiered assignments match learning experiences to preassessment information in order to provide an appropriate level of challenge to each student. Selecting the appropriate tier for students is made easy when you preassess to determine who already knows the content or can demonstrate the skills—and at which levels. The appropriateness of assigning a particular tiered lesson to specific students is totally dependent on the match between what the student knows about the topic and the opportunity the learning experiences provide the student with to learn at an increasingly higher level. The purpose of the match is to facilitate all students making continuous progress. After all, the goal of school is to produce lifelong learners.

Learning experiences need to be challenging but not too challenging, not frustratingly challenging. It is useful to think about providing learning experiences that are challenging enough to have students thinking and working hard to successfully complete the assignment yet well within their capability to do so. Vygotsky (1978) described the Zone of Proximal Development as the distance between a student's independent level and the level at which he needs assistance. That is the optimal level of challenge that all students need.

Note that it is not the same level of challenge for all students but a level of challenge appropriate to provide rigor for all students; *rigor* is a relative term. It is the match of the learning experience to where the student or students provide evidence that they are ready to learn with regard to the content that the class is studying. In order to continue to learn, there must be an appropriate level of challenge for all students. This doesn't mean 22 separate lessons as you will group or cluster students who demonstrate similar levels of readiness to learn the specific content you are teaching. Think back to the How Do You Learn It? Activity in Chapter 3. All students who were expert, advanced, or distinguished in playing an instrument were not at those highest levels in tennis, baking cookies from scratch, or all other activities, nor will they likely be at those levels in every topic they will be studying.

Tiered lessons scaffold instruction, providing support to take students from one level to the next. Teachers plan the scaffolding to enhance learning. They determine what content and skills are required for reaching the next level of understanding. This scaffolding allows the teacher to plan what learning experiences are appropriate for reaching learning outcomes at the level of mastery. Then he can do backward planning to tier instruction for those students who need additional support in order to be ready to be successful reaching the mastery level. Scaffolding doesn't stop with planning learning experiences for students who are on target to achieve at grade level or those who need more to reach mastery; it also informs the teacher in his planning for students who are already at or near mastery in order for them to make continuous progress. Tiering instruction is a practical way to provide appropriate challenge, and tiered lessons depend upon scaffolding both content and skills.

TIERING: A FAMILIAR EXAMPLE

Let's start with an example that is familiar to most people: purchasing a car. Of course, individuals have different levels of interest in cars. Some consumers may be at tier one. They don't know a lot about automobiles and have little interest beyond wanting a car that works well, looks good, and costs as little as possible. A consumer at tier two may be interested in a few different factors—size of the engine, fuel economy, environmental protection, safety, and stylish features. This tier two consumer will likely have consulted *Consumer Reports* to know the safety and best-buys of cars being considered for purchase. Tier three car consumers may want to know facts and figures related to electronics that are available for crash avoidance, autonomous driving, and/or other advances in automobile construction, safety, technology, or fuel economy, including advances that are currently being worked on or are possibilities for the future. Consumers at these three different levels share an interest in buying an automobile, but their interests and knowledge about buying cars are vastly different.

Preassessing learners reveals differences about potential car purchasers' knowledge and interests in cars. Of course, these car buyers are really your students, and their interest and knowledge of cars parallels the concept you're teaching. Once the preassessment information has been gathered, what you do with the information will depend upon the learning outcome you have established. If the goal is to prepare a better consumer, you will tier learning experiences to take the potential car purchasers to the next level of knowledge about what is important when purchasing a car.

Information and interest in cars vary greatly among consumers (mirroring what will often be the case in your classroom). Likewise, the learning experiences are designed to move the individuals to the next level of knowledge. If this were for a classroom setting, learning experiences could be tiered to facilitate doing so—that is, each person should be able to make continuous progress. The teacher could design tiered learning experiences and match them to the level of interest and knowledge that the students displayed:

- Tier 1 Learners: Individuals select one issue about safety, fuel economy, or another aspect about which potential purchasers should be well versed and prepare (a) a 5-minute speech with or without technology, (b) an iMovie, or (c) a dialogue or a skit.
- Tier 2 Learners: Individuals select one or more features about cars that should be "musts" for consumers to consider prior to purchasing a car with the rationale to support their recommendations. Prepare (a) a persuasive or informative speech with or without technology, (b) an iMovie, or (c) a presentation with a poster or illustrations.

- Tier 3 Learners: Individuals will select, highlight, and explain a unique feature or features some automobiles have or a feature that is currently under study but may become available in the future in (a) a 5-minute informative or persuasive speech with technology or a poster, (b) an iMovie, or (c) a product of choice.

When the learning tier is matched to what students know about cars and their interests when purchasing one, each student is engaged in learning about what targets becoming a better consumer of cars. Yet, the learners are not all engaged in the same learning assignments, as they had different starting places. Each learner is making continuous progress or learning new material. Students have a choice of products at the tier to which they are assigned. Choice of product is often motivating, and it is the content that is most important rather than the manner in which students present the content. All students will share their products with the class, and all will learn from what others share. Through tiered instruction, everyone is learning at levels of difficulty and complexity beyond their starting knowledge and skills; all are learning about factors that may influence decision making with regard to purchasing a car. Choice of product provides variety that has two benefits: It is motivating to the student to select a product that uses her strengths and interests, and it provides variety to the class when students share what they have learned.

Tiered learning experiences provide the opportunity for all students in a classroom to make continuous progress. Tiers combine content, process, and product to create learning experiences that can be scaffolded to match student interests, strengths, and levels of readiness.

LEVELS OF READINESS, INTERESTS, AND STRENGTHS

The first consideration when matching the instructional tier to the student or cluster of students is the level of readiness. Who already knows, understands, or can use the content or demonstrate the skills? Who needs additional support in order to know, understand, and/or demonstrate the skills? That is the preassessment question presented in Chapter 1. Students can't learn what they already know. Neither can students learn what is too difficult without scaffolding the knowledge and skills to reach the learning goal. Assessing the level of readiness is the starting point for matching instruction to students in order to facilitate continuous progress.

Interests can be the students' interests in the topic being studied or they can refer to their interests in school and in their lives outside of school. When teachers capture student interest, they often increase student motivation and engagement in learning. If you are studying World War II, you may have students who are most interested in life on the home front, warfare, aircraft, or alliances.

Strengths often tie closely with interests. Strengths can describe students' preferred ways of learning that often reflect talents. Perhaps those talents are in drawing, acting, debating, planning, or myriad other areas. Remember that the more you know about your students, the better equipped you are to match learning experiences to students.

Levels of readiness, interests, and strengths will be referenced repeatedly in this book as they provide ways to match learning experiences to students. Teachers preassess student levels of readiness, interests, and strengths.

CONTENT: WHAT STUDENTS MUST KNOW, UNDERSTAND, AND/OR BE ABLE TO DO

The *content* is the "what" that you want the students to learn, whether that be the three states of matter and their characteristics or the author's use of diction and syntax to illustrate the theme. Content may be tied to one or more disciplines and must be significant, because time is such a precious commodity in classrooms. You simply can't open the text to Chapter 1 in the fall and believe that students' learning needs will be met by the end of the spring semester as you cram in those last precious chapters. You must focus carefully on content. Planning the concepts to be taught for the year must be intentional; there is no time to waste. That means that you as the teacher must plan carefully to ensure that students have opportunities for important learning throughout the school year. The curriculum decisions you make are very powerful, because you will determine the opportunities young people in your classroom have to learn significant content at appropriately challenging levels. It sounds a bit overwhelming, doesn't it?

So, where do you find the content for the academic year? State standards that often are the Common Core State Standards (CCSS) provide the starting point for the content you teach, and the curriculum standards in the specific disciplines are the second important source of curriculum in grades K–12. Note the different levels found in most standards. All concepts specified in the standards can be taught at a basic level, and most can be taught at a complex level. For example, students can learn the basics about the cell in elementary school; however, the cell (even one specific type of cell) can be the focus of study in graduate courses in molecular biology. Or, if a student has mastered the level of state history that meets grade-level standards, you have the opportunity to extend the study for a student or students to study the impact of immigration on the economy of the state or another topic to expand learning about state history. That is how tiering learning opportunities can address the learning needs of all students—not with the one-size-fits-all curriculum plan but with scaffolded or tiered lessons. Significant content abounds to ensure that all students are learning new information and skills on an ongoing basis. You remove the learning ceiling as you provide content that is challenging to each learner engaged in the study. You don't change the topic for Tier 3, but you extend the topic beyond what is expected for Tier 2. Because most states are requiring standards-based teaching, the starting point must be state and national standards.

Another way to look at content is to use the knowledge dimension that is described in *A Taxonomy for Learning, Teaching, and Assessing: A Revision of Bloom's Taxonomy of Educational Objectives* (Anderson et al., 2001). Substituting the word *knowledge* for *content*, the authors divide the dimension into four levels: factual knowledge, conceptual knowledge, procedural knowledge, and metacognitive knowledge. The content that appears in the center section of the Bloom Chart (a tiering strategy discussed fully in Chapter 6) can be broken down into the different knowledge categories as shown in Figure 5.1.

The key consideration with the content is that it must be important to know. Consequently, it must be important enough to spend planning time on tiered assignments, so all students will have opportunities to learn the content at the highest level they are ready to learn. Tomlinson and McTighe (2006) state, "Virtually all students should consistently experience curricula rooted in the important ideas of a discipline that requires them to make meaning of information and think at high levels" (p. 84). Rich curriculum is for all students, and the tiering matches the learning experiences to students' levels of readiness, strengths, and interests in the topic being studied.

So how does tiering assignments relate to content? Content can be basic or complex. Basic content is often at the level of facts, concepts, principles, and generalizations. But concepts, principles, and generalizations can also include complex content. Content becomes more complex when it focuses on issues and problems related to the concepts. For example, study of a concept can be basic and complex. Basic study of civil rights will include understanding the concept itself, knowing the history and interpretation of civil rights in the United States, and examples of how these rights are protected by the judicial system. A study of civil rights can focus on complex content as well. It may include studying issues related to civil rights, such as issues involving civil rights around the world, a study of civil rights court cases with regard to the interpretation (there would be no court cases if civil rights were always clear cut), or projecting civil rights of the future. Matching the tier to the level at which the students are ready to learn allows for continuous progress. An example of tiering lessons with the topic of

Major Types and Subtypes	Examples
A. Factual Knowledge–The basic elements students must know to be acquainted with a discipline or solve problems in it	
Aa. Knowledge of terminology	Technical vocabulary, musical symbols
Ab. Knowledge of specific details and elements	Major natural resources, reliable sources of information
B. Conceptual Knowledge–The interrelationships among the basic elements within a larger structure that enable them to function together	
Ba. Knowledge of classifications and categories of ownership	Periods of geological time, forms of business
Bb. Knowledge of principles and generalizations	Pythagorean theorem, law of supply and demand
Bc. Knowledge of theories, models, and structures	Theory of evolution, structure of Congress
C. Procedural Knowledge–How to do something, methods of inquiry, and criteria for using skills, algorithms, techniques, and methods	
Ca. Knowledge of subject-specific skills and algorithms	Skills used in painting with watercolors, whole-number division algorithm
Cb. Knowledge of subject-specific techniques	Interviewing techniques, scientific method and methods
Cc. Knowledge of criteria for determining when to use appropriate procedures	Criteria used to determine when to apply a procedure involving Newton's second law, criteria used to judge the feasibility of using a particular method to estimate business costs
D. Metacognitive Knowledge–Knowledge of cognition in general as well as awareness and knowledge of one's own cognition	
Da. Strategic knowledge	Knowledge of outlining as a means of capturing the structure of a unit of subject matter in a textbook, knowledge of the use of heuristics
Db. Knowledge about cognitive tasks, including appropriate contextual and conditional knowledge	Knowledge of the types of tests particular teachers administer, knowledge of the cognitive demands of different tasks
Dc. Self-knowledge	Knowledge that critiquing essays is a personal strength, whereas writing essays is a personal weakness; awareness of one's knowledge level

Figure 5.1. Levels of knowledge. From *A Taxonomy for Learning, Teaching, and Assessing: A Revision of Bloom's Taxonomy of Cognitive Objectives* (p. 29) by L. W. Anderson and D. R. Krathwohl (Eds.), 2001, New York, NY: Longman. Reprinted with permission.

civil rights is provided later in this chapter. Remember, scaffolding the content will help you tier learning experiences.

PROCESS: WHAT STUDENTS MUST BE ABLE TO DO COGNITIVELY

In a learning experience, what you want the student to do cognitively is known as the *process*. The process that the student engages in can be at the knowledge level, but it also can be elevated to a more challenging level if the student already knows the information. For example, some students are new to probability while other students have studied the concept and are ready to start applying what they already know about this concept. All students will be learning about probability, but they will begin at different levels due to their demonstrated prior learning or readiness. You are sure of this because you have preassessed and can document the students' starting points for the unit.

One of the assets of studying the same concept or topic but at different levels with tiered lessons is that every student can join the discussion. In the discussion of the three branches of government, for example, all students engage in talking about key elements even though some may have looked at basic responsibilities of the legislative branch while others analyzed effective ways to lobby for a bill. Nonetheless, all students can join in and contribute to the discussion of the legislative branch. They will learn from each other's contributions.

So how do you tier instruction to emphasize process? You ensure that students who have mastered or are close to mastering the learning outcomes don't waste their time going over material they know and understand. As you tier the process, you plan learning experiences that require high-level thinking.

Process can be categorized in various ways. The *Taxonomy of Educational Objectives: The Classification of Educational Goals. Handbook I: Cognitive Domain* (Bloom, 1956) provides a well-known and easily understood framework for planning differentiated learning experiences (although that wasn't the purpose of the book). This frequently used taxonomy had the following levels: knowledge, comprehension, application, analysis, synthesis, and evaluation. Although you are probably familiar with this taxonomy, you may or may not be familiar with the latest interpretation of it.

More than a decade ago, a small group of cognitive psychologists, curriculum theorists, instructional researchers, and testing and assessment specialists worked together to re-examine the original taxonomy. This group, which included Krathwohl, who worked with Bloom on the original taxonomy, took a second look at it. Anderson et al. (2001) edited a book that describes the updated taxonomy. They kept the six levels but changed the names and switched two of the

Original	Revised
Evaluation	Create
Synthesis	Evaluate
Analysis	Analyze
Application	Apply
Comprehension	Understand
Knowledge	Remember

Figure 5.2. Original and revised versions of Bloom's Taxonomy of Cognitive Objectives.

positions. Switching the descriptors of the categories from nouns to verbs (verbs tie into the cognitive process), they presented the following levels: remember (formerly knowledge), understand (formerly comprehension), apply, analyze, evaluate, and create. The emphasis on the cognitive process (the verb usage), as well as the convincing argument for switching the last two levels, inspired us to use this revised taxonomy of cognitive objectives in this chapter. Figure 5.2 presents the original taxonomy and the revised taxonomy. Bloom's taxonomy will help you design learning experiences to differentiate for the wide range of learners in a classroom. The new look of the taxonomy is fresh; it is Bloom with a new twist—but one that makes sense.

Of course, Bloom's taxonomy represents only one way to write the process dimension of learning experiences. You could choose to focus on other thinking skills. Perhaps you want to build creative thinking skills. Torrance (1963) described *fluency, flexibility, originality,* and *elaboration* as key skills used by creative thinkers. Creativity can be incorporated into thinking about content from new perspectives and developing products that are unique.

Tiering by process involves using verbs that prompt thinking at varying levels. All students need to engage in thinking; however, they do not all have to do so on the same level on the same schedule. Tiering by process has the goal of making students critical and creative thinkers, both of which are key to problem solving and decision making. The 21st-century skills include thinking skills—critical thinking, creative thinking, problem solving, and decision making.

PRODUCT: HOW STUDENTS WILL DEMONSTRATE OR SHOW WHAT THEY HAVE LEARNED

Teachers have always relied on student products to demonstrate what students have learned. The most frequently used products have been written or oral, with pen-and-paper tests leading the way. Essays, speeches, paragraphs, and reports are among the most frequently used products, and they are important. No doubt it is essential for students to be able to write and speak the English language as well as possible. Still, there are other products that tap the talents and pique the interests of students. Think of the talented art student who would be delighted to draw portraits of the characters in *Macbeth* to show personality traits instead of writing about them. That delight could equate in a better understanding of the characters of Macbeth and MacDuff than a written analysis ever could. Other products motivate students to learn the content. Sometimes just knowing that the student will be able to show you what she's learned by something other than a test will encourage her to study a subject that didn't really interest her at first. Take products that utilize technology. Using the computer to produce a PowerPoint presentation or to make a pamphlet may make learning some key concepts about chemistry or English literature a priority to them if they can do it in a way that they enjoy.

Many different types of products exist, and various educators have categorized products in numerous ways. Each of those could have—and most have had—product lists developed with them. Those lists prove invaluable and are definitely worthy resources. But, a product list alone won't make you totally comfortable with (much less an expert in) providing multiple products. Let's make it a bit more meaningful. Figure 5.3 provides a list (certainly not an all-inclusive one) that shows a range of products. After looking over the list, take a few moments and decide on categories that you can use to group products. Name the categories (you establish the categories so that it makes sense to you), and put the products in those categories that you select. The reason that having a system to categorize products is important is that you have students with different levels of readiness as well as varying interests and strengths.

Once you have thought about how you can cluster these products, the next step is to mark products that you expect students to complete throughout a school year. For example, you may want the students to create maps and graphics to accompany oral and written reports to address the geography standards. For local history, you may require the students to develop a walking tour and to present their plan in a map with illustrations and explanations. Standards will inform your decision about products that should be included in your curriculum. What are the skills that standards specify that can be honed through engaging students in product creation? This list now evolves into your list of products that you expect your students to be able to use during the course of a school year. Please don't limit yourself to the products on the list. Be sure to ask yourself some questions:

- What variety in products do I provide?
- What products could I add to my list that would extend the potential ways that my students can demonstrate what they have learned?

Advertisement (online)
Advertisement (print)
Advertisement (radio)
Advertisement (television)
Biography
Blog
Blueprint
Board Game
Book Cover
Bulletin Board
Cartoon
Case Study
Chart
Children's Book
Choral Reading
Collage
Collection
Column
Commercial
Computer Graphic
Computer Program
Costume
Dance
Debate
Demonstration
Diagram
Dialogue
Diorama
Document-Based Question
Documentary
Dramatic Presentation
Drawing
Editorial
Essay
Exhibit/Display
Experiment
Feature Article
Game
Graph
Graphic Organizer
Greeting Card
Illustrated Story
Interview (live)
Interview (recorded)
Interview (written)
Invention
Journal
Lesson
Letter (business)
Letter (friendly)
Letter to Editor
Mask
Matrix
Mathematical Formula
Mentorship
Mime
Mock Trial (attorney)
Mock Trial (defendant)
Mock Trial (judge)
Mock Trial (plaintiff)
Model
Monologue
Movie
Mural
Museum Exhibit
Musical
News Article
Newscast
Newsletter
Op-Ed Article
Open Response
Oral Presentation
Outline
Painting
Pamphlet
Peer Evaluation
Photo
Photo Essay
Plan
Play
Podcast
Poem
Political Cartoon
Poster
PowerPoint
Prezi
Press Release
Public Service Announcement (radio)
Public Service Announcement (television)
Puppet
Puppet Show
Questionnaire/Survey
Research Paper
Review (Film, Book, etc.)
Science Fair Exhibit
Sculpture
Scrapbook
Script
Service Learning Project
Short Story
Simulation
Skit
Song
Speech (oral)
Speech (written)
Story Telling
Technical Report
Timeline
Venn Diagram
Video Game
Volunteer Activity
Webpage
Wiki
Workshop
Written Report

Figure 5.3. Product list.

- What products could I use to motivate students by appealing to their interests and strengths?
- What products could I include that would lead to real-life learning because they are products that adults use in their professions?

There is no "right answer" as to the categories for products; rather, choose the way that makes the most sense to you. There are numerous ways to categorize them from learning profile to resources required to time needed. The important point to remember is that some students enjoy certain products, tolerate some, and loathe others. Because students differ in their interests, strengths, and abilities as well as their experience with various products, these differences show up in the products that they like or dislike being assigned; all students will not equally enjoy creating the same products. That's why product choice may be a huge motivator. Remember that when you allow students to develop different products, you are more concerned with what they've learned than how they're showing you what they've learned. Let us repeat: You are the decision maker; you plan to give students a choice of products when *what* they are to learn is more important than *how* they show you what they have learned. An interesting byproduct may be increased motivation to learn.

On the other hand, you will want all students to be able to write, whether it is beginning writing in elementary school with complete sentences and paragraphs or an analytical essay in secondary school. When a written product (or speech or experiment) is necessary, then students do not have a choice as to which product they will produce. Once again, the word *intentional* comes into play. What is the intent of the learning experience? You must make a conscious choice as to the product or products—which products your students will focus on for the year, which ones they must complete for a particular learning experience, and which ones will be available for individual choice. If learning the content is the goal of the learning experience, then allowing students to choose their own product will likely work well. If learning the content and perfecting a specific product are the goals, then providing product choices is not appropriate. Choice works well but not all of the time.

Products provide real-world learning opportunities. Adults create and use quality products, so they pave the way for success beyond high school. Therefore, the assessment of products can and should be authentic, and it should provide multiple opportunities to create products that move toward being professional in quality.

Tiering instruction with products can be accomplished by providing rubrics that are increasingly more sophisticated. Rubrics can be written to focus at increasingly higher levels of challenge: They are tiered. The rubric guides the student as he develops the product as well as the one who will assess the product.

Also, the student will use the rubric to self-assess the finished product as well as what she learned as she created the product. The one-size-fits-all rubric limits student growth, so it is important to use rubrics that prompt students to work at increasingly challenging levels.

Tiering instruction certainly applies to products. Rubrics are essential for communicating expectations. Rubrics guide students to create high-quality products. Expectations are assigned to students for the product they are working on, and those expectations differ based on the experience the student has had working on that particular product, whether it is a poster, essay, monologue, or experiment. Product choice appeals to interests and strengths, yet those choices must be matched to students to ensure that they are appropriately challenged. Doing so requires the teacher to match assignments of specific rubrics to specific students based on information he has gleaned about their past performance on that specific product. In case the thought of producing multiple rubrics for offering choice of products is intimidating, in Chapter 10 you will learn about a protocol for assessing products, the Developing and Assessing Product (DAP) Tool, which has three tiers for each product with different levels of expectations and increasing sophistication at each tier.

You are the decision maker, and you are the one to assign tiers for products to students. You match the tier to the student, and, by doing so, you facilitate continuous progress with scaffolded learning experiences. That is what tiering directs in your classroom—continuous progress.

An example of a tiered lesson can be seen in this lesson on civil rights:

- Tier 1: Individuals inform others about one specific civil right guaranteed by the U.S. Constitution by selecting one of the following and preparing (a) a poster, (b) a PowerPoint presentation, or (c) a dialogue or a skit.
- Tier 2: Individuals select an issue related to the interpretation of one civil right guaranteed by the U.S. Constitution. Prepare (a) a persuasive or informative speech with or without technology, (b) an iMovie, or (c) a presentation with a poster or illustrations.
- Tier 3: Individuals will select, highlight, and explain a potential U.S. civil right of the future in (a) a 5-minute informative or persuasive speech with technology or a poster, (b) a pamphlet, or (c) the product of your choice.

Note that the product choices are offered to appeal to student strengths and interests (some of the product choices were used in the tiered example of purchasing a car while others are new to these tiered assignments). Engaging product choices aren't saved for the Tier 3 choices, but rather product choices are equally interesting and engaging at all three levels. How the students demonstrate what that have learned (the product) in this tiered assignment isn't as important as what the students learn. The important consideration with the tiered assignments is to match the tier to the student's level of readiness to study the topic: in this case, civil rights. It is very important that all of the students are working to reach the learning outcomes at levels that tie in with their current knowledge and understanding of the topic being studied.

CONCLUDING THOUGHTS

Tiering involves ratcheting up the content, process, and product in the learning experience. As you tier assignments, you have the entire class studying the same concept or topic, so all are ready to participate in the discussion. No one is left out of the opportunity to talk about what they have been learning from a variety of resources (based on readiness levels) and by creating products that vary (based on strengths and interests). All of the students participate in learning with all involved in experiences that are equally engaging but not identical—after all, the students don't have identical levels of readiness, interests, or strengths.

Another critical point is that teachers expect to differentiate, so they are not disappointed when preassessment results reveal large learner differences. It is normal to plan learning experiences for students who need support to master grade-level learning outcomes as well as for those who are on target to reach the grade-level outcomes. But it is also normal and to be expected to have advanced learners for whom you need to prepare tiered assignments. Tiered instruction allows all students to make continuous progress. The next chapters will show several strategies to tier assignments.

IMPORTANT TAKE-AWAYS

- Tiering instruction involves scaffolding in order to level the learning experiences.
- Tiered learning experiences are matched to levels of readiness, interests, and strengths to provide appropriate challenge to each learner.
- Tiering learning experiences is appropriate for all grades and in all content areas.
- Usually, it is best to design the tier for students who are ready to master the grade-level standard before planning the tier for students who need support to move toward meeting the standard and the tier for students who have already met the standard.
- Content is the *what* that you want the students to learn, and it can be tiered to be basic or complex.

- The process is what you expect the students to do cognitively, and the process can go from remembering and understanding to higher level processing of the content.
- The product is how you want students to demonstrate what they have learned, and the products can be tiered in their levels of difficulty.
- Rubrics guide the student's development of the product as well as the assessment of the product by the teacher and the self-assessment of the product by the student. Rubrics can be tiered.

CHAPTER
6

Tiering Learning Experiences With Bloom's Taxonomy

> The artist is nothing without a gift, but the gift is nothing without work. —Émile Zola

You've preassessed and now have documentation indicating which students know what, as well as some information on what they would like to learn about the topic or concept and how they would prefer to learn. But, you know that completing a preassessment isn't good enough. The next step is to take those results and modify the lesson or the unit. You are now ready to address the third essential question: "What can I do for him, her, or them so they can make continuous progress and extend their learning?"

Planning learning experiences to address a wide range of learner needs is key to helping students make continuous progress. However, most of us haven't had direct training in differentiation; therefore, we're unfamiliar with strategies that can help us address our students' levels of readiness, interests, and strengths. But, I think it's a safe bet to say that we have had experience (and probably repeated training!) in Bloom's Taxonomy of Cognitive Objectives (Bloom, 1956).

Initially described in Chapter 4 were the original Bloom's (1956) taxonomy and the revised taxonomy by Anderson and Krathwohl (2001). The revised taxonomy will be used in this book. Specifying verbs that can be used for each level of the taxonomy expands the ease with which you can plan questions or learning experiences at varying levels of complexity.

Let's look at that familiar concept as a strategy for differentiation, particularly tiering assignments. One simple way to differentiate is to design learning experiences using a Bloom Chart.

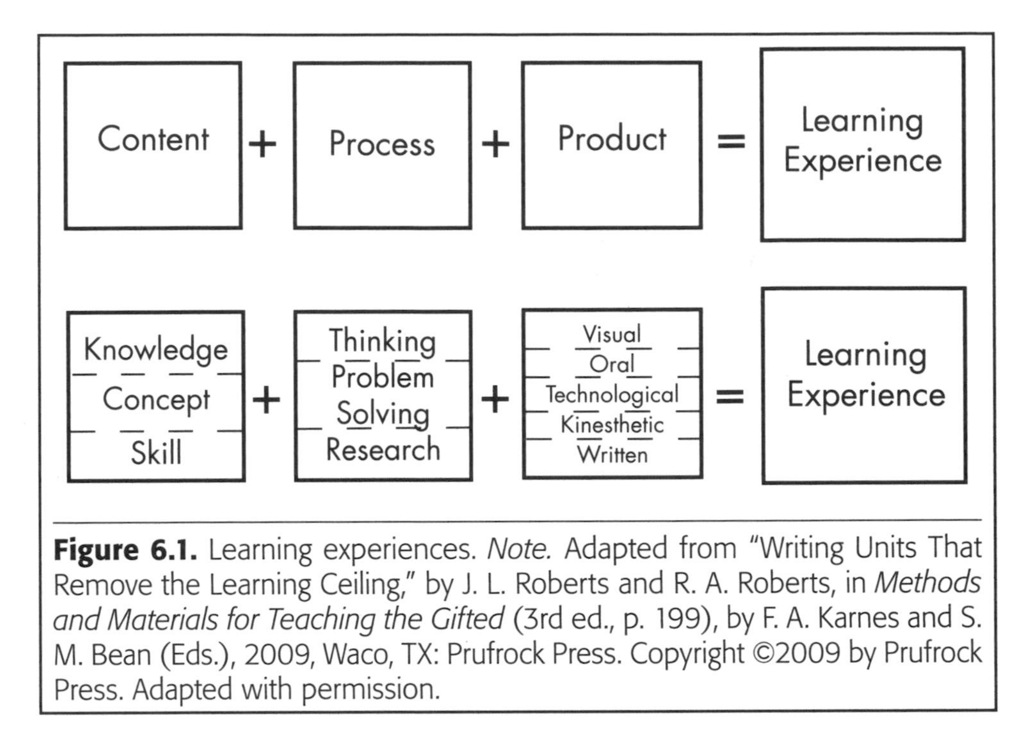

Figure 6.1. Learning experiences. *Note.* Adapted from "Writing Units That Remove the Learning Ceiling," by J. L. Roberts and R. A. Roberts, in *Methods and Materials for Teaching the Gifted* (3rd ed., p. 199), by F. A. Karnes and S. M. Bean (Eds.), 2009, Waco, TX: Prufrock Press. Copyright ©2009 by Prufrock Press. Adapted with permission.

WHAT IS IT?

Very simply, you can offer a variety of learning experiences on the same topic or concept by varying the process (verb), content (basic or complex), and/or product choices. No one skips over essential concepts or skills; however, students who already have mastered the content or skills engage in learning experiences that are matched to what they already know and are able to do. No one is left running in place when she could be learning new things—making continuous progress.

Learning experiences combine content, process, and product (see Figure 6.1). Teachers are really good at designing learning experiences—and with a little practice with a familiar concept, they will be good at planning learning experiences that are differentiated to ensure that each student is challenged to learn. Let's look closer at what we mean by content, process, and product.

- Content—What do you want the students to learn?
- Process—What do you want the students to do cognitively?
- Product—How do you want the students to show or demonstrate what they have learned?

As you plan differentiated learning experiences with a Bloom Chart, you will include content, process, and product. Remember from Chapter 5 that the content is what you want students to learn—the concept or topic. The process is what you want students to do cognitively—the level of thinking. The product is

The Six Categories of the Cognitive Process Dimension

1. REMEMBER—Retrieve relevant knowledge from long-term memory
2. UNDERSTAND—Construct meaning from instructional messages, including oral, written, and graphic communication
3. APPLY—Carry out or use a procedure in a given situation
4. ANALYZE—Break material into constituent parts and determine how parts relate to one another and to an over-all structure or purpose
5. EVALUATE—Make judgments based on criteria and standards
6. CREATE—Put elements together to form a coherent or functional whole, reorganize elements into a new pattern or structure

Figure 6.2. The six categories of the cognitive process dimensions. *Note.* From *A Taxonomy for Learning, Teaching, and Assessing: A Revision of Bloom's Taxonomy of Educational Objectives* (p. 31), by L. W. Anderson et al. (Eds.), 2001, New York: Longman. Copyright ©2001 by Longman. Reprinted with permission.

how you want students to show or demonstrate what they have learned. Figure 6.2 provides the six categories of the cognitive dimensions of the revised Bloom's taxonomy.

A word of caution: You must be very careful when creating learning experiences. You may think that you are challenging your students to think at high levels, but you may actually have them doing more hands-on than minds-on tasks. Check out the examples on Figure 6.3. At which level of Bloom's taxonomy are the learning experiences? Look carefully at the thinking level, not the actual verb used. If you only looked at the verb, you may have marked many of them at the highest level. In actuality, they are all at the lower levels of the taxonomy. Figure 6.4 shows a leveling-up of one of the activities. Notice how much more thought goes into the learning.

The *create* level of the cognitive taxonomy is most difficult to plan, especially when you realize making a creative product (such as writing a story or composing a song) does not make the process reach the create level necessarily. The *create* part comes from thinking creatively, such as through prediction or envisioning the content in a new way.

The process dimension provides the way to make the learning experiences more difficult or more complex using the Bloom strategy for differentiating (tiering). Figure 6.5 goes into greater detail with the six cognitive levels and skills that

BLOOM PREASSESSMENT

Write the level of Bloom's taxonomy for each learning experience:

R—remember	U—understand	AP—apply
AN—analyze	E—evaluate	C—create

_____ 1. Create a brochure explaining the president's duties and the duties of the cabinet.

_____ 2. Design and construct a poster defining quadrilaterals. Include at least five examples.

_____ 3. Develop an artistic mobile that contains 10 facts about the chemical element of your choice.

_____ 4. Dressing as a character in the story, describe yourself and the role you play in the story to the class.

_____ 5. Using an online tool, design an avatar that will carefully explain the Pythagorean Theorem. Be sure to include visuals as well.

_____ 6. Using an online collage/tag cloud generator, create a collage or tag cloud that details the elements of art.

_____ 7. Write song lyrics that delineate the three states of matter and their molecular structure.

_____ 8. Create a flowchart that outlines the steps a court case must take in order to reach the federal Supreme Court.

_____ 9. Make a labeled diagram of the human heart. Be sure to include all of the vocabulary words from the unit.

_____ 10. Write and illustrate a children's book explaining the parts of speech. Books will be presented to the third-grade class.

Figure 6.3. The Bloom preassessment

can be developed under each level. This listing of the cognitive process with subskills and examples will be useful as you plan learning experiences for your class.

The process dimension is so important for challenging your students in their thinking. A bonus is that critical thinking is key to students reaching 21st century goals.

WHAT DOES IT LOOK LIKE?

The Bloom Chart provides an easy way to design learning experiences that allow the content to remain the same while altering the process and the product

Dressing as a character in the story, describe yourself and the role you play in the story to the class.

Dressing as a character in the story, explain why you acted the way you did in a pivotal point in the story.

Dressing as a character in the story, imagine that you acted the opposite way you did in a pivotal point in the story. Predict how this would have changed the outcome.

Dressing as a character in the story, analyze the relationship you had with two others characters. Explain why your relationships were the way they were.

Figure 6.4. Leveling up.

to provide challenge and choice. Think about that for a moment. This strategy involves all students thinking about the same topic or concept—they're just doing so on different levels and showing what they know in different ways. It's pretty simple. Information from the preassessment tells you who already knows and understands the content. It tells you who doesn't need to spend time learning the basics because he already understands those core concepts and is ready to advance in his thinking about the content. As you well know, you can't learn what you already know, so an array of learning experiences designed using the same content allows every student to continue learning about that particular concept—students who are new to it, as well as students who know quite a bit about the concept before the unit begins. Preassessment data also tell you who needs to start at the beginning and who needs to start with a more complex level. Within a classroom, students differ greatly on what they know and understand about a concept or a topic before a unit is taught. Teachers can save valuable time when they preassess what students know before they get started teaching a particular unit. Making assumptions about which students are at particular levels with regard to the specific content is risky at best, because a social studies student may know a lot about state government yet be a beginner in the geography of the region.

How do you use the learning experiences you plan on a Bloom Chart? Does everyone in the class have to complete each one? Once again, the key word is *intentional*. The teacher matches the learning experience to the student through information gained on the preassessment. No, every student will not complete each learning experience, but rather each student will engage in learning experiences that allow him to continue learning about the concept or topic being studied at an appropriately challenging level.

Let's use the example of the Warriors of Xian activity to examine how the Bloom Chart works (see Figure 6.6). Some students in the class may never have heard of the Warriors of Xian. For them it is appropriate to engage in learning

Process Categories	Cognitive Processes and Examples
1. Remember–Retrieve relevant knowledge from long-term memory.	
1.1 Recognizing	(e.g., Recognize the dates of important events in U.S. history)
1.2 Recalling	(e.g., Recall the dates of important events in U.S. history)
2. Understand–Construct meaning from instructional messages, including oral, written, and graphic communication.	
2.1 Interpreting	(e.g., Paraphrase important speeches and documents)
2.2 Exemplifying	(e.g., Give examples of various artistic painting styles)
2.3 Classifying	(e.g., Classify observed or described cases of mental disorders)
2.4 Summarizing	(e.g., Write a short summary of the events portrayed on videotapes)
2.5 Inferring	(e.g., In learning a foreign language, infer grammatical principles from examples)
2.6 Comparing	(e.g., Compare historical events to contemporary situations)
2.7 Explaining	(e.g., Explain the causes of important eighteenth-century events in France)
3. Apply–Carry out or use a procedure in a given situation.	
3.1 Executing	(e.g., Divide one whole number by another whole number, both with multiple digits)
3.2 Implementing	(e.g., Determine in which situations Newton's second law is appropriate)
4. Analyze–Break material into constituent parts and determine how parts relate to one another and to an overall structure or purpose.	
4.1 Differentiating	(e.g., Distinguish between relevant and irrelevant numbers in a mathematical word problem)
4.2 Organizing	(e.g., Structure evidence in a historical description into evidence for and against a particular historical explanation)
4.3 Attributing	(e.g., Determine the point of view of the author of an essay in terms of his or her political perspective)
5. Evaluate–Make judgments based on criteria and standards.	
5.1 Checking	(e.g., Determine whether a scientist's conclusions follow from observed data)
5.2 Critiquing	(e.g., Judge which of two methods is the best way to solve a given problem)
6. Create–Put elements together to form a coherent or functional whole; reorganize elements into a new pattern or structure.	
6.1 Generating	(e.g., Generate hypotheses to account for an observed phenomenon)
6.2 Planning	(e.g., Plan a research paper on a given historical topic)
6.3 Producing	(e.g., Build habitats for certain species for certain purposes)

Figure 6.5. The six categories of the cognitive process dimension and related cognitive processes. From *A Taxonomy for Learning, Teaching, and Assessing: A Revision of Bloom's Taxonomy of Cognitive Objectives* (p. 31) by L. W. Anderson and D. R. Krathwohl (Eds.), 2001, New York, NY: Longman. Reprinted with permission.

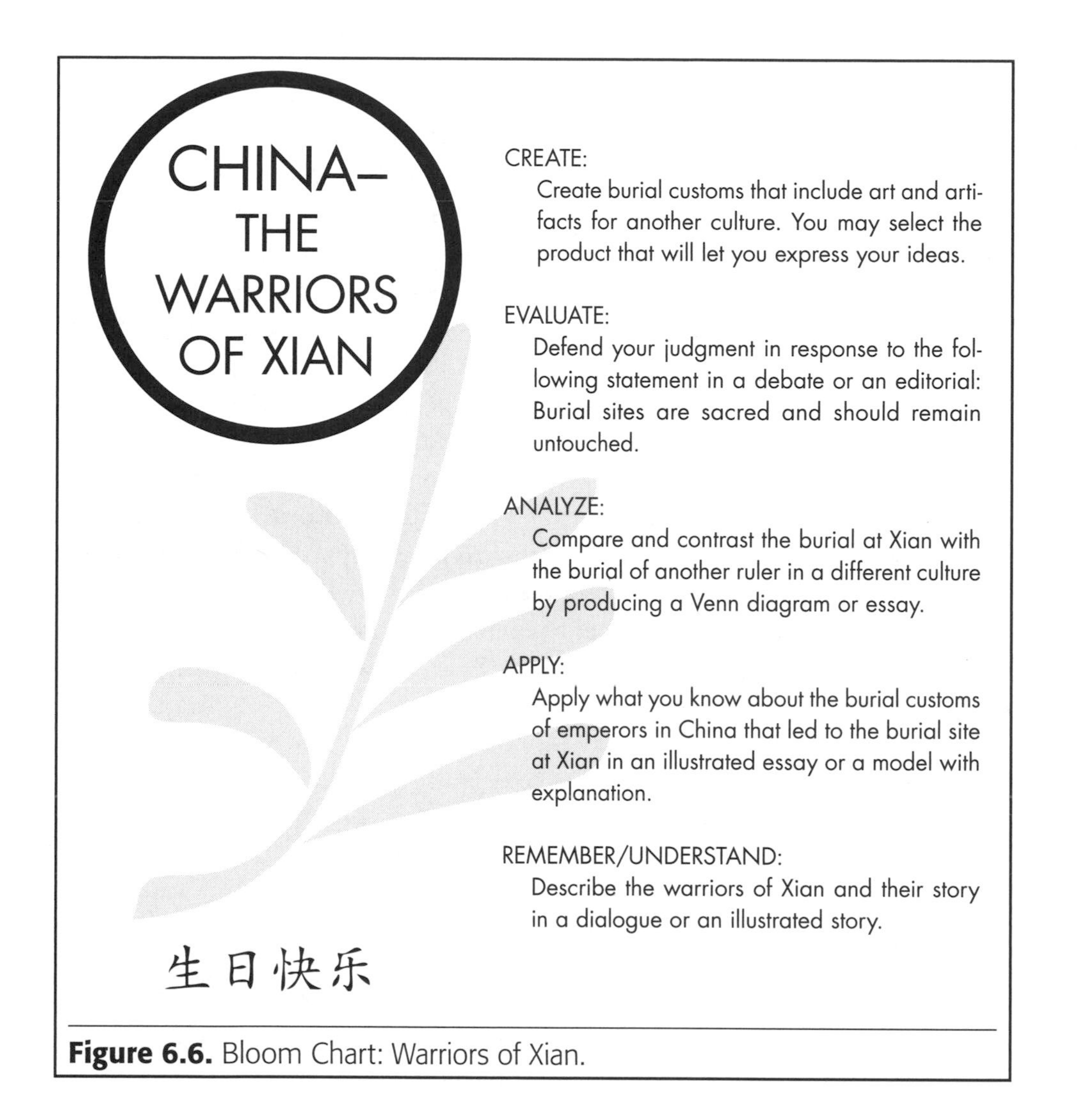

Figure 6.6. Bloom Chart: Warriors of Xian.

experiences that provide an understanding of the treasures that were found there—what they are, the significance of the farmer's discovery, and why the warriors, horses, and chariots were there in the first place. Other students already know and understand the basic facts about the Warriors of Xian and are ready to learn at higher levels. The key is to have everyone in the class engaged in learning about the Warriors of Xian, but at different levels (levels that match what they already know about the topic). When the class discusses what has been learned, every student contributes and they learn from each other. What a win-win situation! Everyone is learning about the Warriors of Xian, but at a level appropriate to their previous experience with the topic or level of readiness to learn this specific topic. They are also demonstrating what they've learned in various ways—again, ways that address their needs, interests in the topic, or levels of readiness.

Juan has read a book about China and is very interested in learning more. He was fascinated as he learned about the discovery of the elaborate soldiers, horses, and chariots that had been buried in the tomb in Xian. It created a genuine interest in learning more about the customs of the rulers of China that would motivate the creation of these figures. Tiffany is fairly unaware of world history, so she is uninterested in the opportunity to study about the Warriors of Xian. The different learning experiences that can be planned and offered on a Bloom Chart can match learning experiences to the student's level of readiness to engage in studying this topic, such as one on a fairly complex level as Juan examines the burial customs of this time and compares them with other customs in other cultures. For some students, the study will build interest, and for others it will further their opportunity to extend the study to more complex issues, such as burial customs as they are seen in art and artifacts of cultures. Everyone learns when learning experiences are not a one-size-fits-all approach—that is, unless the topic is brand new to everyone in the class.

Some of you may question what happens when one assignment such as the Warriors of Xian is given to an entire class. Will Juan, although capable of thinking about the topic on a very high level, decide to take the easy way out and simply describe the warriors' story in a dialogue? And how will Tiffany keep from being very frustrated if she tries to defend the statement that burial sites are sacred and should remain untouched if she isn't even really aware of what the Xian burial site was? Both of those examples would be inappropriate, and little learning would occur. The key, then, to using the Bloom Chart is to match the options to the students. For example, two Warriors of Xian sheets could be created—one that lists Analyze, Evaluate, and Create learning experiences for students like Juan, and one that lists Remember/Understand, Apply, and Analyze options for learners like Tiffany. Remember the word *intentional* that has been used so frequently in this book? You must be intentional about the choices given to students—the match is the key.

The learning experiences that you create with a Bloom Chart are easy to use. They are also relatively easy to design. In fact, each time you complete a Bloom Chart, you are more efficient than the previous time. If you work with one or more of your colleagues, you increase the number of ideas and the fun of doing it. Yes, it really can be fun to design these learning experiences. If you complete two learning Bloom Charts on the same concept/topic, you create more choices of learning experiences for your students—choices at each of the levels of the revised Bloom's taxonomy. Later you can talk together about which ones worked well and which ones you want to modify for next time.

WHEN DO I USE IT?

The Bloom Chart can be used in many different ways, but each way presented here ensures differentiation.

TIERING TO DIFFERENTIATE LEARNING EXPERIENCES

Tiering involves planning and offering learning experiences at increasing levels of difficulty. Since the Bloom Chart varies the process, the learning experiences provide opportunities for thinking at increasingly higher levels. Tiering provides opportunities for all students to study one particular concept or topic but at varying levels, basic to complex. It is not random as to whom the different learning experiences are assigned. Instead, you assign the levels to students based on the evidence that they provided in their preassessments. Remember, continuous progress is the goal.

The Bloom Chart provides an easy way to differentiate learning experiences. Students who showed on the preassessment that they haven't mastered the concept will have the opportunity to choose among the three learning experiences that are at the know, comprehend, and apply levels. Other students will be ready to start with levels to analyze, evaluate, and create.

IN-CLASS ACTIVITY

The learning experiences may last for only one class or for a 2- to 3-day time period. The more engaging the learning experience, the more motivated the students will be, and learning experiences should be equally engaging at all levels. A variety of products and the opportunity to have a choice of products motivate students to work on learning the content—sometimes even when the content isn't a high priority for them. Although students might consider it easy to revisit content that they already know about and understand, the teacher won't give the students that choice. Our goal isn't to review material we already know; our goal is continuous progress for each student. Student choice comes into play only among learning experiences that will challenge the student. That's where the intent comes in—you design your Bloom Chart with options appropriate for continuous progress, and you limit those choices depending on the preassessment results.

Figure 6.7 is a Bloom Chart on fractions. The knowledge of fractions varies greatly in the class. For example, Elizabeth knows a lot about fractions. Based on the preassessment, she will be given a choice of completing two of the three upper level learning experiences on fractions. Jacob is still trying to master the basics of fractions, so his assignment is to complete two of the learning experiences that involve knowing, understanding, and applying. Both Elizabeth and Jacob are learning new information about fractions, but they each are doing so at a level

	PROCESS	CONTENT	PRODUCT
CREATE	*Create*	*Fractions*	*Open Product/ Your Choice*
	Create examples of an interesting, unusual way to use fractions or to teach someone else about fractions. Select the product to present your ideas.		
EVALUATE	*Justify*	*Fractions*	*Persuasive Essay or Debate*
	Justify learning about fractions in a persuasive essay or debate.		
ANALYZE	*Compare*	*Fractions*	*Venn Diagram or Poster*
	Compare fractions and decimals on a Venn diagram or poster.		
APPLY	*Organize*	*Fractions*	*Number Line*
	Organize fractions on a number line.		
UNDERSTAND	*Explain*	*Fractions*	*Discussion or Role Play*
	Explain fractions in a discussion or a role play.		
REMEMBER	*Identify*	*Fractions*	*Chart or Pictures*
	Identify fractions on a chart or with pictures.		

Figure 6.7. Bloom Chart: Fractions. *Note.* Adapted from *Enrichment Opportunities for Gifted Learners* (p. 24), by J. L. Roberts, 2005, Waco, TX: Prufrock Press. Copyright ©2005 by Prufrock Press. Adapted with permission.

challenging to them personally—and they have options in how they demonstrate that learning. The content is constant (fractions), but the process and product are altered to make certain that each student is still learning something new. Note that all students are studying fractions while on different levels.

CENTERS

Most educators consider centers to be a strategy for primary or elementary school children, but centers can actually be an incredible tool for differentiation at all levels. Centers or learning stations are designed for students to be engaged in learning as individuals or in small groups, and often the directions for center activities are located throughout the classroom. Students can engage in center learning experiences during a designated center time or when they have completed their assignments. The center may be the location in the room for learning activities, or it may be the designated place to pick up directions and materials needed for the learning experience and then students return to their tables or seats to complete them.

When using a Bloom Chart with centers, the actual learning experiences may be typed (or written) and placed on file folders, which can be laminated to reduce wear and tear. Folders come in two colors: one for learners who need to process the topic at a higher level of the taxonomy, and one for learners who need to process the content at lower levels. Students know their color as they move from center to center. They still have choice of learning experience, but each learning experience is commensurate with their readiness level as demonstrated by the preassessment. On the next topic to be studied, their readiness level may be different from what it is on the current one. This matching of learning experiences to the student's level of readiness qualifies as tiered learning experiences. Centers also can house both the materials and technology needed to complete the learning experiences. If the center focuses on poetry, Charles can take his love of poetry and develop skills at higher levels when he is steered toward the more challenging learning experiences by requiring him to complete three of the six learning experiences, two of which must be at the three highest levels on a Bloom Chart. Deepa is not ready for the more advanced learning experiences with poetry, so the teacher would contract with her to complete the learning experiences at the knowing and understanding levels plus one higher level activity of her choice. You just want to guarantee that each student will be successful, and you also want each child to be working at a level of challenge. Each student should be able to successfully fulfill the assignments and feel good about what he or she is learning. Each one should be learning new content and skills. That is how we build confidence among learners.

Although the Monet example in Figure 6.8 provides multiple options for each learner, all levels could have more choices if more than one Bloom Chart were planned for the same topic. You could get with a colleague to design two or three Bloom Charts on this topic to allow even more possibilities. Students who demonstrated in the preassessment that they didn't know much about Monet could have a choice of several learning experiences at each level of knowing, understanding, and applying, whereas students who knew quite a bit about Claude Monet and his Impressionist paintings could have multiple choices at the analyzing, evaluating, and creating levels. Based on preassessment results, you could contract with individual students about which choices they have. Everyone must be challenged to stretch mentally. The learning experiences could be written out and presented at a table located on one side of the room. During the next 10 days, the students would have the opportunity to complete three learning experiences during center time or to choose two out of the three learning experiences at the assigned level—those learning experiences must be matched to the preassessed levels of readiness and interest. Once again, every student is learning new content and skills.

John DeLacey, a principal, remarked in a personal correspondence about using the Bloom chart to plan and implement centers:

> Coming from an elementary setting and now being in a middle school setting, a point that I loved is that centers do not have to be just for primary. They can serve a great purpose for differentiation and independent learning or small group learning if planned appropriately. The Bloom Chart is one way the student centers can be planned to work well.

If the most important consideration is every student learning about the topic/concept being studied, let's think of different ways to offer learning experiences. Learning stations may well work if you give it a try, even in intermediate, middle, and high school classrooms.

A resource that provides numerous examples of centers is *Differentiating Instruction With Centers in the Gifted Classroom* (Roberts & Boggess, 2012). Examples of centers include using the Bloom Chart as well as Think-Tac-Toes that you will read about in Chapter 8.

UNIT ASSESSMENT

The learning experiences in a Bloom Chart also can be the blueprint for the final assessment of a unit. The goal is learning about a specific concept or topic, so having students work on different learning experiences is not a problem. In fact, it adds interest for you as the teacher because you don't have to grade 24 or 120 versions of the same product. It works well for the students, too, because each one is working on a product at the level of cognitive challenge at which he will be stretched, as well as successful.

	PROCESS	CONTENT	PRODUCT
CREATE	*Create*	*Impressionism/ Monet*	*Choice*
	Create a new style of art that incorporates Monet's Impressionism and moves in a new direction.		
EVALUATE	*Take a Position*	*Impressionism/ Monet*	*PowerPoint Presentation or Presentation With Illustrations*
	Take a position on the rejection of the art of the Impressionists from the salons of Paris and then present it.		
ANALYZE	*Compare and Contrast*	*Impressionism/ Monet*	*Choice*
	Compare and contrast the basic elements of Monet's Impressionism and Seurat's Pointillism in a product of your choice.		
APPLY	*Apply*	*Impressionism/ Monet*	*Impressionist Painting*
	Apply the elements of Monet's Impressionism in a painting.		
UNDERSTAND	*Describe*	*Impressionism/ Monet*	*Short Story or Essay*
	Describe the basic elements of Impressionism in a short story or essay using Monet as the example.		
REMEMBER	*Compile*	*Impressionism/ Monet*	*Illustration or Poster*
	Compile facts about Monet's Impressionism and present them in a series of illustrations or a poster.		

Figure 6.8. Bloom Chart: Monet and Impressionism.

After reading Harper Lee's *To Kill a Mockingbird*, students can think about the theme of prejudice and discrimination on very different levels and then demonstrate that thinking through a skit, a PowerPoint presentation, or even a children's book (see Figure 6.9). Regardless of the product, if choices are targeted to learning based on preassessment data, each student is challenged in his thinking. The learning experiences require higher level thinking as they move up from knowing, understanding, applying, analyzing, evaluating, to creating. Based on assessing students, they are assigned to complete their project or projects at the level matching their readiness on the topic of prejudice and discrimination. Tiering allows students to complete this unit assessment at varying levels in order to challenge them all at levels at which they can be successful—yet at levels that will stretch them.

Another example of learning experiences is planned for concluding a study of East and West Germany (see Figure 6.10). In an Advanced Placement European history class, the teacher assigned students specific learning experiences with a choice of completing two of three at the analyze, evaluate, or create levels or at the remember, understand, or apply levels. Final products will be shared with the class, providing variety and a potential great discussion of the topic from various perspectives. The result is enriching for the students and teacher.

These Bloom Charts with learning experiences that are tiered provide examples of ways you can design learning experiences for units of study that allow students to address standards. They are not frivolous, but rather these learning experiences are ones you plan to facilitate reaching learning outcomes with a high level of student engagement.

OPTIONAL LEARNING EXPERIENCES

What happens to the student who has already mastered the content you plan to teach? For example, the class has been studying insects. Jerome has been interested in bugs since he was a little boy and has spent a lot of time with a grandfather who has knowledge of insects of various types. He may choose to look at social insects while the class is studying basic information on insects, and his Bloom Chart may be similar to the one in Figure 6.11. The entire class is learning about insects; however, based on preassessment information, Jerome is studying a topic that is more specific and perhaps he is moving along rapidly enough to learn about social insects at complex levels and with higher level thinking. If all children are ready for that experience, then they all should be learning at complex levels and at higher levels of thinking. If all children aren't ready, let's not hold Jerome back. He deserves to make continuous progress in an area of interest in which he has had lots of experience.

Students can learn to challenge themselves with learning experiences when they find that what they are being asked to do is not challenging enough for

Bloom Chart: *To Kill a Mockingbird*

	PROCESS	CONTENT	PRODUCT
CREATE	*Create*	*Prejudice and Discrimination*	*Skit*
	Create the jury deliberation exemplifying the roles of prejudice and discrimination that resulted in their guilty verdict in a skit.		
EVALUATE	*Advocate*	*Prejudice and Discrimination*	*Speech*
	In a speech, advocate a position on a controversial issue steeped in prejudice and discrimination. Use the novel as support.		
ANALYZE	*Analyze*	*Prejudice and Discrimination*	*PowerPoint*
	Analyze the key scenes from the novel that reflect the themes of prejudice and discrimination. Present the analysis in a PowerPoint presentation.		
APPLY	*Relate*	*Prejudice and Discrimination*	*Talk Show Script*
	Relate the themes of prejudice and discrimination in the novel to modern events by writing a television script for a talk show. Interview three people.		
UNDERSTAND	*Describe*	*Prejudice and Discrimination*	*Song*
	In a song, describe examples of prejudice and discrimination from the novel.		
REMEMBER	*Illustrate and Label*	*Prejudice and Discrimination*	*Children's Book*
	In a children's book, illustrate and then label examples of prejudice and discrimination from the novel.		

Figure 6.9. Bloom Chart: *To Kill a Mockingbird.*

Bloom Chart: East and West Germany

	PROCESS	CONTENT	PRODUCT
CREATE	*Create*	*East and West Germany*	*Committee Report*
	Based on events as they were in 1988, create a solution that would result in the reunification of Germany. Remember, you must appease all political groups within both East and West and ease the fears of neighbors like France who might not want a strong, reunified German Federation. Present your solution in a format suitable for a UN conflict resolution committee.		
EVALUATE	*Critique*	*East and West Germany*	*Speech*
	Critique the method of governance in either East or West Germany, using specific evidence from both nations to back up your assertions in a speech.		
ANALYZE	*Compare and Contrast*	*East and West Germany*	*Essay*
	Compare and contrast the ideas of equality of opportunity and equality of condition in an essay, using evidence from the case of East and West Germany to back up your ideas.		
APPLY	*Relate*	*East and West Germany*	*Your Choice*
	Relate the history of East and West Germany to that of another nation (like Korea or Vietnam) separated by Cold War hostilities in a product of your choice.		
UNDERSTAND	*Explain*	*East and West Germany*	*Poster/PowerPoint*
	Explain how geopolitical circumstances following the end of WWII and the beginning of the Cold War led to the creation of East and West Germany in a poster or PowerPoint presentation.		
REMEMBER	*Describe*	*East and West Germany*	*Venn Diagram*
	Describe the political, economic, and social characteristics of East and West Germany in a Venn Diagram.		

Figure 6.10. Bloom Chart: East and West Germany. *Note.* Used with permission by Katherine Booth, high school teacher.

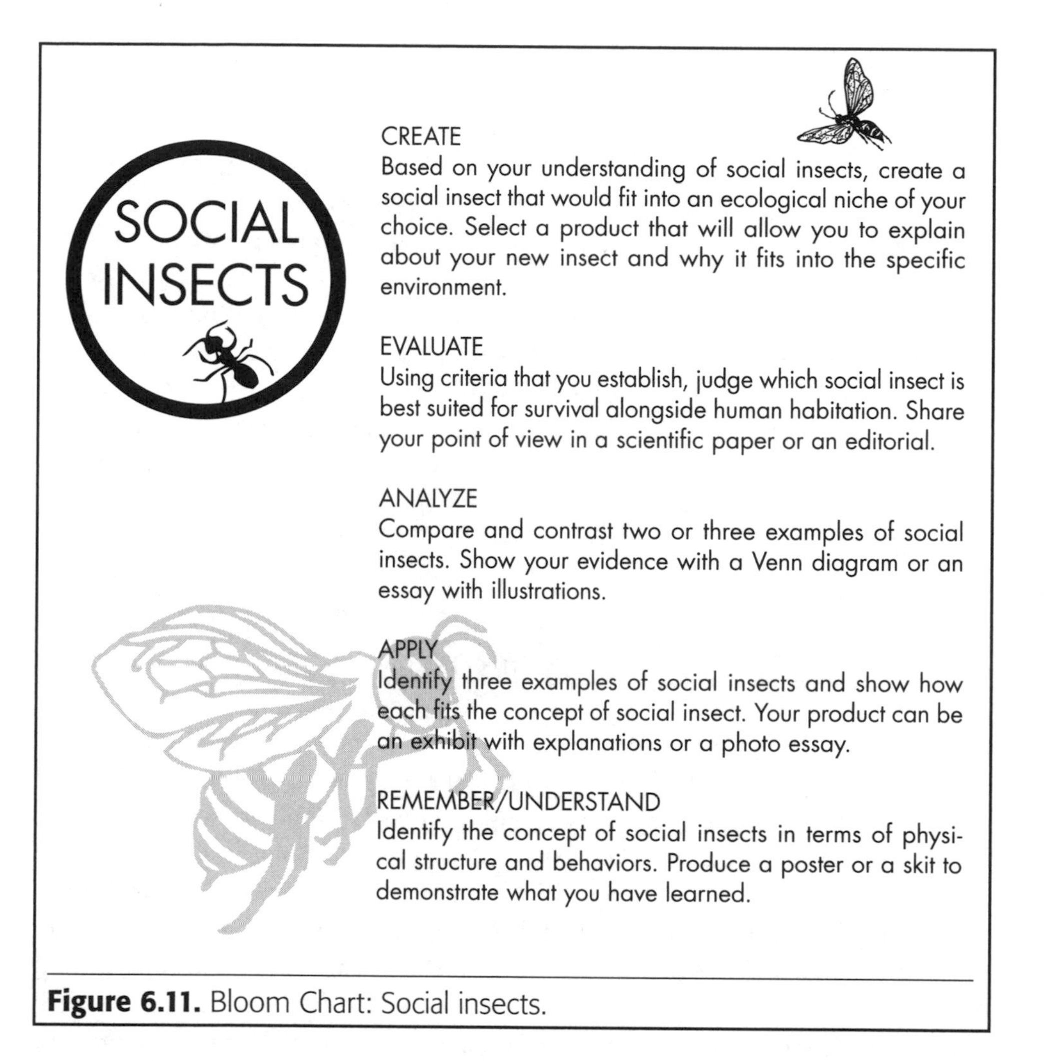

Figure 6.11. Bloom Chart: Social insects.

them. Tell your students that designing their own learning experiences around the content you determine would be great; however, they must get your approval before starting. Once again, information from the preassessment will guide you in the decision you make.

Katherine Booth, a secondary teacher, highlighted in a personal correspondence the relevance for planning learning experiences with the Bloom Chart as the organizer:

> My thought as I made my Bloom's-based lesson was that efficiency would be greatly increased if I utilized this tool for each unit. Each student would, minimally, be given the opportunity to process the content at a basic remember-and-understand level. Those who'd already met those levels would be able to *immediately* begin processing the content at a higher level. Instead of spinning the wheels of the class moving ALL

students through basic, scaffolding-up understanding to analysis or creation, time would be saved as each student worked at his or her current level. Quick students would find no limit to their learning, even if they started at a lower level based on preassessment and those students who needed basic information would spend their time making gains at a level appropriate to them. As I made my chart, I felt the opportunity of "time not wasted" opening up, and I am honestly excited about how using these charts will open up time in the year for more synthesis at the end of a unit for ALL students, so that all can hopefully reach into the higher levels of Bloom's. Time is a teacher's most precious resource and, as a teacher constantly guarding and jealous of the time I have with my students and my content, I am ready to utilize any tool that will provide more of that most scarce of resources.

HOW DO I DIFFERENTIATE WITH THE BLOOM CHART?

Ask yourself: What is it that I want everyone to know, understand, or be able to do when they walk out the door? All students will be held responsible for that concept or topic—on varying levels. In the *To Kill a Mockingbird* unit mentioned earlier (see Figure 6.9), everyone is expected to understand the role that prejudice and discrimination play in the novel. That idea is reflected in the middle column for each level of the taxonomy. So, if LaKeisha is able to relate that idea to current events in Africa or the Middle East, she is still thinking about the concept, but on a more complex level. Matthew may still be processing the theme of prejudice and discrimination found in the novel on a lower level of thought: He may try to understand which scenes in the book exemplified the theme. But, the bottom line is that every single student in the class is thinking about the same theme. When the class discusses this theme, all students can contribute in a meaningful way. No one is working on assignments that are way too easy or way too difficult. Instead, each student is learning at a level that provides challenge—just the right amount of challenge to facilitate learning. (See Appendix D for a template of the Bloom Chart.)

DEVELOP RESPECTFUL, ENGAGING TASKS FOR EACH LEVEL

One key to differentiating learning experiences successfully (i.e., everyone learns) is to have tasks that are engaging. It is not appropriate to have one group of students working on a worksheet while others are involved in hands-on learning. Respectful tasks are ones in which all children have opportunities to learn new things and at a level of challenge that will require mental stretching to reach. It is a bonus and a motivator if they are working on products that interest them and that highlight their strengths. Of course, you will provide the support so that the students are ready and willing to stretch their minds to reach higher standards than they have reached before.

DIVIDE TASKS INTO CHOICE OPTIONS AND THEN PURPOSELY ASSIGN OPTIONS

Be sure to use preassessment information when assigning options for students. Allow for student input. To ensure that your students are challenging themselves (not taking the easy way out or overwhelming themselves with the impossible), you as the educated professional must limit their options. They get to choose, and that pleases and motivates them. Whether they choose from two or three options is immaterial. Please remember that all students don't complete all of the learning experiences in a Bloom Chart. You base their options on preassessment information, and you offer choices for them to make—and remember that each choice must challenge that student. Offer choices within limits. For example, Alita, who demonstrated that she knows quite a bit about ecosystems, can choose two out of the three learning experiences in the create, evaluate, and analyze levels. She's happy because she has a say in her learning. The teacher is happy because she knows that Alita is being challenged. Bailey's preassessment indicated that ecosystems are new to him, therefore, his choices will come from the remember, understand, and apply levels. You know that continuous learning will occur regardless of the choice he makes. It is best to limit choices to two or three. You may ask students to choose one from the higher level choices and one from the lower level. We suggest that you do not label the levels. Simply offer choices and let the students begin learning.

Don't forget that some students may want to switch products from those on the Bloom Chart; perhaps they'd prefer developing a model to designing a pamphlet. Encourage that freedom whenever possible. As long as the student is working on a challenging level, the actual product choice often is irrelevant. If alternatives are allowed, make sure those kids opting for other products provide rubrics or scoring guides. Or offer them a Developing and Assessing Products (DAP) Tool (you will learn more about DAP Tools in Chapter 10).

DISTRIBUTE RUBRICS OR SCORING GUIDES FOR EACH

Rubrics or scoring guides are essential for establishing criteria for students to develop and you to assess products. In order to keep your sanity, you will find it useful to use rubrics that can be used again and again without revising them when the same product is assigned again but with different content. Students need to have rubrics that will guide them to the next level of expertise—another way to stretch a student by notching up the expectation if she is ready to make a shift to the next level with the product, whether it is a technical report, a model, or a monologue. You will see a discussion of the scoring guide called the DAP Tool in Chapter 10. Because experts in various fields use many of the products that students develop to show what they have learned, the level of performance has no ceiling. DAP Tools will lift the ceiling and inspire students to perfect their products from assignment to assignment. The rubrics set the expectations, and your feedback to the students helps each ratchet up the production the next time the product is assigned or is offered as a choice to show what he has learned.

THE INTENTIONAL USE OF BLOOM

Using Bloom's taxonomy for differentiation is not new. Engine-Uity (http://www.engine-uity.com) has numerous examples of units that have been planned for students from primary through high school using Bloom's taxonomy to organize learning experiences. Roberts and Roberts (2009) provide examples in a textbook chapter called "Writing Units That Remove the Learning Ceiling." Samara and Curry (1994) have used the taxonomy in designing units that challenge all learners. Numerous examples are available to provide a starting point with units using Bloom's taxonomy, and these examples could easily be adapted to the revision, as well. You are the decision maker. You must intentionally match the level of content, process, or product with each student's interests, needs, abilities, or skill levels.

DIFFERENTIATING THROUGH PROCESS

When using Bloom's taxonomy to differentiate, be sure to keep the following points in mind:

- Any time a question is asked the second time (e.g., on a test), that question is one involving remembering—regardless of the wording or the original level.
- Knowledge is very important. It is impossible to apply, analyze, evaluate, or create if you don't have knowledge about the topic or concept. Every time students apply, analyze, evaluate, and create, they increase their knowledge base. Figure 6.12 illustrates how the cognitive levels interact to increase the knowledge base.
- Process verbs may be used at more than one level; however, the following list will guide you in choosing verbs that are likely to prompt students to think at and engage in learning at various levels of the revised taxonomy.

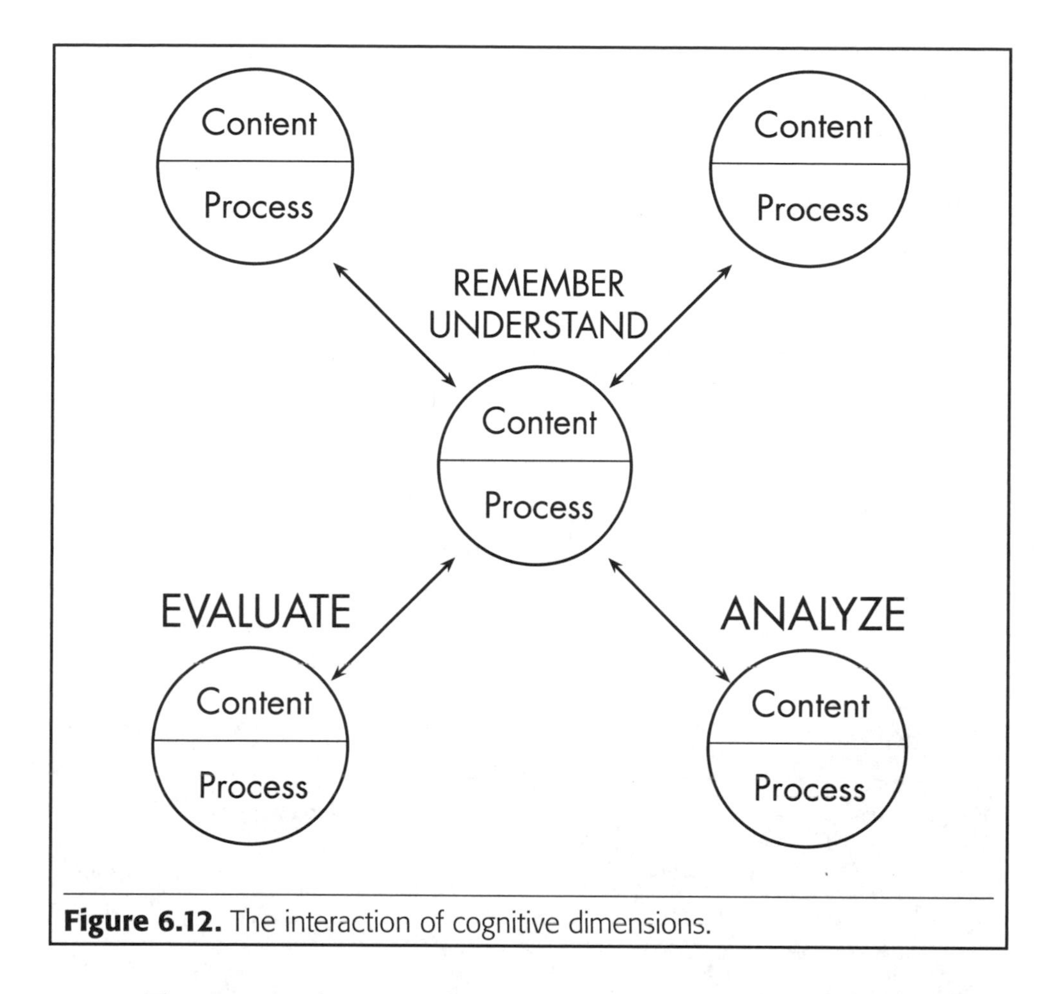

Figure 6.12. The interaction of cognitive dimensions.

- The create level requires the student to think creatively about the content. The thinking is not at this level just because the product is one deemed to be creative like writing a story or drawing illustrations.

CREATE:
predict, hypothesize, design, construct, create, compose

EVALUATE:
interpret, judge, justify, criticize, decide, verify, conclude

ANALYZE:
compare, contrast, take apart, specify, dissect, deduce, determine, differentiate, distinguish

APPLY:
organize, group, collect, apply, order, classify, model, use, construct, relate

UNDERSTAND:
explain, translate, restate, connect, conclude, summarize, describe, show, paraphrase

REMEMBER:
list, observe, describe, uncover, recognize, tell, recall

CONCLUDING COMMENTS

Differentiating the process dimension of learning experiences works to keep all students studying the same concept but at cognitive levels matching their readiness. All students are studying the same concept or topic—just at a level matched to where they are in their learning on that concept or standard. Everyone contributes to the discussion of the concept or topic from the vantage point of various learning experiences. Bloom's taxonomy is but one way to differentiate. Additional differentiation strategies are discussed in the following chapters.

IMPORTANT TAKE-AWAYS

- The Bloom taxonomy (original and revised) provides a system for organizing learning experiences according to process—the cognitive process.
- Tiering with learning experiences organized using a cognitive taxonomy allows for matching students to learning experiences with appropriate levels of challenge.
- Learning experiences combine content, process, and product.
- The Bloom Chart is the planning document, but you will present the learning experiences in other formats for your students.

CHAPTER 7

Tiering With Venn Diagrams

> When teachers differentiate, students who have gifts and talents are more likely to show themselves and be recognized. —Susan Johnsen

Differentiation options can take many forms: products, process, content, and/or assessment. The key is intent—why are you, as a professional educator, modifying this content, process, product, or assessment for this particular learner or cluster of learners? How does that modification link to the student's interests, strengths, abilities, or readiness? If you can answer those questions with confidence stemming from proof (i.e., preassessment), then the student is on her way to continuous progress.

The more familiar a strategy is, the more likely a newcomer to differentiation is apt to utilize it. That's why Venn diagrams can be used so successfully to differentiate. Many of us have manipulated those two intertwining circles in our own assignments as students, and we realize the analytical value and high levels of thought possible in the exercise. Englishman John Venn introduced this diagram in his 1881 work *Symbolic Logic* as he demonstrated mathematical and logical relationships, both higher levels of thought. Many fields outside of education also have embraced these diagrams. Lannie Kanevsky (2003) explored Venn diagrams in relation to differentiation and tiered assignments and focused on ensuring challenge for children and young people who are ready for advanced learning. Venn diagrams are an easy way to create tiered assignments in every classroom.

WHAT IS IT?

In its simplest form, the Venn diagram provides students with alternate ways of cognitively understanding the concepts and varying tiers of complexity by which to process the information. Whereas Think-Tac-Toes in Chapter 8 mesh well with product differentiation, the Venn diagram strategy is an excellent vehicle for process and content differentiation.

In order to differentiate, however, multiple circles (or ovals in our version; they're more user-friendly) are needed. More ovals increase the complexity of the process and content. A few students are capable of processing the information in only the most basic ways. For them, one oval can be used as a graphic organizer for one concept. Later then, if appropriate, those one-oval concepts can be compared and contrasted in two ovals. Many learners are probably ready to compare and contrast at the same time. For these students, two overlapping ovals indicate that the two concepts or sets of information have some things in common, but not all. Looking at only two concepts, though, will prove too simplistic and elementary in thinking for some students. Three overlapping ovals for these learners indicate that sets of information have some unique characteristics, some things in common with another set, and other things in common with all three. But, for some students, even three ovals can't readily explain the complexity of their thought regarding the concept. These gifted young people are able to make connections and think abstractly. Four overlapping ovals indicate that sets of information have some unique characteristics, things in common with another set, other things in common with three, and some common elements in all four.

For those mathematicians out there, we realize that the mathematically correct four-item Venn differs from the Venn-like graphic organizer (known as Venn variation here) we use for comparing four items. The mathematically correct four-item Venn allows for comparison of all variations of pairings in one shape, but it is somewhat cumbersome to use because spacing is very limited. The end result may be very challenging to read, plus the process of creating it also may be confusing. However, if we were to select one version of the mathematically correct four-item Venn, it would be the flower. Please see Appendix E for examples.

The beauty of this strategy for tiered assignments is that all students, regardless of their complexity of thought on the topic, can contribute equally to the discussion. Whether the concept is characterization in a novel, chemical reactions, or types of government, all students have thought about the concept and have something of value to say.

Another great benefit of using Venn diagrams deals with time. If students are preassessed correctly, each student should devote roughly the same amount of time to the exercise—regardless of the number of ovals. For example, if a fifth-grade class is studying the states of matter, the students will vary in their ability to think about the states of matter. Their experience with the topic will also vary. Figure 7.1 shows the four different Venn diagrams that would be used for this unit. On a sheet with just one oval, a few students will analyze the characteristics and examples of one state of matter; in fact, they could choose which one to explore: gas, solid, or liquid. More learners will compare and contrast two states

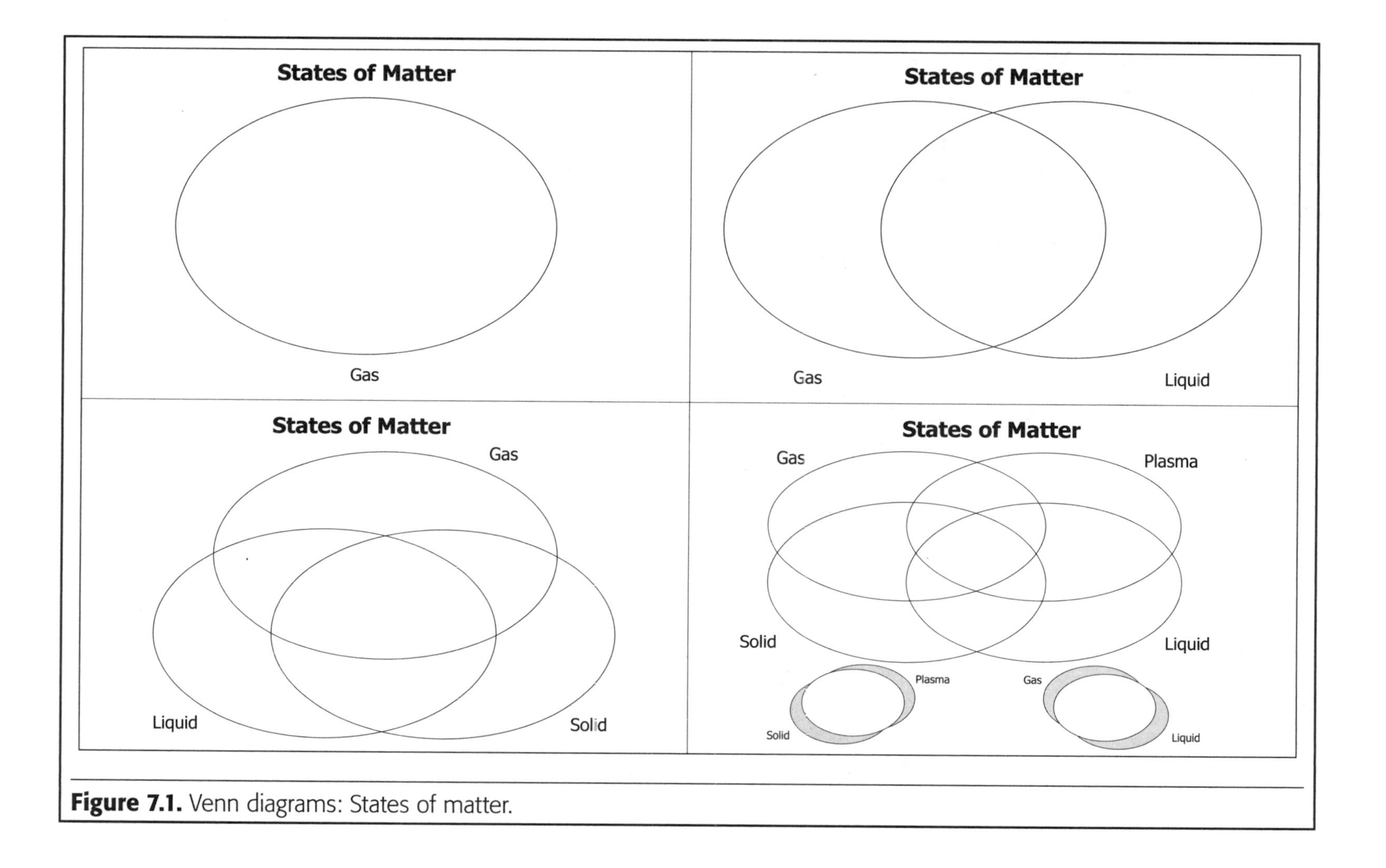

Figure 7.1. Venn diagrams: States of matter.

of matter—for example, gas and liquid—in a traditional Venn diagram on their paper. Some others will analyze all three states of matter. Finally, a few students will add the concept of plasma to the mix using four ovals on their paper. Please note the additional ovals at the bottom that allow the student to compare gas to liquid and solid to plasma.

If the professional educator (that's you!) has done well matching the student's ability to the content level, the entire exercise should take 40 minutes (or whatever time you determine)—regardless of the number of ovals. Then, the rest of the time can be spent in whole-group discussion of the main concepts. Everyone tackles the same concepts, but on his or her own level—that's differentiation. Another easy way to add interest to this assignment would be to let the students choose which states of matter to analyze.

Kanevsky (2003) argued that requiring the same number of items, details, and characteristics in total for the ovals also simplifies the exercise. For example, the fifth graders in the previous example were instructed to think of 10 characteristics and/or examples of states of matter. Students working with one oval would need to generate that many characteristics/examples for gas (or a state of matter of their choice). The students assigned to work on two ovals need 10 total; they may find three examples that are unique to either gas or liquid, plus an additional four that are shared between the states of matter. The configuration is up to them. Students working with three ovals may find two examples for gas alone, one for solid, two for liquid, one that gas and solid share, two that gas and liquid share, one that solid and liquid share, and then one that all have in common—or any other configuration as long as the examples total 10. The four-oval students list 10 examples using any of the 15 spaces. The variations are almost endless. Kanevsky encouraged students to meet a minimum number but let them know additional examples are appreciated and rewarded (be that through extra points or public display). In a differentiated classroom, students experience a climate that encourages and celebrates differences. But, no one wants an assignment that requires him to do four times as much work as others. The key to differentiation is not *more* but *different*. When the same number of examples is required of everyone, students who are advanced or of high ability or who know a lot about this particular content do not feel penalized, nor do students who are struggling feel patronized. Each is getting a challenging assignment that strengthens her brain and provides continuous progress.

This tiering strategy, just like using Bloom Charts (see Chapter 6) and Think-Tac-Toes (see Chapter 8), has many possible uses in the classroom.

WHAT DOES IT LOOK LIKE?

Here is an example of how this strategy might look in a sixth-grade classroom. This class has been reading the Harry Potter books and is analyzing the characters. Figure 7.2 shows examples of the Venn diagrams that might be produced by students.

Some students will look at one character of their choice, listing adjectives or descriptors that best characterize the person. Others will compare and contrast two characters. Some learners will be ready to analyze three characters in relation to each other, and a few, maybe just one or two, will be ready for four. No matter the number of ovals, each student writes down 12 descriptors. After the exercise is complete, then all students (whether they manipulated data with simplicity or complexity) can participate in the discussion of characterization in the Harry Potter series.

Continuing with the Harry Potter theme, it is easy to encourage students to try the next challenging level by making a modification. A word list can be just the assistance a learner needs to bump from one to two or two to three ovals. See Figure 7.3.

Replacing the student with one of the characters adds critical thinking (See Figure 7.4.). Imagine the learner finding similarities with both the protagonist and antagonist. Many will relish the Harry Potter similarities, but they would be surprised to note any Voldemort likenesses. Figure 7.5 bumps the thinking to the highest level of Bloom's taxonomy: Create. Here students predict what the pre-13-year-old Harry was like as well as the post-50 Harry. The Venn diagram used in this way can stimulate and challenge all learners, including those with gifts and talents.

WHEN DO I USE IT?

DIFFERENTIATING PROCESS IN AN IN-CLASS LEARNING EXPERIENCE

When the entire class is learning the same topic in a class period, Venn diagrams can be used to tier the level of complexity of the learning experience. A fourth-grade math class, for example, is studying fractions based on Common Core State Standard (Council of Chief State School Officers & National Governors Association for Best Practices, 2010) *Understand decimal notation for fractions, and compare decimal fractions.* During the class period, then, all students would explore the expression of quantities that aren't whole numbers and the way in which the numbers are expressed in relation to other numbers; however, each

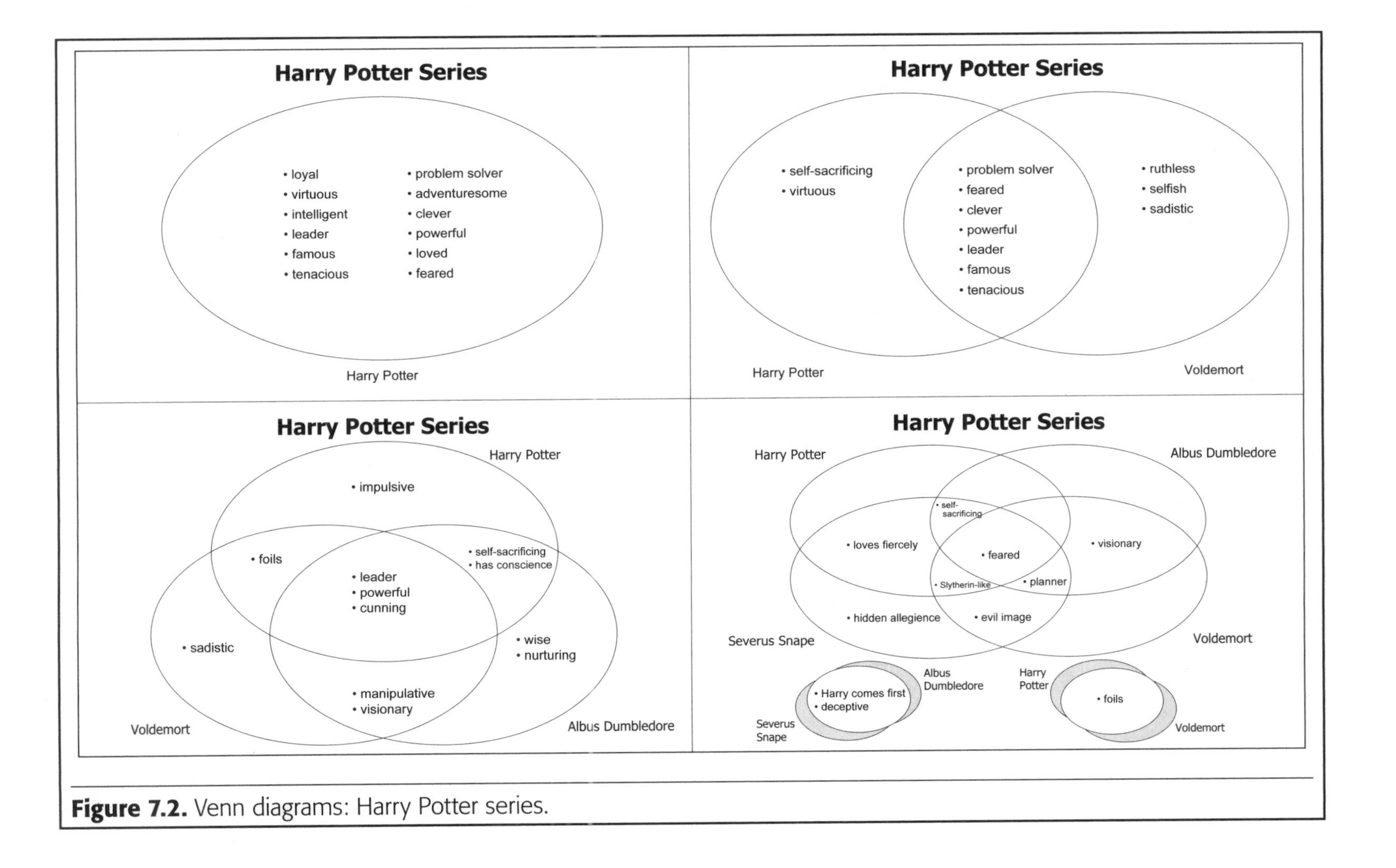

Figure 7.2. Venn diagrams: Harry Potter series.

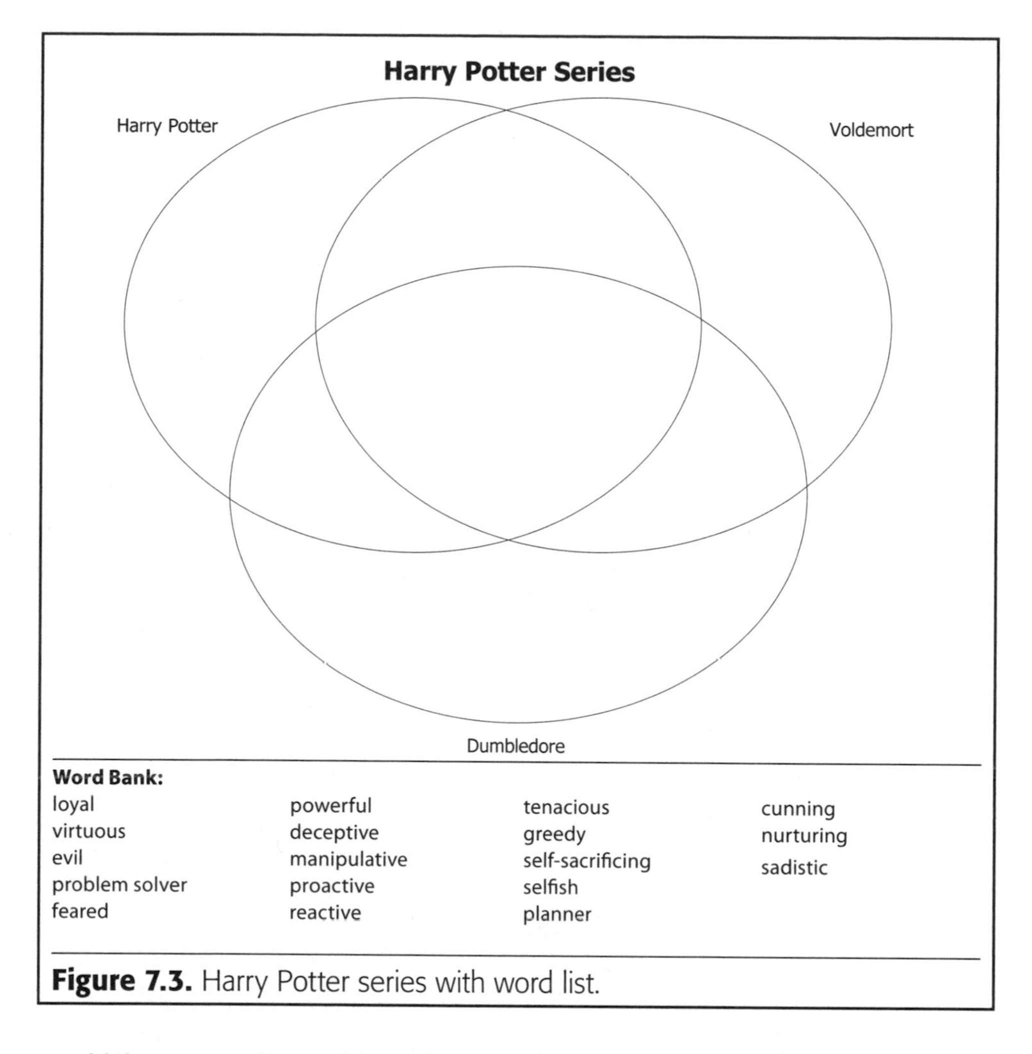

Figure 7.3. Harry Potter series with word list.

would do so according to his readiness as determined by a preassessment. Figure 7.6 shows examples of those varying levels. After individual work, the teacher would lead a class discussion comparing and contrasting fractions, decimals, ratios, and percentages. The debriefing is the most important part of the process. Each student, then, examines the parts of numbers on varying tiers of complexity.

INDIVIDUAL AND/OR GROUP ACTIVITIES

Remember the variation of the T-W-H Chart discussed in Chapter 4? It's not "What did you learn?" but rather "How do you want to learn?" This strategy encourages flexibility in grouping and an open learning environment. Venn diagrams lend themselves readily to group or solo work. To illustrate, in the character analysis example given earlier, you may have four students all working on the one-oval level. Each student could tackle characterization for a different character. They could then group together in partners combining their one oval

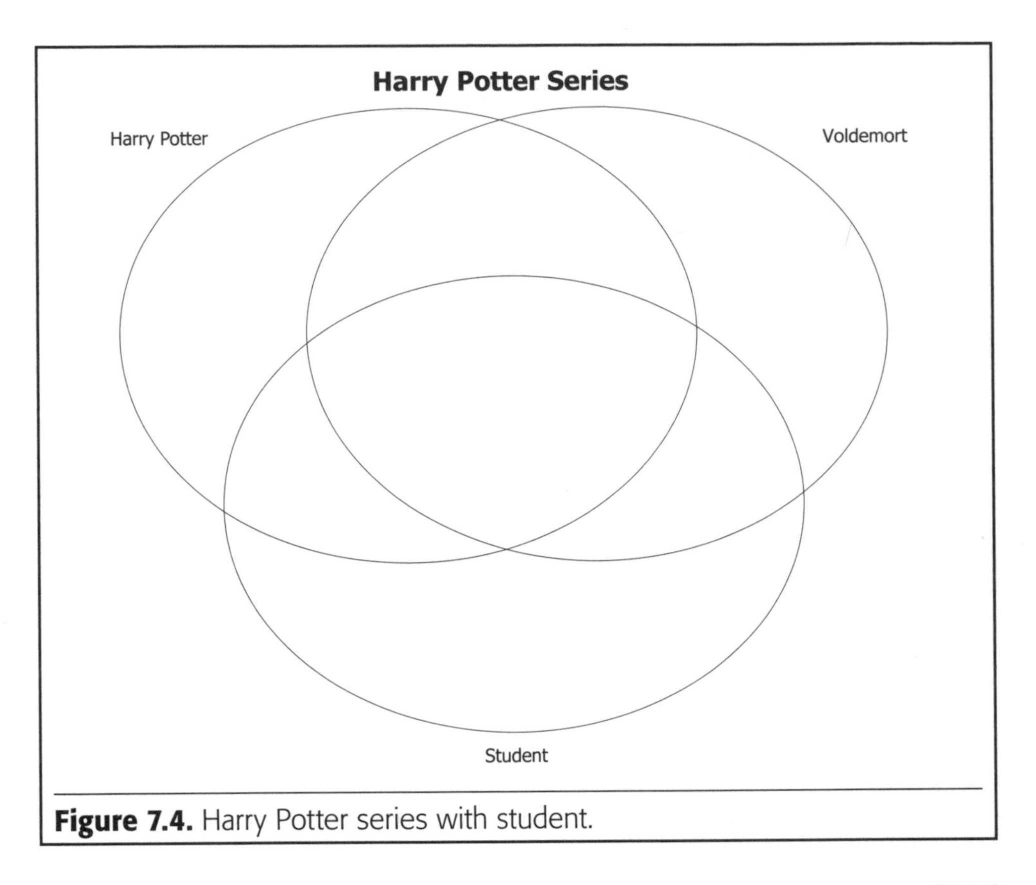

Figure 7.4. Harry Potter series with student.

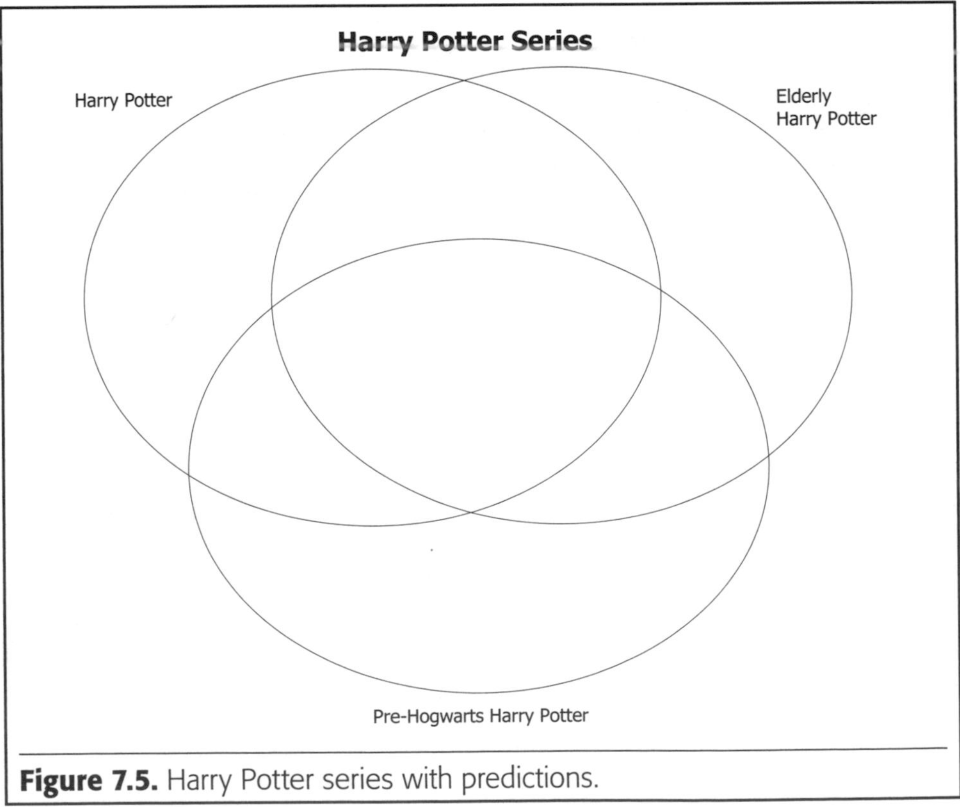

Figure 7.5. Harry Potter series with predictions.

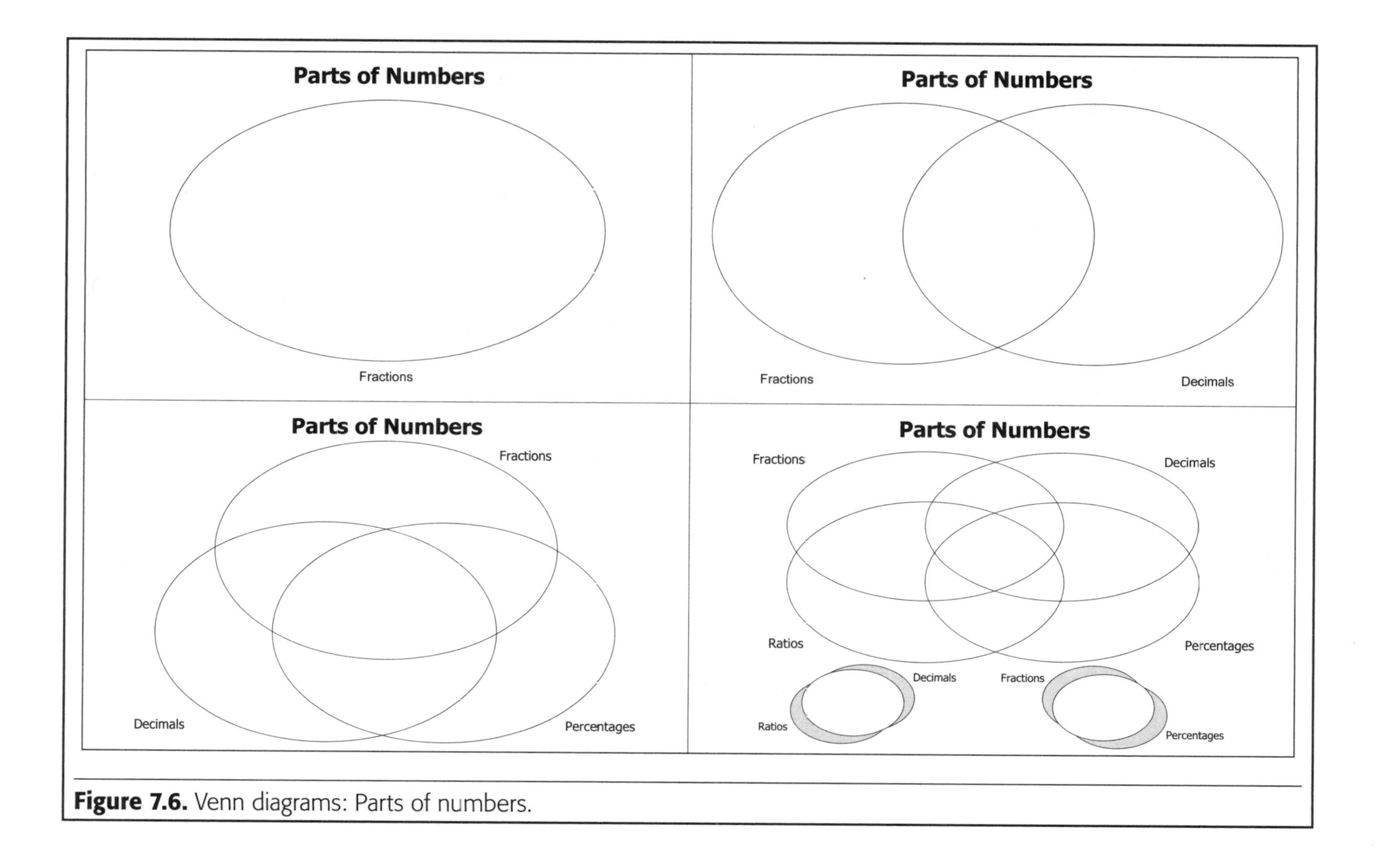

Figure 7.6. Venn diagrams: Parts of numbers.

into two, and eventually those two groups can merge, creating a four-oval Venn comparing and contrasting four characters. You would have students working at their own levels, and, with the help of others, thinking at even higher levels. Venn diagrams easily can be adapted to group or individual work—the choice, the intentional decision, is yours.

For example, a geometry class has been studying quadrilaterals. The pretest indicated varying levels of understanding regarding characteristics of quadrilaterals. An in-class exploration using Venn diagrams proves to be an excellent strategy that will provide continuous progress for every student. Each student receives a sheet with the appropriate number of ovals. Those with one oval will work in pairs so that each student separately can fill out one quadrilateral's characteristics in full, and then work together to complete the compare and contrast version (see Figure 7.7). The others may work alone or in pairs.

DIFFERENTIATING PROCESS IN AN OUT-OF-CLASS LEARNING EXPERIENCE

If Venn diagrams are assigned as homework, the whole-class discussion must still occur. This brings validity to each assignment regardless of the number of ovals. Look at the high levels of thought in the high school example on world religions (see Figure 7.8). Students working with one oval will be challenged just as much as those working with two, three, or four as long as the teacher has preassessed correctly. The complexity of thought does indeed increase as the number of ovals increases. Note the amount of detail in the examples in Figure 7.8.

GRAPHIC ORGANIZERS FOR PREWRITING

Because Venn diagrams are so structured, they serve as excellent graphic organizers for learners to develop and organize their ideas before writing. A self-contained class of gifted fifth graders explored mammals using the Venn this way for a constructed response. Given three ovals, students were to analyze a topic of their choice as they prepared to write. Figure 7.9 is an excellent start to writing that shows great understanding.

This strategy can also be used as a graphic organizer for prewriting for a longer composition. As students brainstorm and develop ideas, Venn diagrams enable them to organize those ideas and elaborate as needed. For example, a class is writing memoirs that focus on a relationship with someone else. Zach wants to write about his grandfather, and he knows that he needs to focus on a few traits of his grandfather that he can develop fully. Figure 7.10 provides examples of four Venn diagrams relating to Zach's topic. If Zach were a novice writer, he would begin with just one oval focusing on a single trait: helpfulness. This prewriting activity would let him focus on multiple examples of his grandfather's helpfulness to flesh out his paper. If Zach fell into an apprentice level in

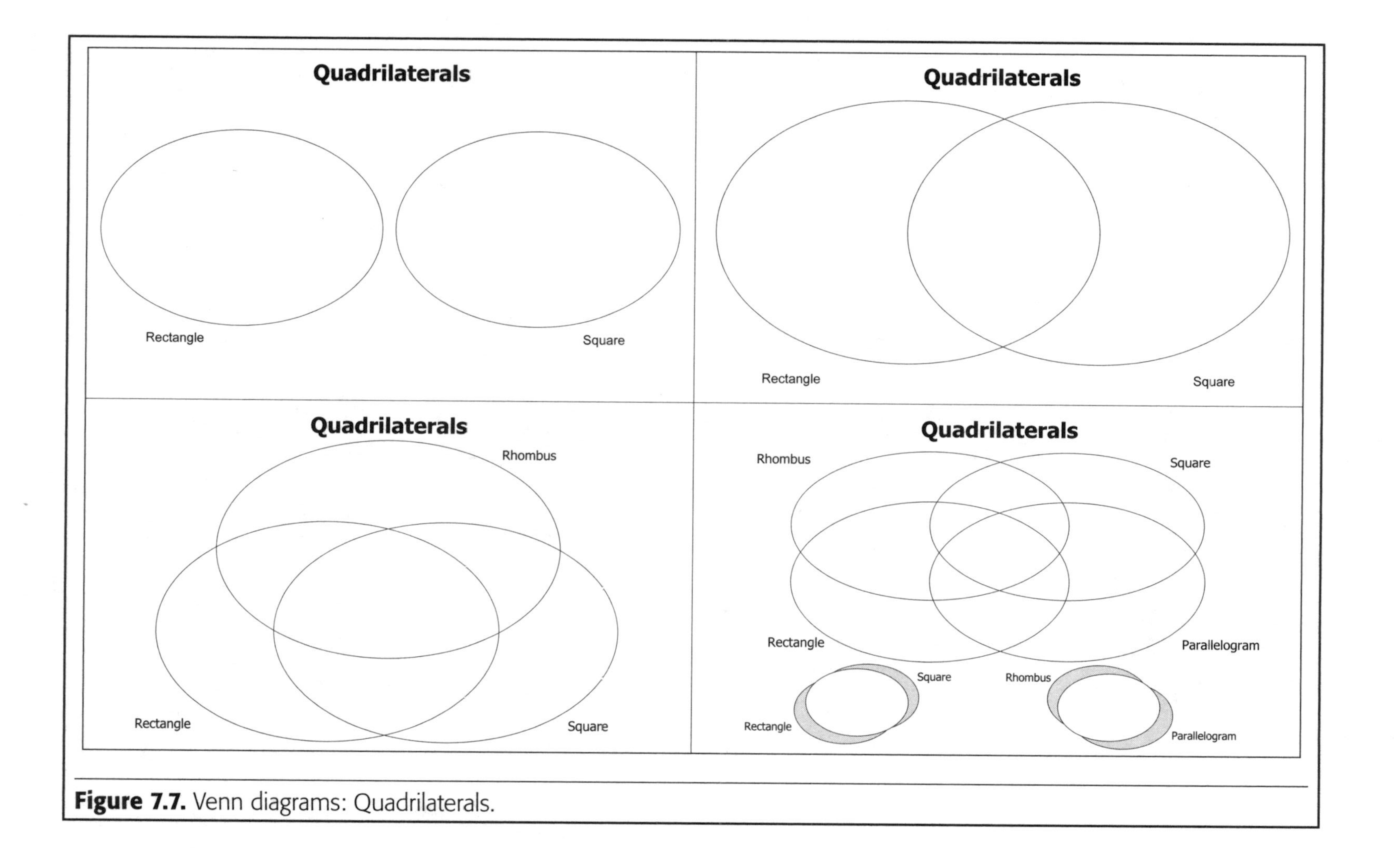

Figure 7.7. Venn diagrams: Quadrilaterals.

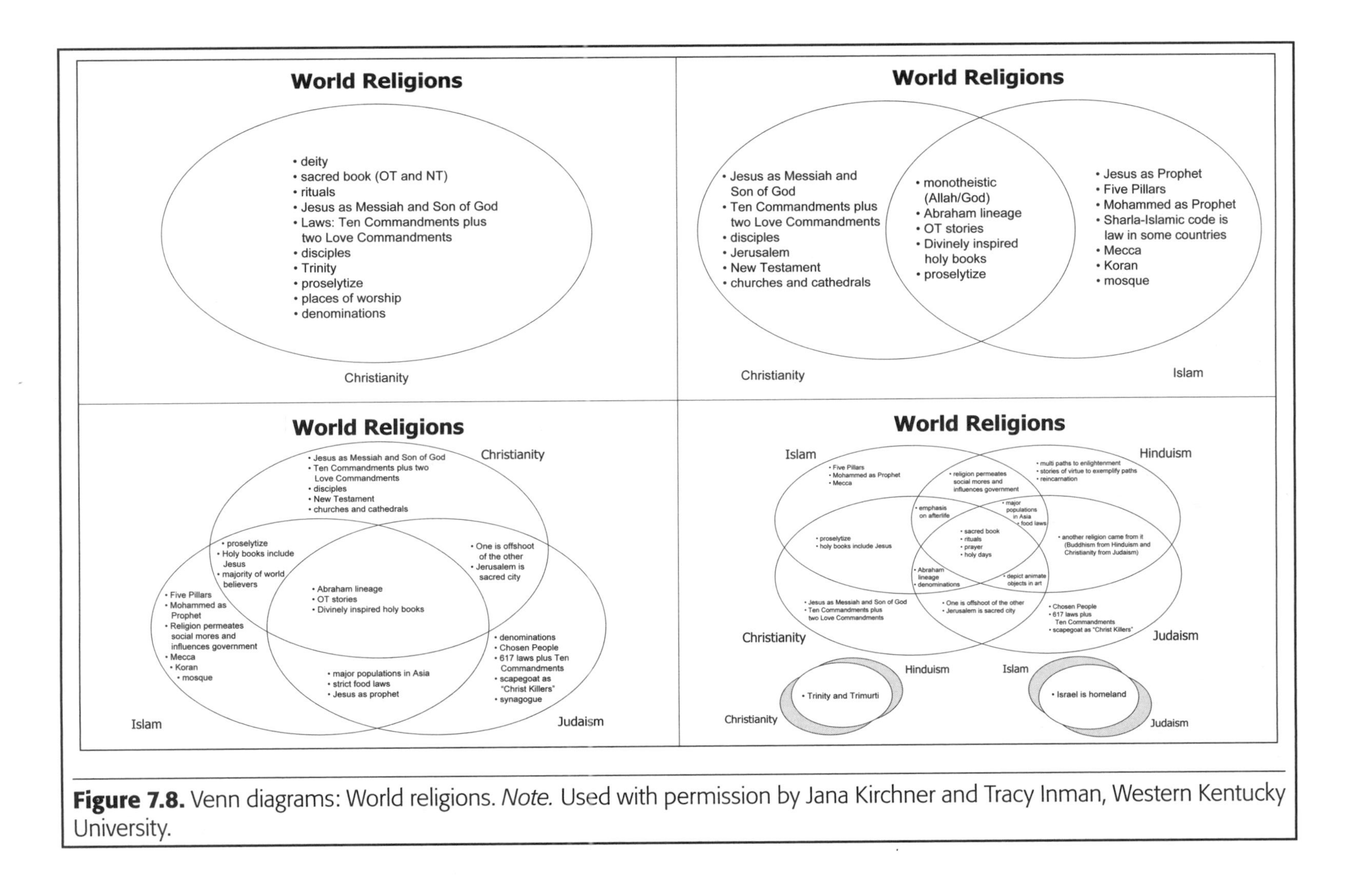

Figure 7.8. Venn diagrams: World religions. *Note.* Used with permission by Jana Kirchner and Tracy Inman, Western Kentucky University.

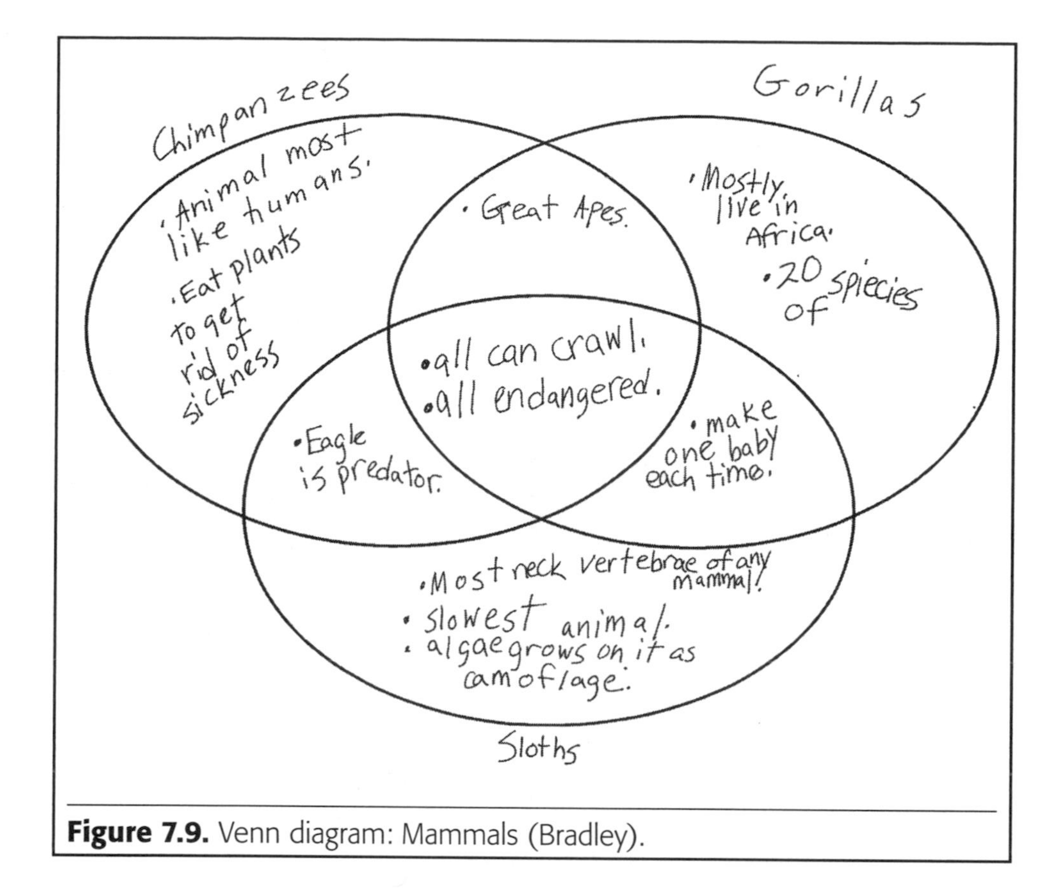

Figure 7.9. Venn diagram: Mammals (Bradley).

writing, he may very well select two traits to develop: helpfulness and being a good sport. By using the traditional Venn diagram, he would find one incident that exhibited both traits: Zach's learning not to get mad at himself in sports by following his grandfather's example. This would serve as an excellent transition between paragraphs or as a closing. Perhaps Zach is a proficient writer capable of more complexity in his writing. In this case, three ovals with an additional trait are more of an appropriate challenge to him. And, if this 10-year-old possesses exemplary writing skills, then four traits better meet his needs. Regardless of the level of ability and complexity, using Venn diagrams as tiered prewriting activities will ensure a strong start to a writing unit.

UNIT REVIEW OR ASSESSMENT

Venn diagrams also work well with a unit review or unit assessment. Again, all students are manipulating the same data or concepts—just on varying levels. Deborah Wyatt, a curriculum, assessment, and instruction consultant, designed a Venn diagram differentiation activity focusing on Kentucky's regions, a social studies exit expectation. In the tasks that follow, please note the varying numbers of characteristics (see Figure 7.11 for visual examples of the activity).

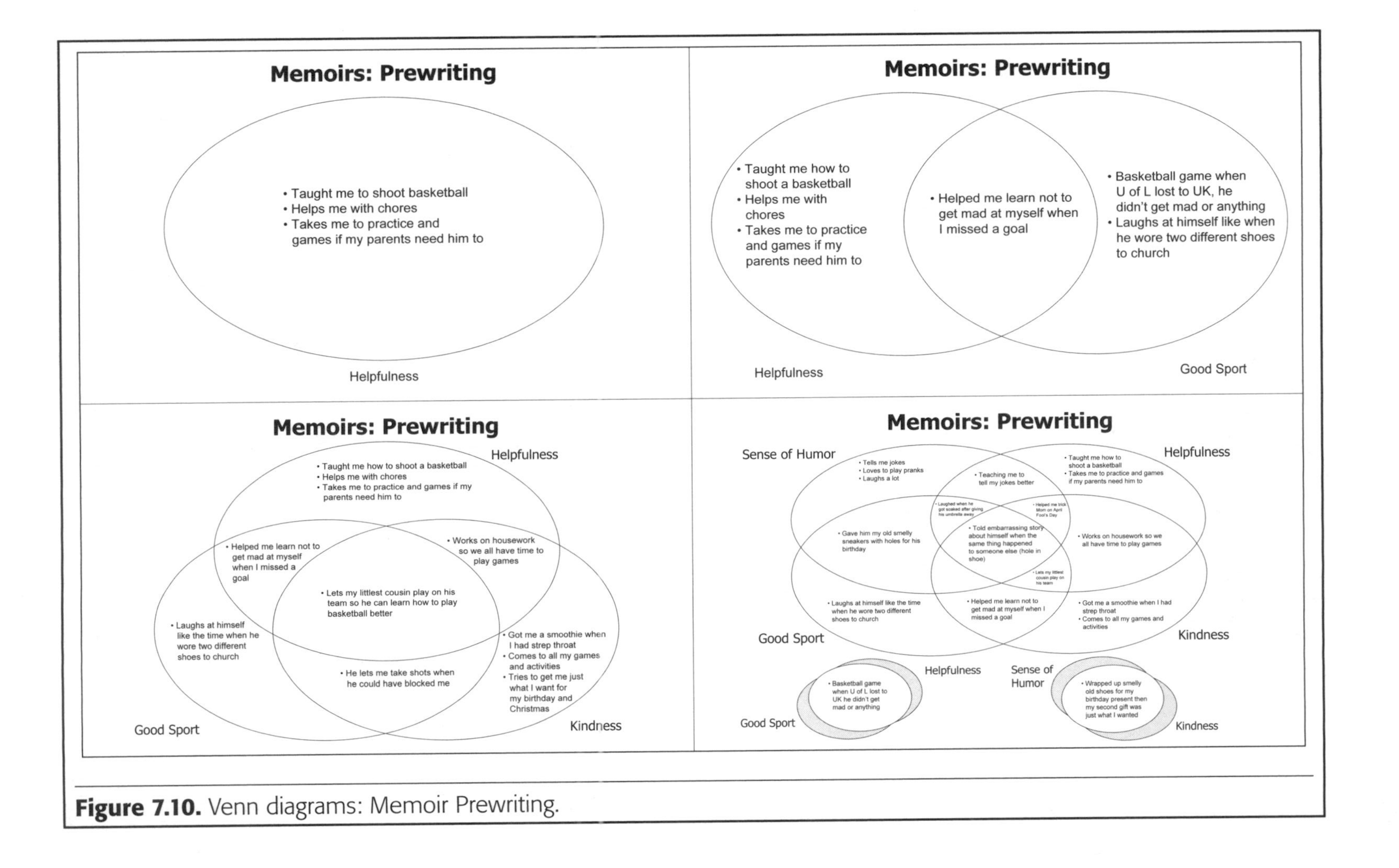

Figure 7.10. Venn diagrams: Memoir Prewriting.

The option of one oval was not provided because Wyatt's preassessment indicated that wasn't needed, but a one-oval analysis is easy to produce:

> Kentucky is divided into six main regions. Choose one of the regions and provide at least 12 characteristics. These may include physical or human characteristics.

Wyatt wrote this prompt for the two-oval version:

> Kentucky is divided into six main regions. Using the Venn diagram with two of the regions, complete each section by providing at least four characteristics for a total of 12. These may include physical or human characteristics.

Wyatt also developed a prompt for a three-oval version:

> Kentucky is divided into six main regions. Using the Venn diagram with three of the regions, complete each section by providing at least 12 characteristics spread among the seven sections. These may include physical or human characteristics.

Finally, Wyatt came up with a four-oval version:

> Kentucky is divided into six main regions. Using the Venn diagram with four of the regions, complete each section by providing at least 12 characteristics spread among the 15 sections. These may include physical or human characteristics.

Wyatt also developed a rubric to assess students' understanding of the topic.

4 Extensive understanding. All information is accurate and complete. Student provides minimum number of characteristics on the diagram in the appropriate place.
3 Appropriate understanding. Most information is accurate and complete. Student provides minimum number of characteristics on the diagram but may have a few errors.
2 Basic understanding. Student attempts to complete Venn diagram. May not provide minimum number of characteristics required. May contain incorrect information or be placed incorrectly.
1 Minimal understanding. Student provides some information on the Venn diagram. May not be complete.

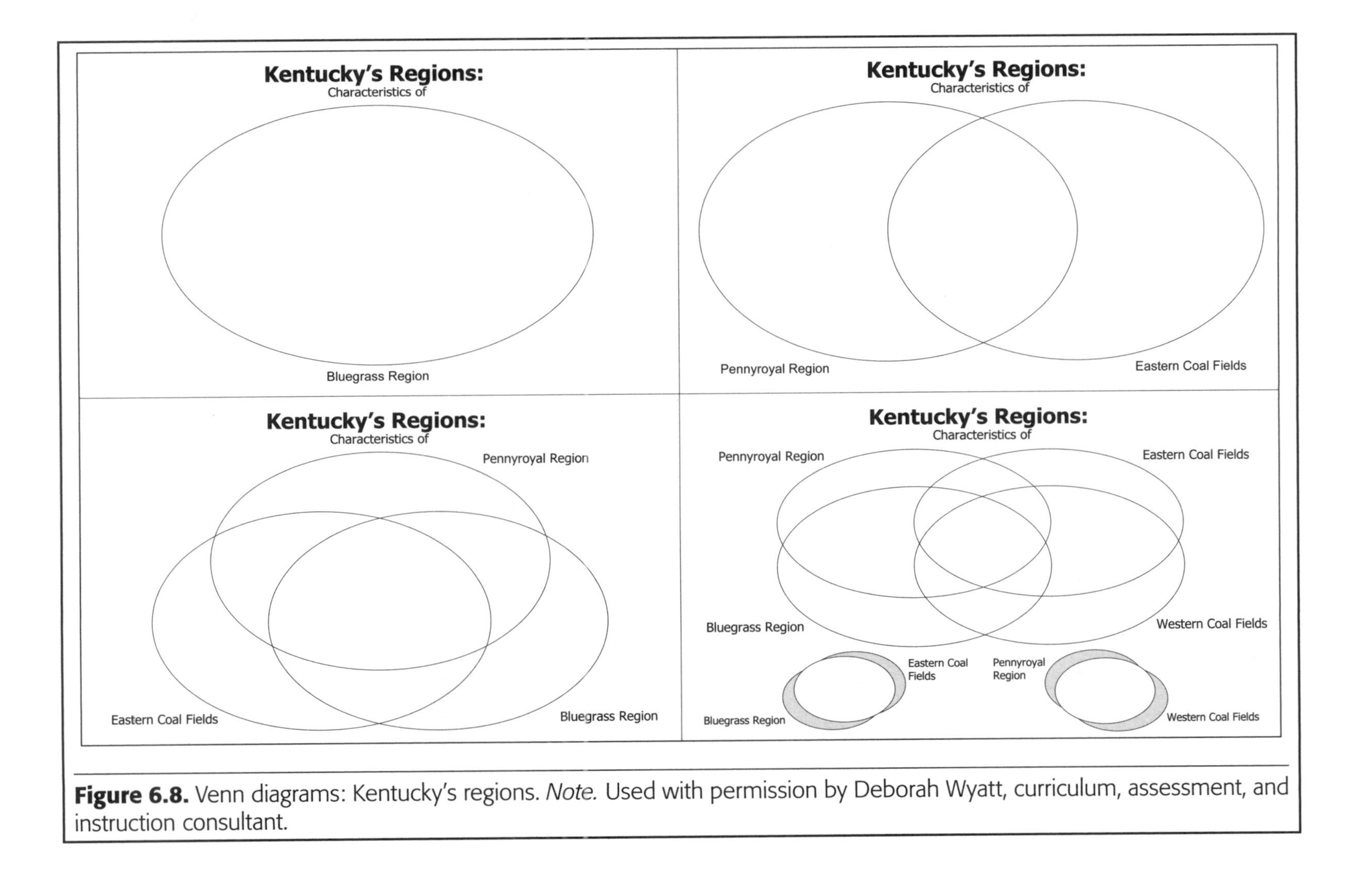

Figure 6.8. Venn diagrams: Kentucky's regions. *Note.* Used with permission by Deborah Wyatt, curriculum, assessment, and instruction consultant.

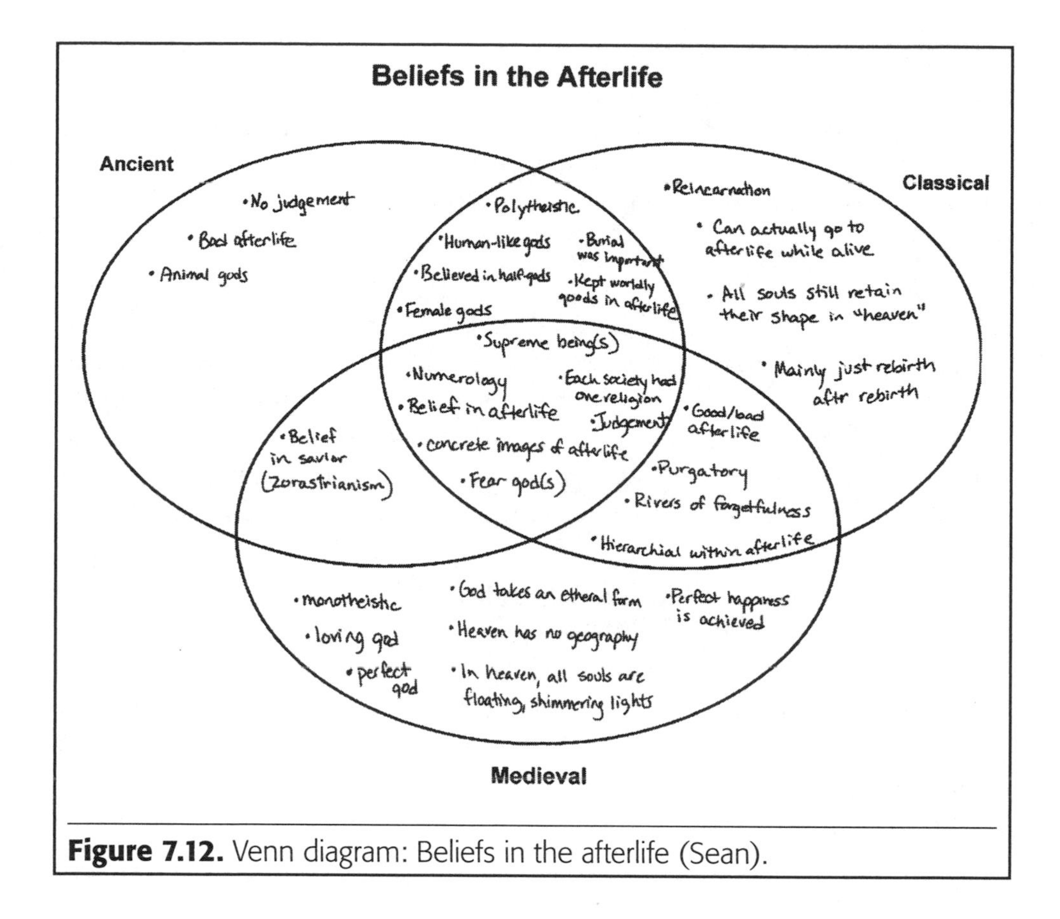

Figure 7.12. Venn diagram: Beliefs in the afterlife (Sean).

0	Information is completely incorrect or irrelevant.
Blank	No response.

If all students are held responsible for the material on varying (and appropriate) levels of complexity, then students experience continuous progress.

A middle school humanities class had been studying different cultural views of the afterlife. Sean's teacher wanted to assess the class's understanding of the material at the end of the unit, so she used Venn diagrams. Figure 7.12 shows Sean's grasp of the unit so far. This served as an excellent assessment tool.

HOW DO I DIFFERENTIATE WITH VENN DIAGRAMS?

Ask yourself: What concept do I want everyone to know and understand when they walk out the door? This is the first question to ask when planning a differentiated or tiered lesson. What is the goal of your lesson? Are you analyzing leadership styles of presidents or causes of revolutions? Are you looking for similarities and differences in artistic styles of Impressionist painters or characteristics of biomes? Perhaps your goal is for students to explore mathematical relationships or character relationships or the relationship between cause and effect. Whatever the concept, be sure that it is multifaceted and complex enough for this tiered assignment.

DECIDE THE FOCUS OF THE CONCEPT

Once you have your concept, consider the ways in which you want students to process it. Are you looking for characteristics? Supporting details? Examples? Causes? Effects? Elements? Relationships? What is it you really want students to know and understand? Once you're clear about what you want, communicate with your students and hold them accountable for your expectations.

HOLD ALL STUDENTS RESPONSIBLE FOR THAT CONCEPT—ON VARYING LEVELS

Design the Venn diagrams so that each learner will be analyzing the concept in the way you intend. For example, if you're analyzing characteristics of animals, you might not want to pair birds and amphibians, and then unrealistically require 20 similarities between the two. Be intentional about your concept and your expectations. (Blank Venn diagram templates have been included in Appendix E for you to reproduce.)

PLACE STUDENTS BY LEVEL

Decide who will work on which level and whether the work will be completed individually, as a group, or as a combination of the two. In order for this to be successful, you must have preassessed your students well (the second question to ask when planning a differentiated lesson). Deciding who will get what number of ovals requires more than guesswork or random distribution. In addition to content, you also may preassess students' learning preferences (e.g., does the student prefer working alone or in a small group?).

ALLOW STUDENTS TO TRY A MORE CHALLENGING LEVEL IF DESIRED

If we want all students to thrive and have continuous progress, then we need to encourage them to stretch their minds and set high expectations. Always allow your students to attempt that next level. Perhaps this would be an optimal time for grouping a student with someone else who also wants to challenge him- or herself more. Be sure to provide plenty of support for those who are taking the risk.

DISTRIBUTE RUBRICS OR SCORING GUIDES

Always make sure that students know your expectations when the assignment is given. Designing the rubrics or scoring guides ensures that you have considered the task carefully and have specific requirements for the grade given. Kanevsky (2003) approached evaluation of the Venn diagram this way:

> Evaluate features of the items in the regions that are most important so students get clear feedback on their strengths and ways they can improve in the future. Accuracy and completeness are essential to pass. Optional criteria can be added as desired to stimulate and reward additional thinking.
>
> - Accuracy—Information in the diagram is correct and placed in correct regions.
> - Completeness—Minimum number of items is provided in each region.
>
> Optional criteria include quantity, quality, and supporting evidence.
>
> - Quantity—Number of times beyond the minimum, or number of items in each region weighted (multiplied) by the number of circles overlapping to create that region.
> - Quality—Subjective rating of the *depth* of reasoning reflected in the richest item(s), or *breadth*, or range of ideas in the items.
> - Supporting Evidence—Presence of evidence and extent to which it supports the item. (p. 44)

DEBRIEF

Make sure that everyone participates in the debriefing discussion. This shouldn't be a problem, because everyone has been analyzing the same concept—at different levels of complexity. The importance of this inclusive participation cannot be stressed enough. It reinforces the respect you have for all learners, wherever they are in their learning journey. Plus, it makes each learner an integral part of your classroom.

WHAT IF VENN DIAGRAMS JUST DON'T WORK FOR YOU?

When you look at more than one oval do your eyes cross? Are you able to think on high levels but just can't figure out where to put what in all those overlapping oval segments? Even if you personally don't have a problem using Venn diagrams, realize that some of your students may. Remember Chapter 3 where we talked about climate and how openness is a critical component of a differentiated classroom? Well, be open to new formats.

Silver, Strong, and Perini (2001) argue there are multiple graphic organizers or tools that help students process information. Various compare-and-contrast organizers accomplish the same task, but they do so in many different designs to appeal to individual learners. For example, their Y organizer may make more sense to someone who needs to compare and contrast than the traditional Venn diagram. Individual characteristics are listed under Topic A or Topic B, whereas shared traits form the bottom of the Y (see Figure 7.13).

If we extrapolate this idea to the ovals concept, one oval is an I (see Figure 7.14), two ovals become the Y, and three ovals are parallel to a Z (see Figure 7.15). The four ovals correspond to a W shape, but it can be messy! Please note the modifications necessary to compare the elements. Appendix F contains examples comparing and contrasting family members using the letter idea.

Silver et al. (2001) also include a box chart for this same type of organization. Here, similar traits go into the box at the bottom (see Figure 7.16 for an example). Blank box charts that can be used to look at two, three, and four concepts also have been included in Appendix F for you to reproduce.

Remember that the Venn diagram (or Y, or box, or whatever visual image you create) is designed to have all learners thinking about the same concept and to hold all students accountable for the same concept but on varying levels of complexity. It's an easy tool to use to tier a lesson.

IMPORTANT TAKE-AWAYS

- Venn diagrams can be used to differentiate process by varying the tiers of complexity.
- If preassessed accurately, the learning experience should take the same amount of time for students whether they are using one, two, three, or four ovals.
- Venn diagrams can be used easily in groups or individually.
- The debriefing is critical; it validates everyone's learning regardless of the complexity of the process.
- Venn diagrams can be used to tier prewriting, unit reviews or assessments, in-class learning experiences, or homework.
- Make sure everyone has the same number of characteristics, qualities, or examples to fill in the ovals. Requiring more for learners ready for complexity is *not* differentiation.

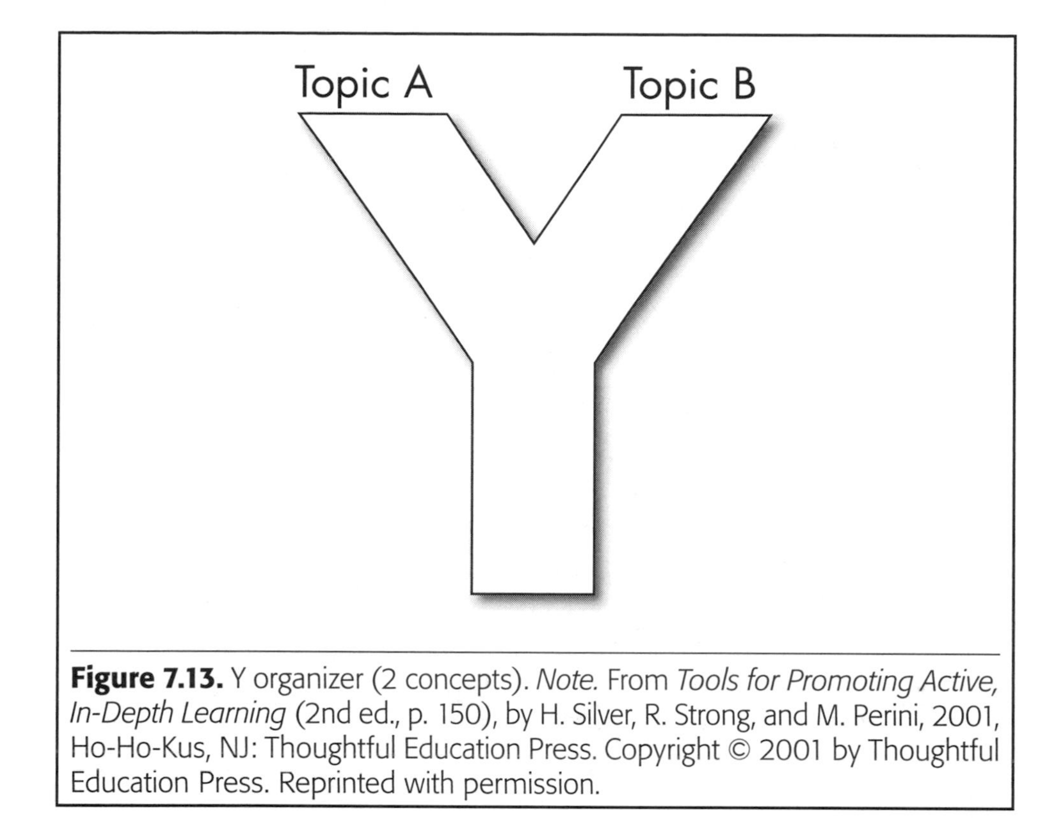

Figure 7.13. Y organizer (2 concepts). *Note.* From *Tools for Promoting Active, In-Depth Learning* (2nd ed., p. 150), by H. Silver, R. Strong, and M. Perini, 2001, Ho-Ho-Kus, NJ: Thoughtful Education Press. Copyright © 2001 by Thoughtful Education Press. Reprinted with permission.

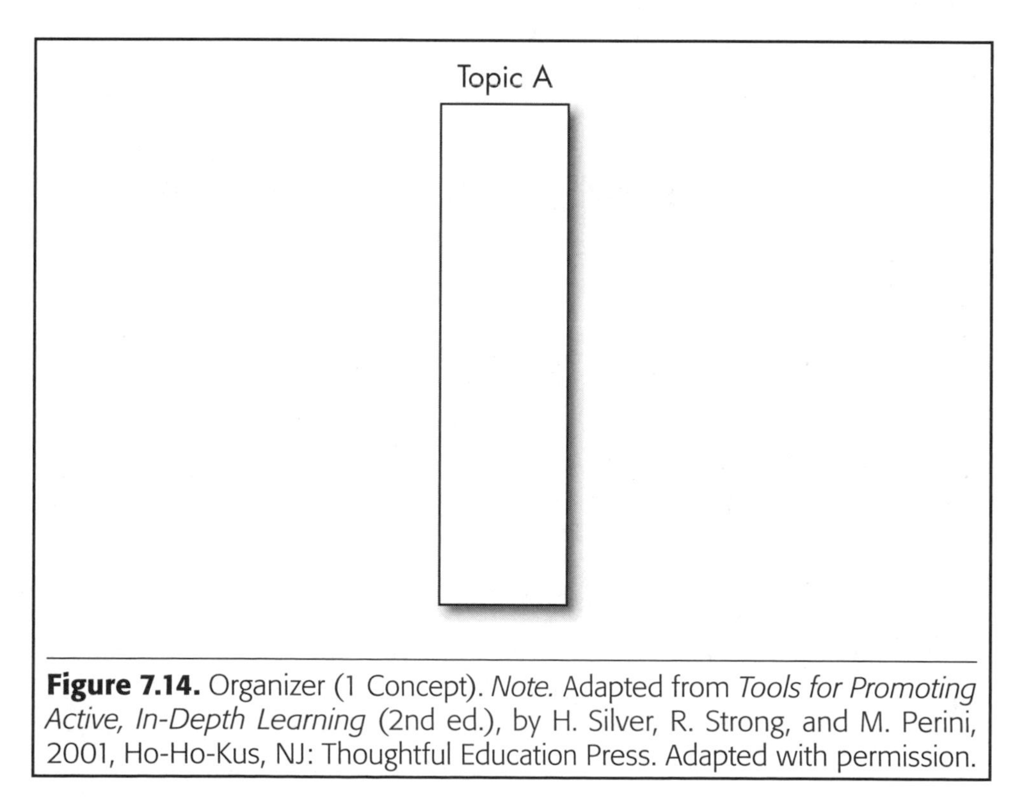

Figure 7.14. Organizer (1 Concept). *Note.* Adapted from *Tools for Promoting Active, In-Depth Learning* (2nd ed.), by H. Silver, R. Strong, and M. Perini, 2001, Ho-Ho-Kus, NJ: Thoughtful Education Press. Adapted with permission.

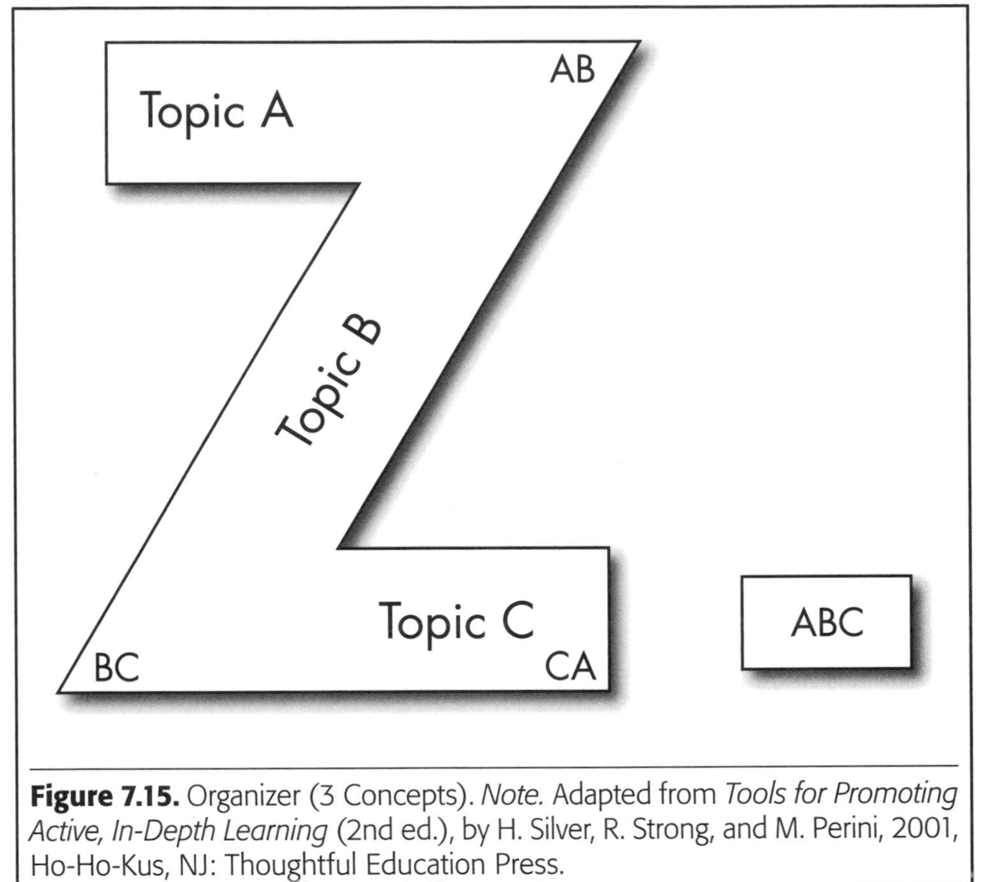

Figure 7.15. Organizer (3 Concepts). *Note.* Adapted from *Tools for Promoting Active, In-Depth Learning* (2nd ed.), by H. Silver, R. Strong, and M. Perini, 2001, Ho-Ho-Kus, NJ: Thoughtful Education Press.

Topic A: City Living	Topic B: Country Living
• Apartments • Office work • Neighborhood stores • Walk most places • Taxis, buses, or subways • No yards • Lots of schools • Buy food	• Houses • Work on farms or in small towns • Stores in town • Cars • Lots of space • Ride bus to school • Maybe one school per county • Grow some of own food
• Playgrounds • Families • Work • Hospitals • School	

Figure 7.16. Box chart: City living versus country living. *Note.* Adapted from *Tools for Promoting Active, In-Depth Learning* (2nd ed.), by H. Silver, R. Strong, and M. Perini, 2001, Ho-Ho-Kus, NJ: Thoughtful Education Press.

CHAPTER
8

Think-Tac-Toe
An Effective Tool for Tiering

The readiness is all. —William Shakespeare

Differentiation is not simply giving students choices. The educational professional must be very intentional about the options provided. Perhaps the options reflect varying levels of readiness. Maybe the activity is designed to address interests. Regardless of the intent, the options must be purposefully selected so that needs, strengths, interests, or abilities of students are taken into consideration.

Many educators recognize the value of this next strategy, calling it by different names such as Think-Tac-Toe or menu (Coil, 2004; Smutny, Walker, & Meckstroth, 1997; Tomlinson, 2003; Winebrenner, 2001). In fact, Westphal (2007, 2009, 2011) has written 12 books filled with menus, broken down by grade level and subject matter. Not only is the Think-Tac-Toe simple to design and use, but it could also increase student motivation because of the control they have over the assignment (i.e., the choices they make). The key to the differentiation angle is intent—the educator's intentional listing of options that match the learning experience to each student. The key to the tiering angle is also intent—the appropriately challenging list of options that match the readiness or ability level of the student according to the preassessment.

WHAT IS IT?

In its simplest form, the Think-Tac-Toe provides multiple options in a tic-tac-toe format for student projects, products, or lessons. Students select one activity from each row to complete. This differentiation strategy encourages choice: *Please allow flexibility in those choices* (in short, don't force them to make a horizontal, vertical, or diagonal line as in the game tic-tac-toe). If a student would rather demonstrate her understanding of acute angles, for example, in a Prezi instead of a puppet show, then more power to her. Rubrics should accompany the assignment and, as always, allow variation in product.

WHAT DOES IT LOOK LIKE?

Think-Tac-Toes may consist of 9, 12, 16, or more (or fewer) squares based on the instructional purpose. Figure 8.1, an example of *Gilgamesh* and Mesopotamia designed for 10th-grade honor students in a World History/World Literature class, provides options in the areas of culture, religion, and literature. For this example, students could be given these instructions:

> As we near the end of our analysis of Mesopotamia and *Gilgamesh*, I want you to show me what you've learned in a way that interests you. Each of you will select one project from each row (category): culture, religion, and literature. The specifics are fleshed out in the accompanying rubrics. Please complete these projects thoughtfully and analytically. They are due in one week.

This assignment ensures that all students are responsible for all three concepts integral to the unit. Please note that this example is not a tiered lesson; there is only one Think-Tac-Toe with a total of nine choices for all students in the class. A tiered lesson might comprise two Think-Tac-Toes, each with nine choices. One has more challenging learning tasks than the other. Each student would receive the appropriate Think-Tac-Toe based on the results of the preassessment; thus, the learning would be tiered based on task complexity and readiness to process the concepts. In this case, because *Gilgamesh* and Mesopotamia are being studied in an honors class, all of the learning experiences are at a higher level of the taxonomy. Each is designed to be intellectually challenging to someone who has been placed in an honors class due to performance or ability.

WHEN DO I USE IT?

Although Think-Tac-Toes can also be used to differentiate in other ways (by interests or learning profiles, for example), the main part of this chapter will be devoted to tiering with Think-Tac-Toes—that is, varying the level of complexity for the students. This mandates at least two Think-Tac-Toes. Just like the Bloom Chart as discussed in Chapter 6, if students were given the choice of multiple learning experiences spanning the range of difficulty in one Think-Tac-Toe, most would choose the easier tasks regardless whether those tasks were most

Culture	Write a survival guide to navigating Mesopotamian culture to be shared with foreign travelers of the time.	Create a skit demonstrating several of Hammurabi's laws incorporated into today's society.	Based on clues from the epic and your understanding of Mesopotamian city-states, predict what Uruk would look like. Create a model using your choice of medium.
Literature	Choose a fictional hero and a hero from real life. Compare and contrast the heroic characteristics of both with Gilgamesh's using a product of your choice.	Compare and contrast Utnapishtim's flood experience with Noah's. Design your own written product.	Create a cuneiform tablet that explicates the theme of Gilgamesh.
Religion	Create a presentation to the priest-king of a city-state explaining why one of the technological advances is needed.	Predict what the Mesopotamian afterlife would be like based on Enkidu's dream. Illustrate that image utilizing your choice of medium.	Write and illustrate a children's book entitled *Religion: The Anchor of Ancient Mesopotamia*. Be sure to defend the title.

Figure 8.1. Think-Tac-Toe: Mesopotamia and *Gilgamesh. Note.* Used with permission by Jana Kirchner and Tracy Inman, Western Kentucky University. Unpublished lesson.

appropriate for the student. Therefore, it is your job as the educational professional to match the list of choices to the student's readiness or ability based on the preassessment.

As mentioned earlier, tiered learning experiences fit beautifully into many classroom scenarios. Tiered Think-Tac-Toes work well in projects accompanying units, unit reviews, or unit assessments. Due to the typical length of project development, you must be careful about using them for a single class period. If you do want to, be very intentional about the time students need to develop a high-quality product.

PROJECT TO ACCOMPANY UNIT

When students are a part of a community of learners where they are accustomed to the fact that not everyone will learn everything in the same way, it becomes commonplace to have different options presented. When a professional educator intentionally (note that word again) creates two Think-Tac-Toes designed for learners of varying ability or readiness levels in order to tier instruction, it's more of a Cracker Jack scenario ("What'd you get?") than a competitive one.

This first tiered example provides options for a K–1 class studying America through its symbols, songs, and places. In addition to whole-group instruction, each child will work on projects that accompany the unit. Figure 8.2 provides a challenge to students who are ready to process the concepts at lower levels. Note how the options all fall under the remember, understand, or apply levels of Bloom's taxonomy. Figure 8.3 provides challenge for those students ready to process concepts at the highest level of Bloom's taxonomy. They will be analyzing, evaluating, and creating in their choices. If preassessed correctly, the match for each child will provide appropriate levels of challenge.

Another example explores the three branches of government. One Think-Tac-Toe (see Figure 8.4) is designed for those students needing less challenge. The other (Figure 8.5) works better for the students who need more challenge.

An intermediate class is studying atoms and molecules. The teacher passes out the appropriately challenging Think-Tac-Toe near the beginning of the unit. Students are to choose two of the four learning experiences to complete by the unit's end. See Figures 8.6 and 8.7.

SEMESTER REVIEWS

Hands-on, minds-on options revolutionize a unit or semester review. Instead of written or oral questions and answers, projects not only provide choice for the student (thus increasing motivation), but the projects also help to encode the information in multiple parts of the brain. Many middle school children, for example, study the elements of art, music, and dance, and they are held accountable for that material on a state exam. Instead of drill and practice, think how meaningful these projects would be—not just for the students completing them, but for those watching others present. For students reviewing the elements of art, music, and dance who need less challenging learning experiences, Figure 8.8 would provide worthy ways to review the important concepts in these content areas. Figure 8.9 provides more complex learning experiences so that the all learners can be appropriately challenged. All students, then, spend time exploring the elements of art, music, and dance as they prepare for the end-of-semester exam.

An elementary science class has been studying Earth and space science all semester. Figures 8.10 and 8.11 provide many learning experiences so that students can choose the ways in which they want to review. Each learning experience is directly linked to a standard, which is italicized. Note that the review is tiered with one set of learning experiences more challenging than the other. The match of Think-Tac-Toe to student provides the individual challenge.

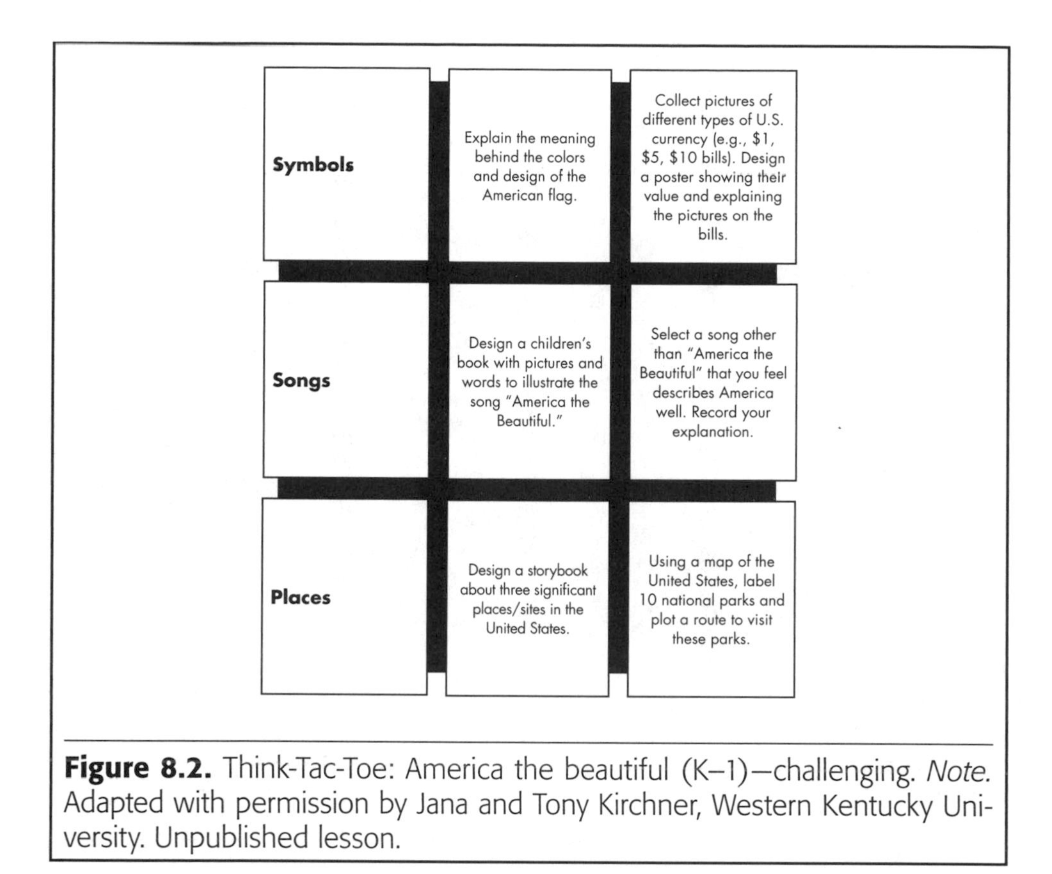

Figure 8.2. Think-Tac-Toe: America the beautiful (K–1)—challenging. *Note.* Adapted with permission by Jana and Tony Kirchner, Western Kentucky University. Unpublished lesson.

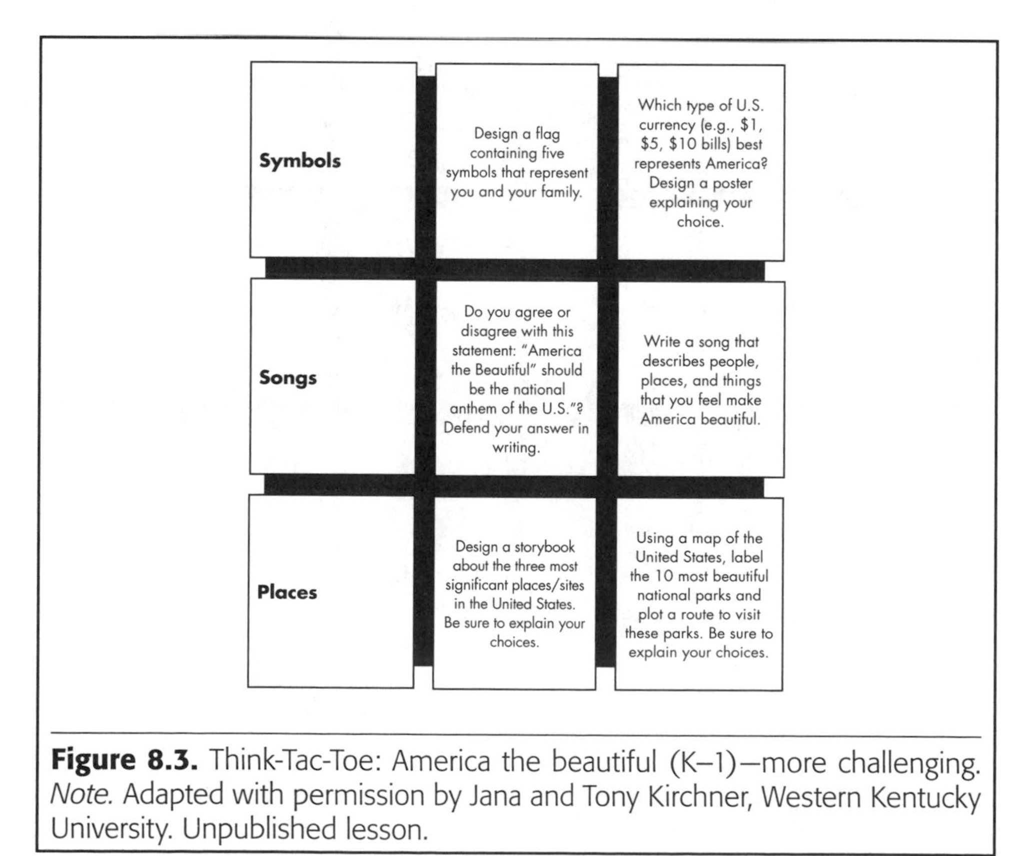

Figure 8.3. Think-Tac-Toe: America the beautiful (K–1)—more challenging. *Note.* Adapted with permission by Jana and Tony Kirchner, Western Kentucky University. Unpublished lesson.

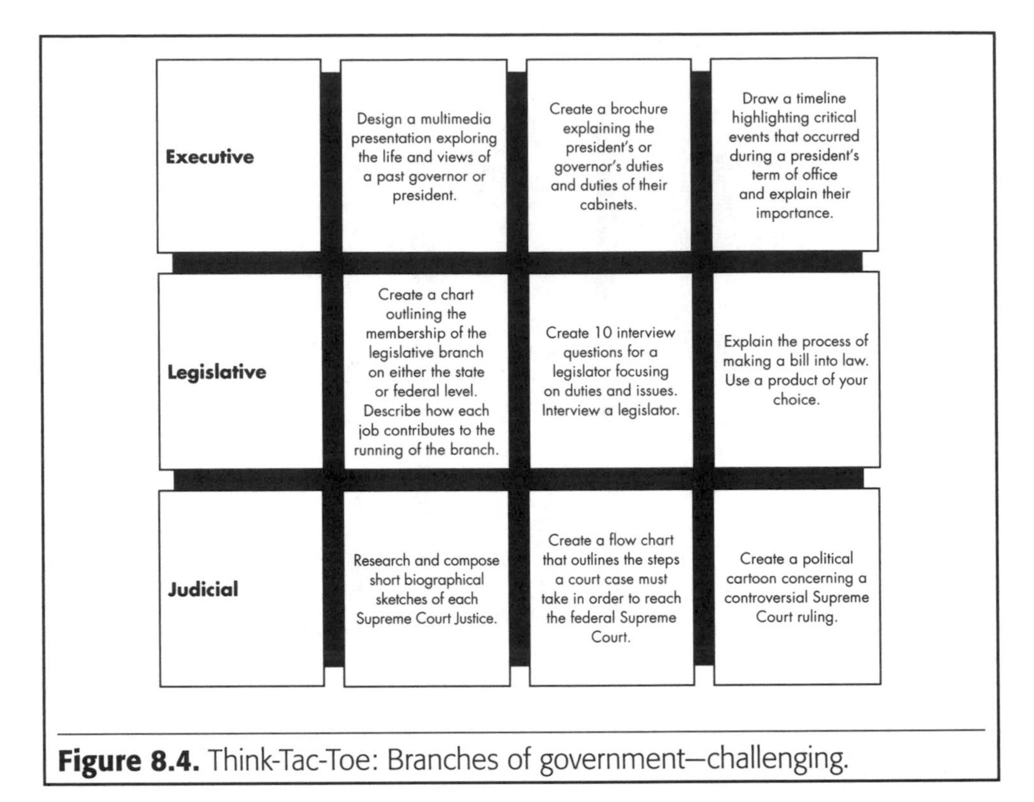

Executive	Design a multimedia presentation exploring the life and views of a past governor or president.	Create a brochure explaining the president's or governor's duties and duties of their cabinets.	Draw a timeline highlighting critical events that occurred during a president's term of office and explain their importance.
Legislative	Create a chart outlining the membership of the legislative branch on either the state or federal level. Describe how each job contributes to the running of the branch.	Create 10 interview questions for a legislator focusing on duties and issues. Interview a legislator.	Explain the process of making a bill into law. Use a product of your choice.
Judicial	Research and compose short biographical sketches of each Supreme Court Justice.	Create a flow chart that outlines the steps a court case must take in order to reach the federal Supreme Court.	Create a political cartoon concerning a controversial Supreme Court ruling.

Figure 8.4. Think-Tac-Toe: Branches of government—challenging.

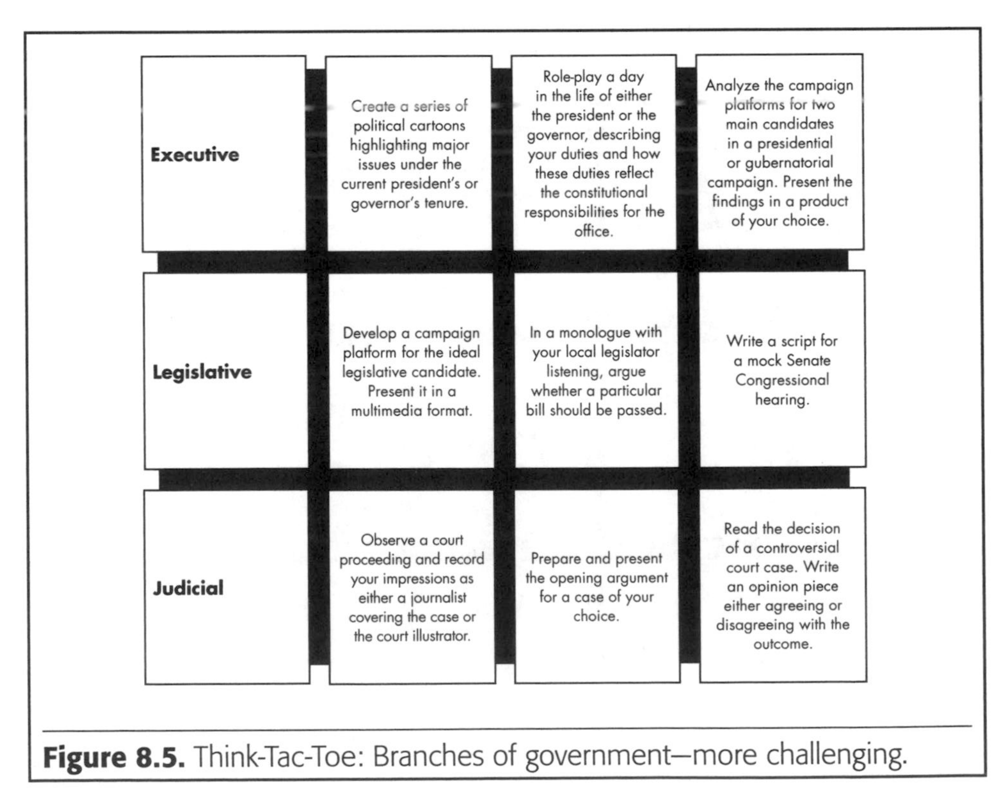

Executive	Create a series of political cartoons highlighting major issues under the current president's or governor's tenure.	Role-play a day in the life of either the president or the governor, describing your duties and how these duties reflect the constitutional responsibilities for the office.	Analyze the campaign platforms for two main candidates in a presidential or gubernatorial campaign. Present the findings in a product of your choice.
Legislative	Develop a campaign platform for the ideal legislative candidate. Present it in a multimedia format.	In a monologue with your local legislator listening, argue whether a particular bill should be passed.	Write a script for a mock Senate Congressional hearing.
Judicial	Observe a court proceeding and record your impressions as either a journalist covering the case or the court illustrator.	Prepare and present the opening argument for a case of your choice.	Read the decision of a controversial court case. Write an opinion piece either agreeing or disagreeing with the outcome.

Figure 8.5. Think-Tac-Toe: Branches of government—more challenging.

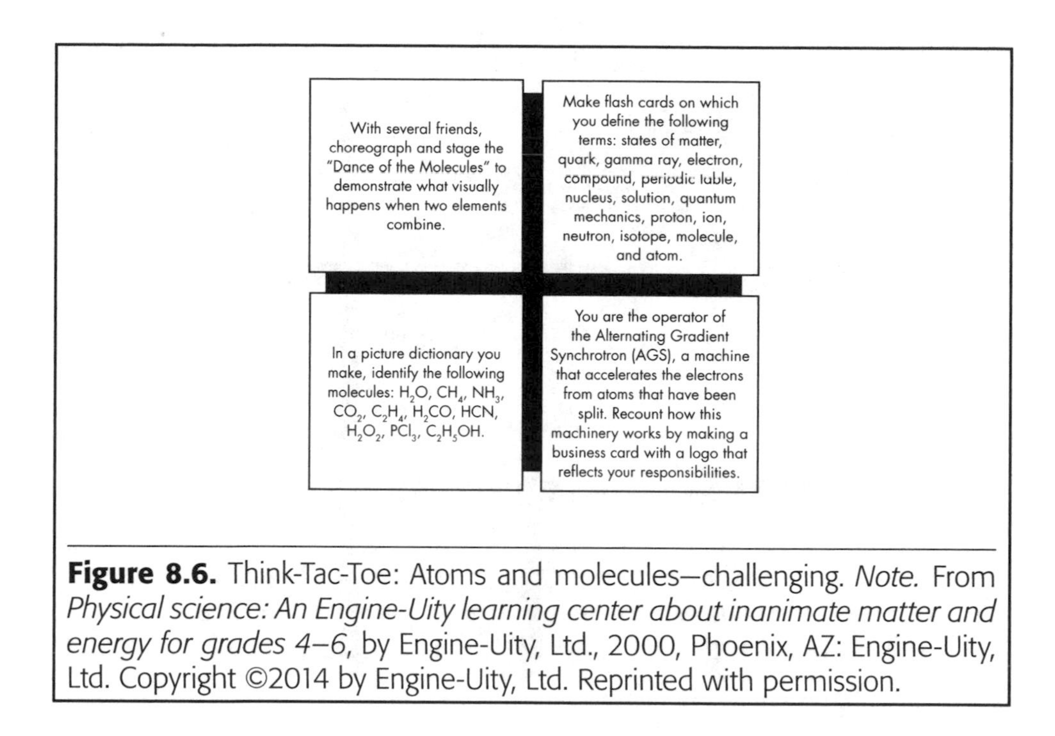

Figure 8.6. Think-Tac-Toe: Atoms and molecules—challenging. *Note.* From *Physical science: An Engine-Uity learning center about inanimate matter and energy for grades 4–6*, by Engine-Uity, Ltd., 2000, Phoenix, AZ: Engine-Uity, Ltd. Copyright ©2014 by Engine-Uity, Ltd. Reprinted with permission.

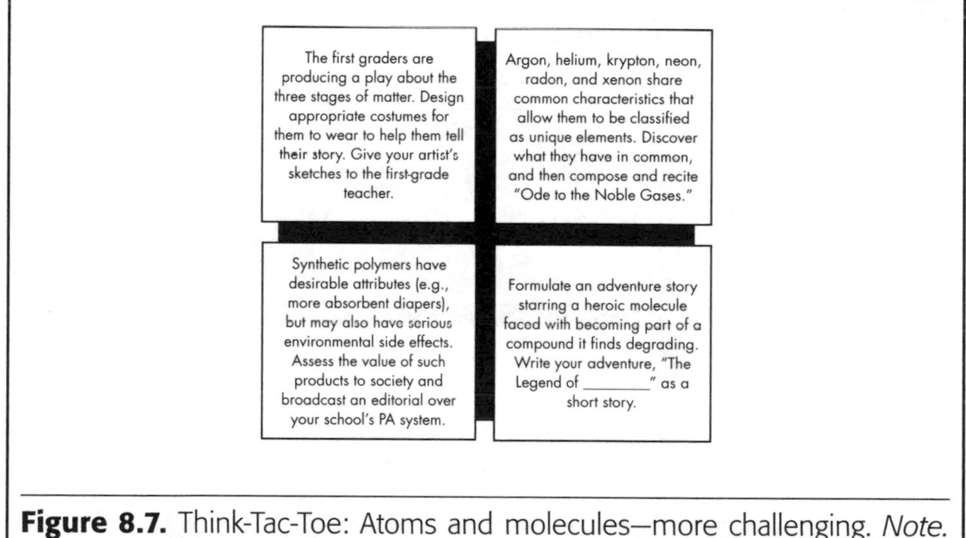

Figure 8.7. Think-Tac-Toe: Atoms and molecules—more challenging. *Note.* From *Physical science: An Engine-Uity learning center about inanimate matter and energy for grades 4–6*, by Engine-Uity, Ltd. 2000, Phoenix, AZ: Engine-Uity, Ltd. Copyright ©2014 by Engine-Uity, Ltd. Reprinted with permission.

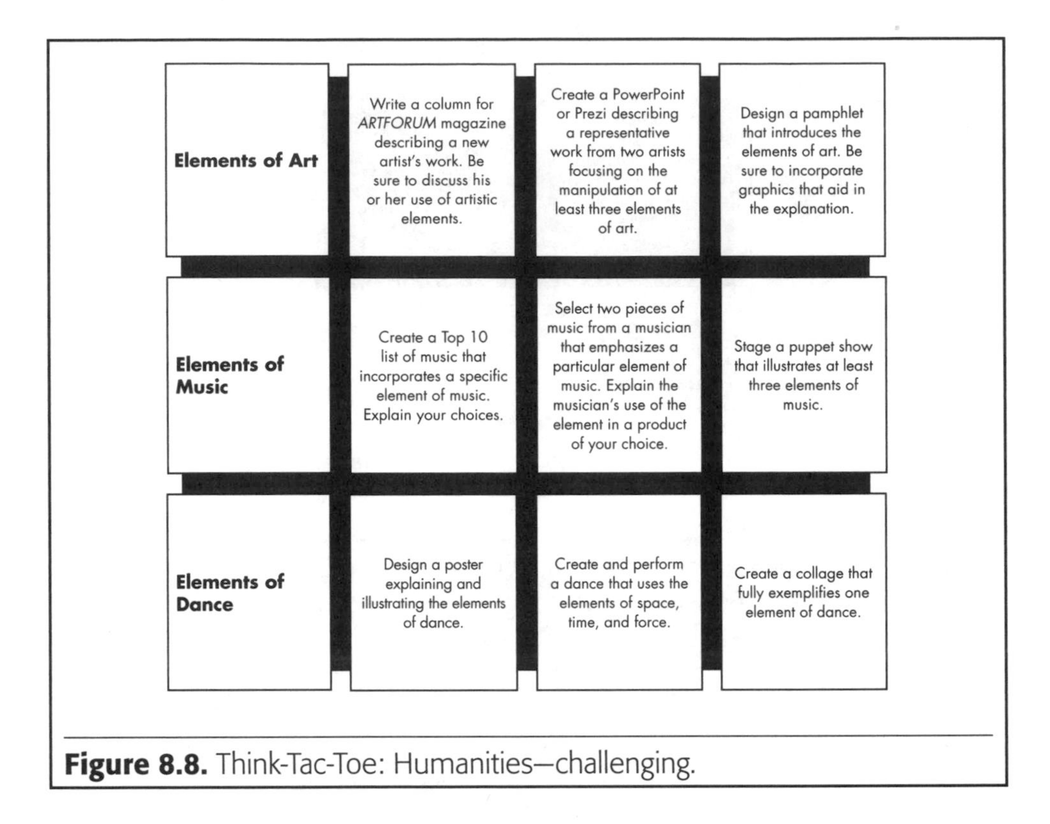

Elements of Art	Write a column for *ARTFORUM* magazine describing a new artist's work. Be sure to discuss his or her use of artistic elements.	Create a PowerPoint or Prezi describing a representative work from two artists focusing on the manipulation of at least three elements of art.	Design a pamphlet that introduces the elements of art. Be sure to incorporate graphics that aid in the explanation.
Elements of Music	Create a Top 10 list of music that incorporates a specific element of music. Explain your choices.	Select two pieces of music from a musician that emphasizes a particular element of music. Explain the musician's use of the element in a product of your choice.	Stage a puppet show that illustrates at least three elements of music.
Elements of Dance	Design a poster explaining and illustrating the elements of dance.	Create and perform a dance that uses the elements of space, time, and force.	Create a collage that fully exemplifies one element of dance.

Figure 8.8. Think-Tac-Toe: Humanities—challenging.

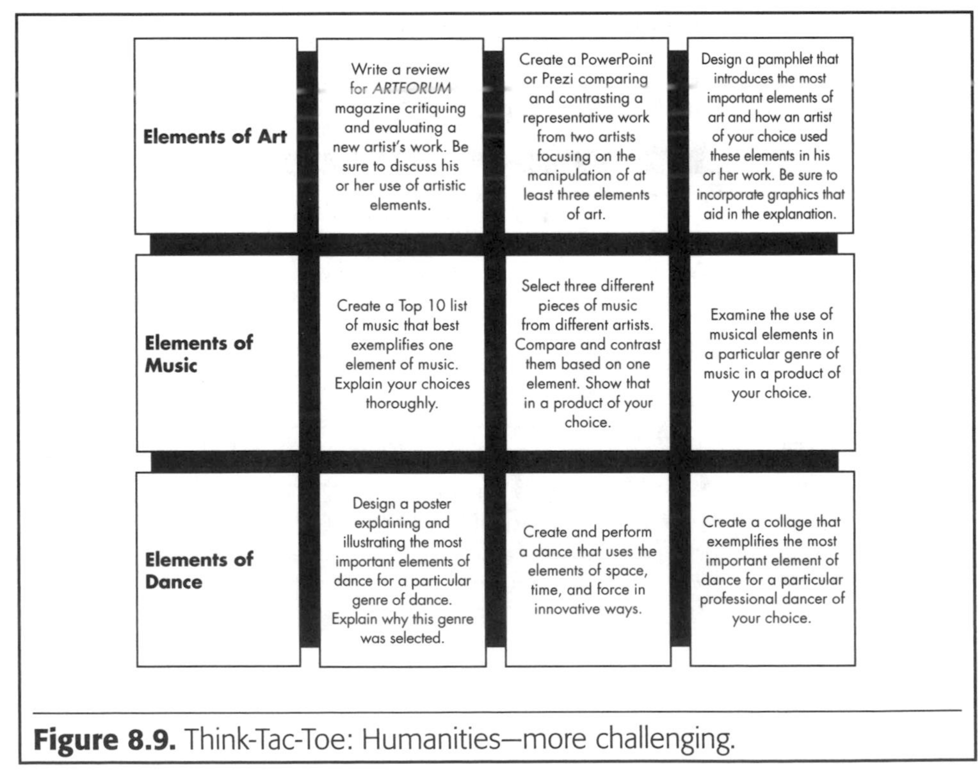

Elements of Art	Write a review for *ARTFORUM* magazine critiquing and evaluating a new artist's work. Be sure to discuss his or her use of artistic elements.	Create a PowerPoint or Prezi comparing and contrasting a representative work from two artists focusing on the manipulation of at least three elements of art.	Design a pamphlet that introduces the most important elements of art and how an artist of your choice used these elements in his or her work. Be sure to incorporate graphics that aid in the explanation.
Elements of Music	Create a Top 10 list of music that best exemplifies one element of music. Explain your choices thoroughly.	Select three different pieces of music from different artists. Compare and contrast them based on one element. Show that in a product of your choice.	Examine the use of musical elements in a particular genre of music in a product of your choice.
Elements of Dance	Design a poster explaining and illustrating the most important elements of dance for a particular genre of dance. Explain why this genre was selected.	Create and perform a dance that uses the elements of space, time, and force in innovative ways.	Create a collage that exemplifies the most important element of dance for a particular professional dancer of your choice.

Figure 8.9. Think-Tac-Toe: Humanities—more challenging.

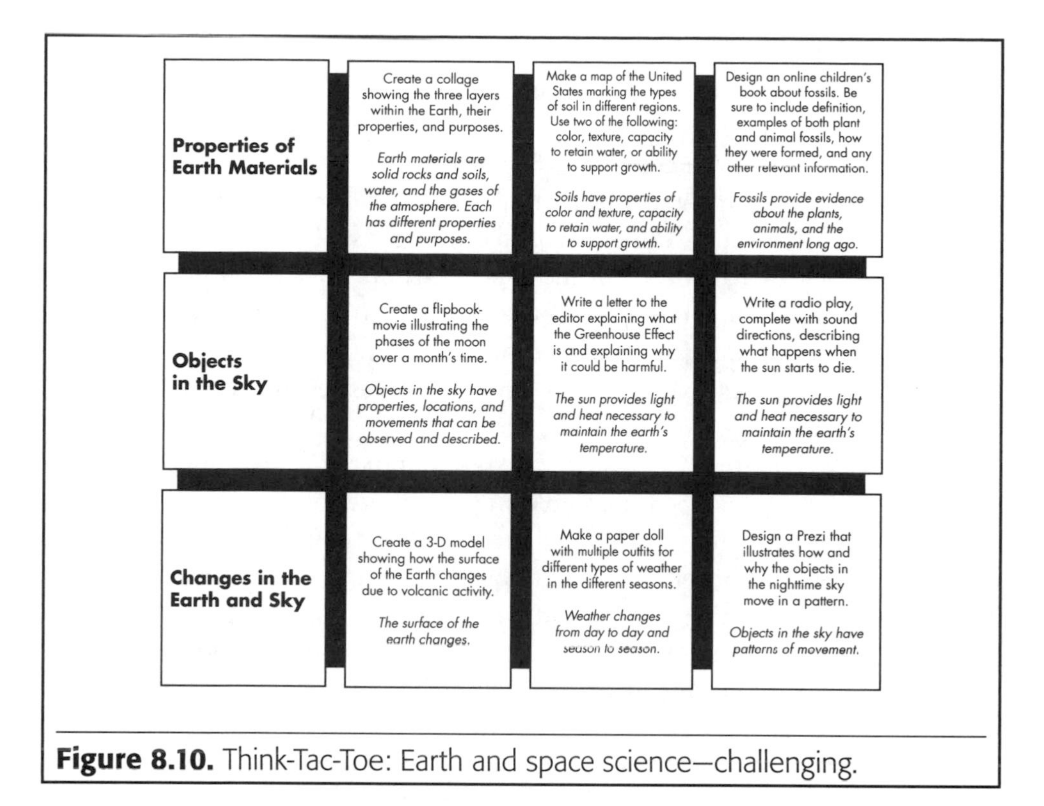

Figure 8.10. Think-Tac-Toe: Earth and space science—challenging.

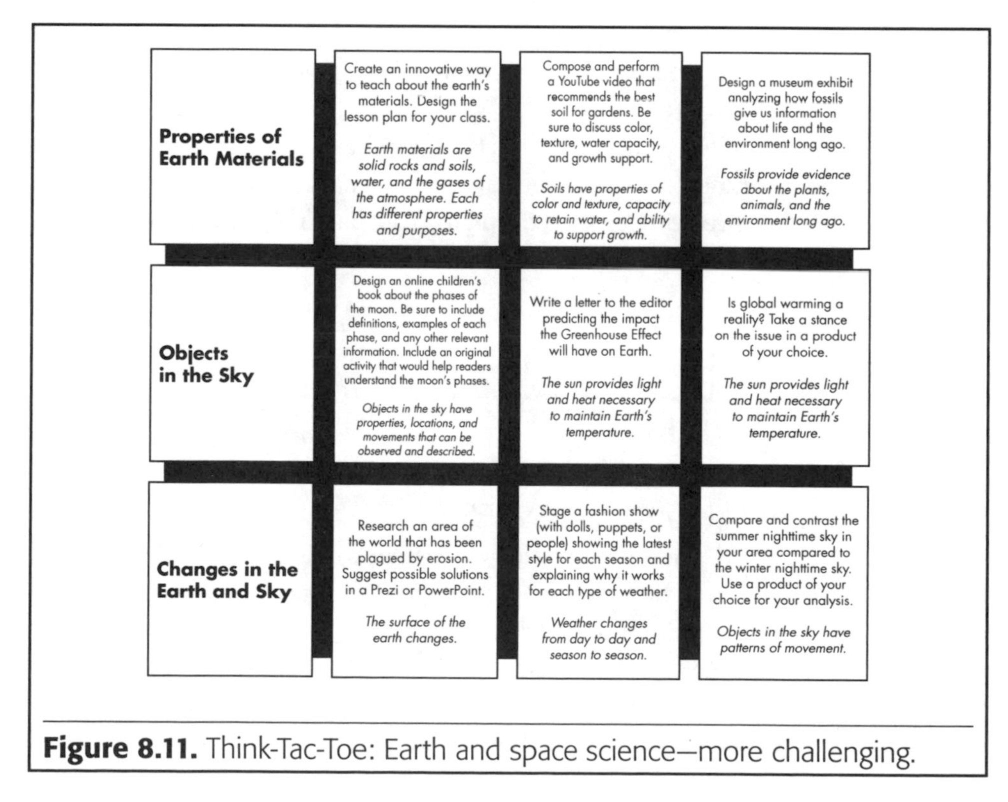

Figure 8.11. Think-Tac-Toe: Earth and space science—more challenging.

UNIT ASSESSMENTS

If the main educational concern of your unit is children learning content (instead of skills such as essay writing or persuasive speaking), then *how* they show they've learned the concept is far less important than *what* they show they've learned. A Think-Tac-Toe, then, is a wonderful alternative to pen-and-paper tests. It allows that young man gifted in the visual arts a chance to show you what he's learned about the theme of *Maniac McGee* in a medium that suits him best, such as an illustration or collage. It proves to be a welcomed motivator. Likewise, if a young woman happens to be a techie, then she can demonstrate her new knowledge of the production elements of theater in a way that ensures success: a Prezi presentation or a webpage.

Don't feel as if you have to sacrifice your standards for summative assessments. Tiered assessments are a viable way to differentiate to address student strengths. Think-Tac-Toes can be designed to be rigorous. If you feel as if you must have a pen-and-paper assessment, then compromise by making the Think-Tac-Toe activities worth 50 points and the other part worth 50 points. Remember that it's your classroom. Just as students have choices, so do teachers. Also, remember that your goal is continuous progress for all students. Alternative unit assessments better meet the needs of your students, at least some of the time. High school students, for example, who have studied a career unit that includes résumé writing and interviewing skills could better demonstrate their learning of the material through such products as those found in Figure 8.12 (for those who need less of a challenge) and Figure 8.13 (for those who need more challenge) than in a traditional written exam.

These next examples (Figures 8.14 and 8.15) can be used in an Algebra II class that has finished a unit on the quadratic equation. As part of the final assessment, students will select two activities to complete. This part is tiered because of the two difficulty levels of the Think-Tac-Toe.

HOW ELSE CAN THINK-TAC-TOES BE USED TO DIFFERENTIATE?

OPTIONAL LEARNING EXPERIENCES

You've preassessed, and two students have already mastered your unit. Winebrenner (2001) noted that 80% or greater proficiency indicates the need to move on. What do you do? You could incorporate a Think-Tac-Toe that explores the subject matter in greater depth or takes a tangential aspect of the content and provides options for study. A graduate course could be taught on almost any single concept, so taking the content and extending it should be very possible. While

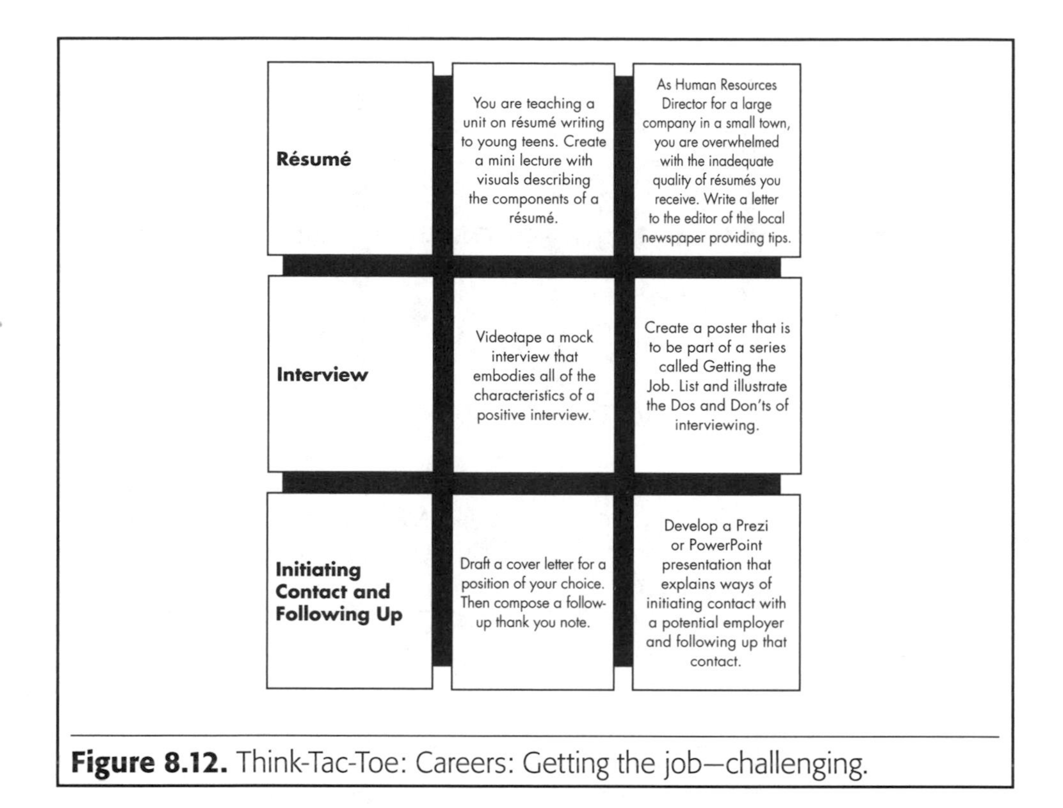

Résumé	You are teaching a unit on résumé writing to young teens. Create a mini lecture with visuals describing the components of a résumé.	As Human Resources Director for a large company in a small town, you are overwhelmed with the inadequate quality of résumés you receive. Write a letter to the editor of the local newspaper providing tips.
Interview	Videotape a mock interview that embodies all of the characteristics of a positive interview.	Create a poster that is to be part of a series called Getting the Job. List and illustrate the Dos and Don'ts of interviewing.
Initiating Contact and Following Up	Draft a cover letter for a position of your choice. Then compose a follow-up thank you note.	Develop a Prezi or PowerPoint presentation that explains ways of initiating contact with a potential employer and following up that contact.

Figure 8.12. Think-Tac-Toe: Careers: Getting the job—challenging.

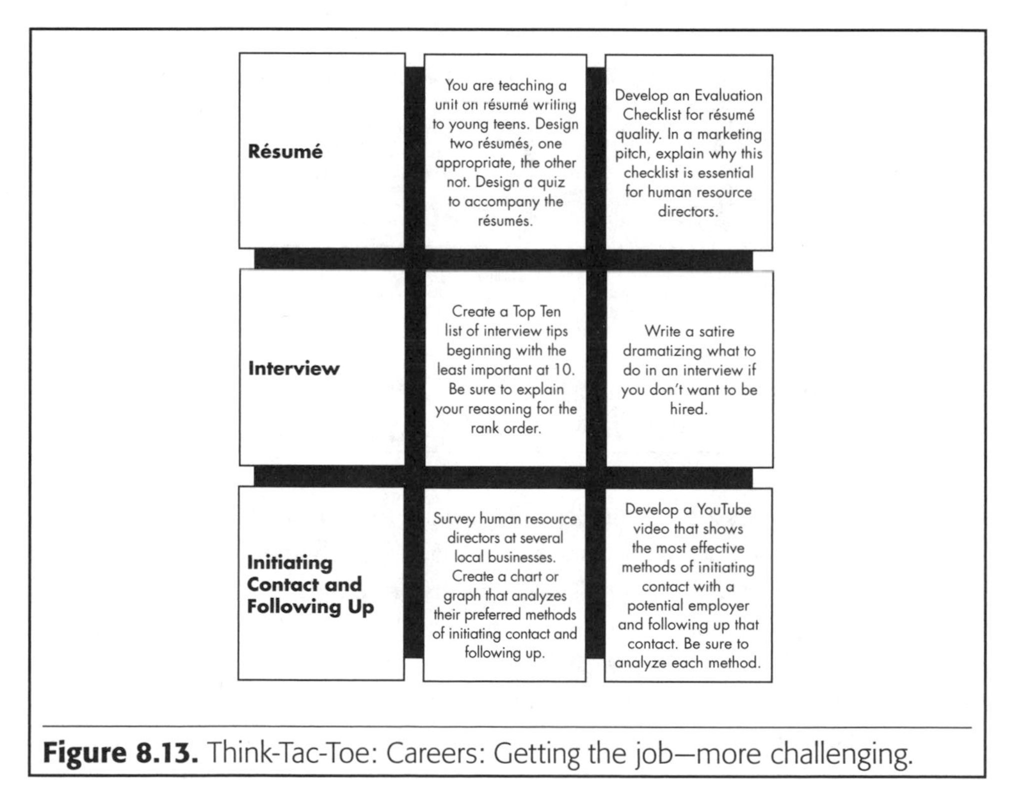

Résumé	You are teaching a unit on résumé writing to young teens. Design two résumés, one appropriate, the other not. Design a quiz to accompany the résumés.	Develop an Evaluation Checklist for résumé quality. In a marketing pitch, explain why this checklist is essential for human resource directors.
Interview	Create a Top Ten list of interview tips beginning with the least important at 10. Be sure to explain your reasoning for the rank order.	Write a satire dramatizing what to do in an interview if you don't want to be hired.
Initiating Contact and Following Up	Survey human resource directors at several local businesses. Create a chart or graph that analyzes their preferred methods of initiating contact and following up.	Develop a YouTube video that shows the most effective methods of initiating contact with a potential employer and following up that contact. Be sure to analyze each method.

Figure 8.13. Think-Tac-Toe: Careers: Getting the job—more challenging.

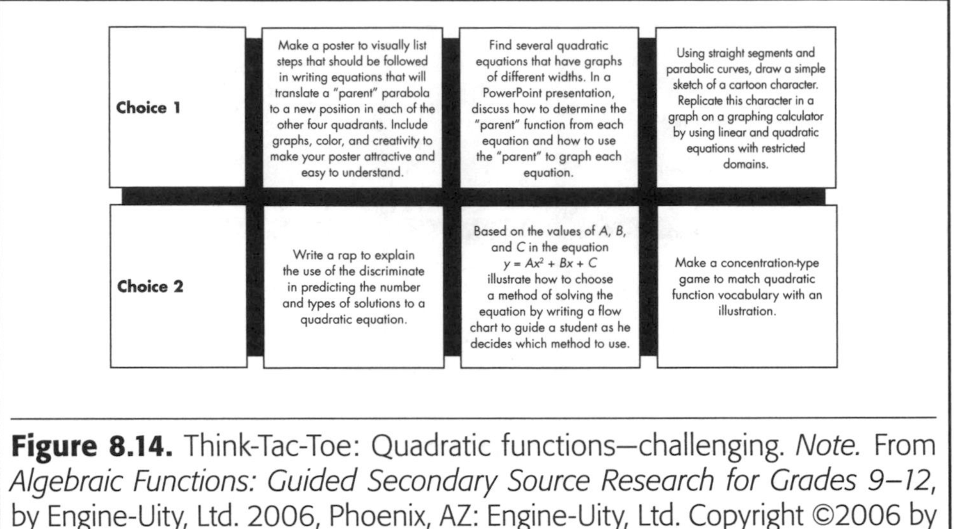

Choice 1	Make a poster to visually list steps that should be followed in writing equations that will translate a "parent" parabola to a new position in each of the other four quadrants. Include graphs, color, and creativity to make your poster attractive and easy to understand.	Find several quadratic equations that have graphs of different widths. In a PowerPoint presentation, discuss how to determine the "parent" function from each equation and how to use the "parent" to graph each equation.	Using straight segments and parabolic curves, draw a simple sketch of a cartoon character. Replicate this character in a graph on a graphing calculator by using linear and quadratic equations with restricted domains.
Choice 2	Write a rap to explain the use of the discriminate in predicting the number and types of solutions to a quadratic equation.	Based on the values of A, B, and C in the equation $y = Ax^2 + Bx + C$ illustrate how to choose a method of solving the equation by writing a flow chart to guide a student as he decides which method to use.	Make a concentration-type game to match quadratic function vocabulary with an illustration.

Figure 8.14. Think-Tac-Toe: Quadratic functions—challenging. *Note.* From *Algebraic Functions: Guided Secondary Source Research for Grades 9–12*, by Engine-Uity, Ltd. 2006, Phoenix, AZ: Engine-Uity, Ltd. Copyright ©2006 by Engine-Uity, Ltd. Reprinted with permission.

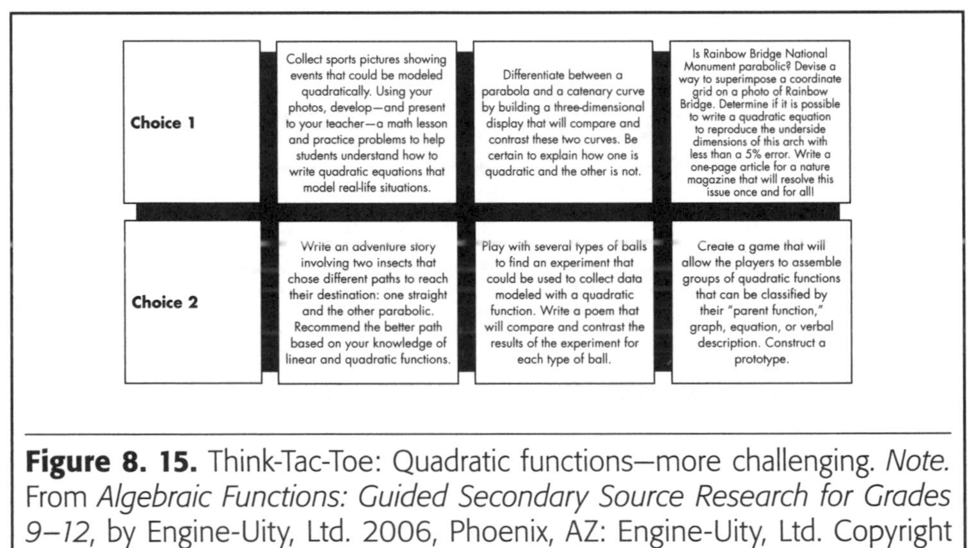

Choice 1	Collect sports pictures showing events that could be modeled quadratically. Using your photos, develop—and present to your teacher—a math lesson and practice problems to help students understand how to write quadratic equations that model real-life situations.	Differentiate between a parabola and a catenary curve by building a three-dimensional display that will compare and contrast these two curves. Be certain to explain how one is quadratic and the other is not.	Is Rainbow Bridge National Monument parabolic? Devise a way to superimpose a coordinate grid on a photo of Rainbow Bridge. Determine if it is possible to write a quadratic equation to reproduce the underside dimensions of this arch with less than a 5% error. Write a one-page article for a nature magazine that will resolve this issue once and for all!
Choice 2	Write an adventure story involving two insects that chose different paths to reach their destination: one straight and the other parabolic. Recommend the better path based on your knowledge of linear and quadratic functions.	Play with several types of balls to find an experiment that could be used to collect data modeled with a quadratic function. Write a poem that will compare and contrast the results of the experiment for each type of ball.	Create a game that will allow the players to assemble groups of quadratic functions that can be classified by their "parent function," graph, equation, or verbal description. Construct a prototype.

Figure 8. 15. Think-Tac-Toe: Quadratic functions—more challenging. *Note.* From *Algebraic Functions: Guided Secondary Source Research for Grades 9–12*, by Engine-Uity, Ltd. 2006, Phoenix, AZ: Engine-Uity, Ltd. Copyright ©2006 by Engine-Uity, Ltd. Reprinted with permission.

the majority of your students are learning the material in your teacher-led class, learning for these advanced students is extended through an in-depth exploration of a topic within a unit. The result: continuous progress for all.

Figure 8.16 is designed for a student in a world history class who, when preassessed, has already learned the majority of information in the ancient civilizations unit. While his fellow classmates are learning concepts he already knows, he will explore the concept of ancient burial customs. (Does part of this look familiar?

It should. The China activities were adapted from the Bloom Chart in Figure 6.6. China: The Warriors of Xian. Realize that different strategies are appropriate at different times. Don't hesitate to alter anything to meet needs!)

An English class is studying Shakespearian tragedy. One student has already read *Romeo and Juliet* (the choice for the whole class's exploration of tragedy), and his preassessment indicates he has processed it at high levels. The Think-Tac-Toe for *Julius Caesar* in Figure 8.17 could be used with this student. He, too, would be reading a tragedy and analyzing theme, character, and setting just like the rest of class.

INTERESTS

Remember that the best way to differentiate according to interests is an interest inventory given at the beginning of a unit of study. Those results guide the Think-Tac-Toe options.

When studying multiples of something—for example, several poems, the seven continents, or even types of cells—encouraging the student to explore just one of those can be very motivating. In a short story unit, for instance, allow the learner to pick a story of her choice to use as the content for the Think-Tac-Toe activities in Figure 8.18. Notice that all of the options are from the mid- to high levels of Bloom's taxonomy. Through this one Think-Tac-Toe, all students analyze setting, plot, and character, but they hone in on a story of their choice. This should prove more motivating to them. And, if some of your students need modifications because the tasks are too difficult, you can also adjust the complexity of the learning experiences.

Another way to incorporate interest in a unit of study is to use a single Think-Tac-Toe that lists a wide variety of learning experiences from which students choose. For example, each discipline has its own unique vocabulary. Exploration of that vocabulary (not just memorization of the definition) not only allows for communication about the subject, but it is fundamental to the understanding and manipulation of the concepts. The example in Figure 8.19 comes from a high school math class studying trigonometry. Each student will be exploring the vocabulary in the unit but will be doing so through a learning experience that particularly interests them. The student chooses one of the nine activities to complete. The Think-Tac-Toe would be passed out on the first day of the one-week unit giving students ample time to complete the activity.

LEARNING PROFILE

In Chapter 3, the learning profile was delineated as four distinct categories of influence on how learners approach learning: gender, culture, intelligence preferences, and learning style (Tomlinson & Imbeau, 2010). Think-Tac-Toes are very natural ways to differentiate both intelligence preferences and learning styles.

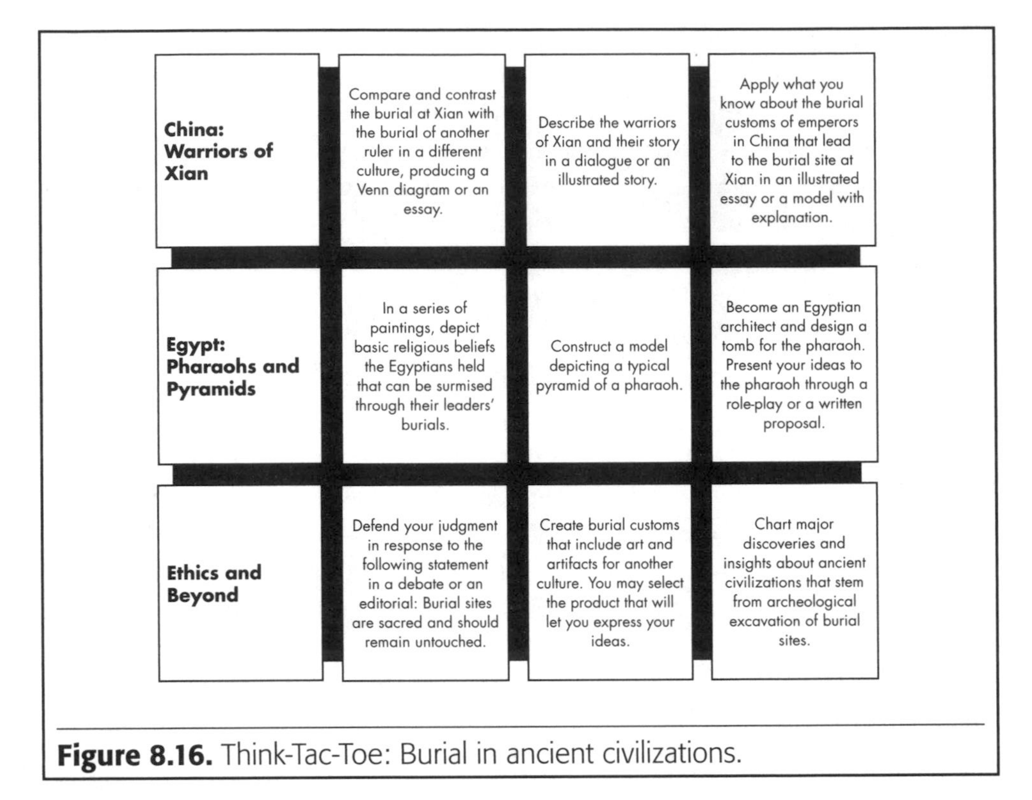

China: Warriors of Xian	Compare and contrast the burial at Xian with the burial of another ruler in a different culture, producing a Venn diagram or an essay.	Describe the warriors of Xian and their story in a dialogue or an illustrated story.	Apply what you know about the burial customs of emperors in China that lead to the burial site at Xian in an illustrated essay or a model with explanation.
Egypt: Pharaohs and Pyramids	In a series of paintings, depict basic religious beliefs the Egyptians held that can be surmised through their leaders' burials.	Construct a model depicting a typical pyramid of a pharaoh.	Become an Egyptian architect and design a tomb for the pharaoh. Present your ideas to the pharaoh through a role-play or a written proposal.
Ethics and Beyond	Defend your judgment in response to the following statement in a debate or an editorial: Burial sites are sacred and should remain untouched.	Create burial customs that include art and artifacts for another culture. You may select the product that will let you express your ideas.	Chart major discoveries and insights about ancient civilizations that stem from archeological excavation of burial sites.

Figure 8.16. Think-Tac-Toe: Burial in ancient civilizations.

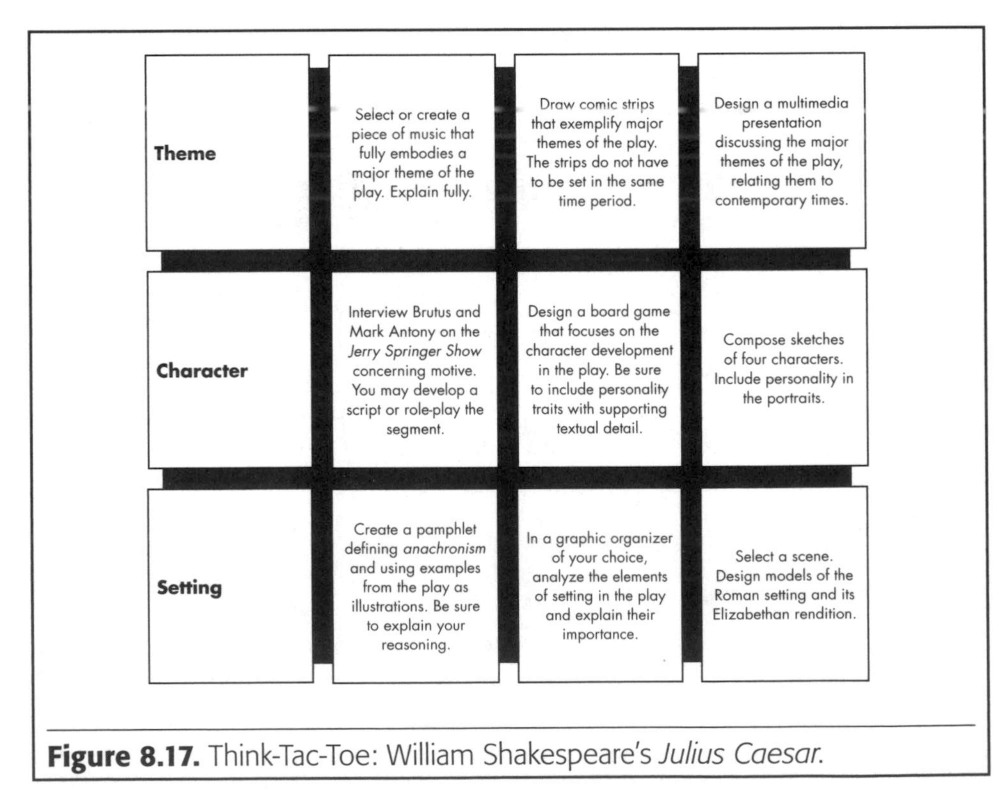

Theme	Select or create a piece of music that fully embodies a major theme of the play. Explain fully.	Draw comic strips that exemplify major themes of the play. The strips do not have to be set in the same time period.	Design a multimedia presentation discussing the major themes of the play, relating them to contemporary times.
Character	Interview Brutus and Mark Antony on the *Jerry Springer Show* concerning motive. You may develop a script or role-play the segment.	Design a board game that focuses on the character development in the play. Be sure to include personality traits with supporting textual detail.	Compose sketches of four characters. Include personality in the portraits.
Setting	Create a pamphlet defining *anachronism* and using examples from the play as illustrations. Be sure to explain your reasoning.	In a graphic organizer of your choice, analyze the elements of setting in the play and explain their importance.	Select a scene. Design models of the Roman setting and its Elizabethan rendition.

Figure 8.17. Think-Tac-Toe: William Shakespeare's *Julius Caesar*.

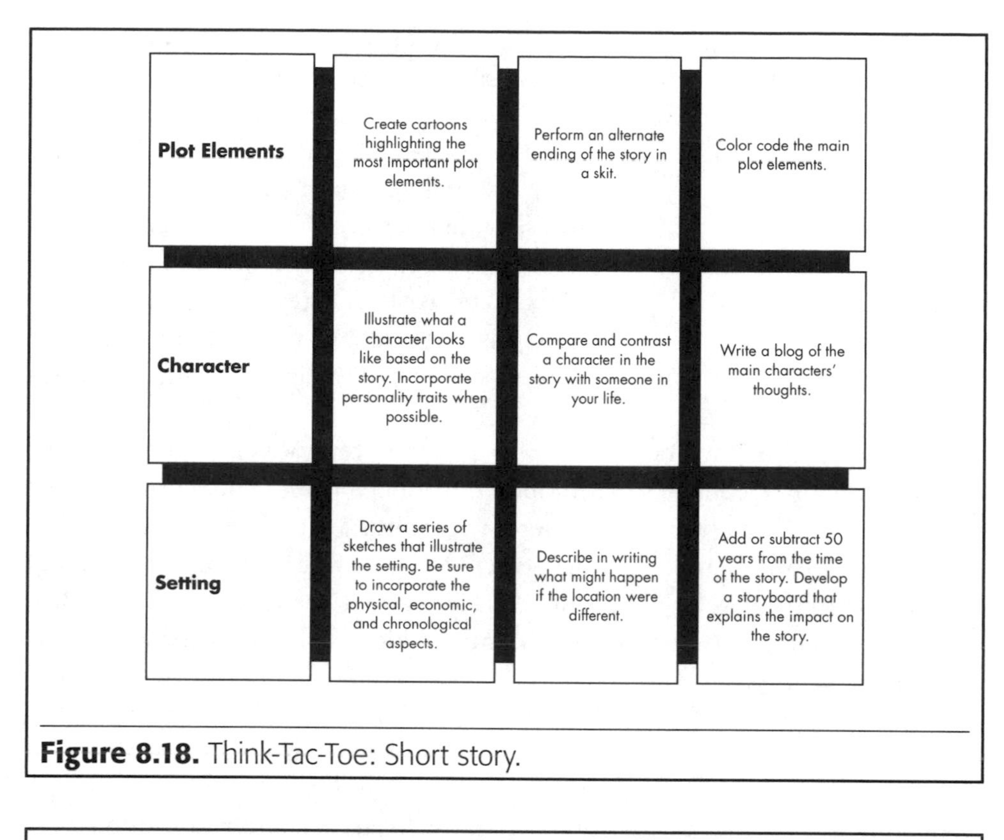

Plot Elements	Create cartoons highlighting the most Important plot elements.	Perform an alternate ending of the story in a skit.	Color code the main plot elements.
Character	Illustrate what a character looks like based on the story. Incorporate personality traits when possible.	Compare and contrast a character in the story with someone in your life.	Write a blog of the main characters' thoughts.
Setting	Draw a series of sketches that illustrate the setting. Be sure to incorporate the physical, economic, and chronological aspects.	Describe in writing what might happen if the location were different.	Add or subtract 50 years from the time of the story. Develop a storyboard that explains the impact on the story.

Figure 8.18. Think-Tac-Toe: Short story.

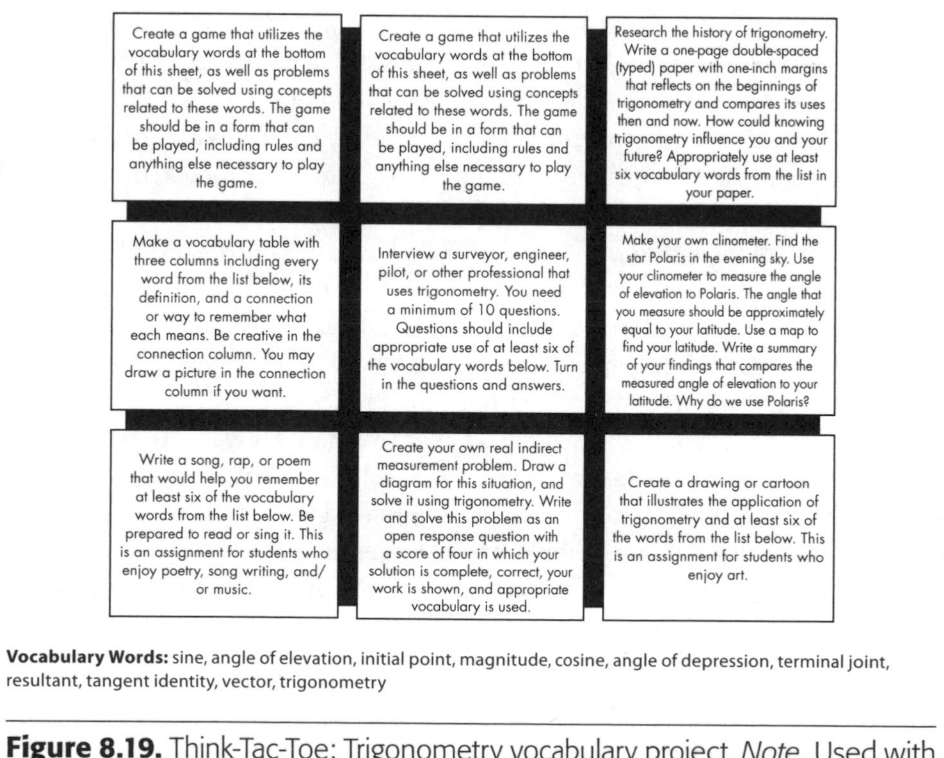

Create a game that utilizes the vocabulary words at the bottom of this sheet, as well as problems that can be solved using concepts related to these words. The game should be in a form that can be played, including rules and anything else necessary to play the game.	Create a game that utilizes the vocabulary words at the bottom of this sheet, as well as problems that can be solved using concepts related to these words. The game should be in a form that can be played, including rules and anything else necessary to play the game.	Research the history of trigonometry. Write a one-page double-spaced (typed) paper with one-inch margins that reflects on the beginnings of trigonometry and compares its uses then and now. How could knowing trigonometry influence you and your future? Appropriately use at least six vocabulary words from the list in your paper.
Make a vocabulary table with three columns including every word from the list below, its definition, and a connection or way to remember what each means. Be creative in the connection column. You may draw a picture in the connection column if you want.	Interview a surveyor, engineer, pilot, or other professional that uses trigonometry. You need a minimum of 10 questions. Questions should include appropriate use of at least six of the vocabulary words below. Turn in the questions and answers.	Make your own clinometer. Find the star Polaris in the evening sky. Use your clinometer to measure the angle of elevation to Polaris. The angle that you measure should be approximately equal to your latitude. Use a map to find your latitude. Write a summary of your findings that compares the measured angle of elevation to your latitude. Why do we use Polaris?
Write a song, rap, or poem that would help you remember at least six of the vocabulary words from the list below. Be prepared to read or sing it. This is an assignment for students who enjoy poetry, song writing, and/or music.	Create your own real indirect measurement problem. Draw a diagram for this situation, and solve it using trigonometry. Write and solve this problem as an open response question with a score of four in which your solution is complete, correct, your work is shown, and appropriate vocabulary is used.	Create a drawing or cartoon that illustrates the application of trigonometry and at least six of the words from the list below. This is an assignment for students who enjoy art.

Vocabulary Words: sine, angle of elevation, initial point, magnitude, cosine, angle of depression, terminal joint, resultant, tangent identity, vector, trigonometry

Figure 8.19. Think-Tac-Toe: Trigonometry vocabulary project. *Note.* Used with permission by Renee Watkins, high school teacher. Unpublished lesson plan.

Think-Tac-Toes that differentiate based on learning style or modality are intentionally designed so that options reflect the varying styles or modalities. Curry and Samara (1991) utilized four learning styles in their curriculum project materials: visual, oral, written, and kinesthetic. Karnes and Stephens (2000) categorized their products according to visual, oral, performance, written, and multicategorical strands. Coil (2004) divided her products into visual, verbal, kinesthetic, and technological sections while Roberts and Inman (2015) used kinesthetic, oral, technological, visual, and written categories. The names of the categories themselves aren't nearly as important as the philosophy behind it (i.e., the provision of multiple product options that appeal to different kinds of learners).

Because Think-Tac-Toes are usually designed topically according to content (e.g., the main concepts of Mesopotamia and *Gilgamesh* in Figure 8.1 were religion, culture, and literature), different modalities need to be represented in each category so that students may optimally express what they've learned about the concept in the way that best suits their individual learning style. Figure 8.20 could be used in an elementary classroom in which students are exploring 2-D and 3-D shapes.

Now look back at Figure 8.16. This Think-Tac-Toe was used as an illustration for an alternative assignment for students who have mastered the majority of concepts in an ancient civilizations unit. Suppose, though, that your entire class were studying the burial rituals in ancient civilizations, and you wanted each student to focus on the burial rites in ancient China and Egypt and the ethical implications of excavation—additionally, you wanted to differentiate based on learning styles. Figure 8.21 shows the learning style of each activity. Note how each row's choices represent different learning styles. In theory, each learner would choose the activity that best matches his preference for learning.

Much has been written about Multiple Intelligences (MI) since Gardner's (1983) landmark work *Frames of Mind: The Theory of Multiple Intelligences*. In fact, it's safe to say that the majority of preservice teachers have studied Gardner and the resulting applications of his theory to education. Whether you consider them to be actual intelligences or alternative ways to consider how a person learns best, MI is a perfect match with Think-Tac-Toes.

One way to incorporate MI is to consider the main concepts to be assessed, create rows based on those aspects, and weave activities that embody the various MI throughout the grid. The actual MI does not need to be listed at the end of the activity necessarily; students should naturally select their areas of strength. For middle school students exploring the structure and functions in living systems, the Think-Tac-Toe example in Figure 8.22 provides them many choices as to which products they want to create. Figure 8.23 encourages elementary students to consider their MI when studying parts of speech.

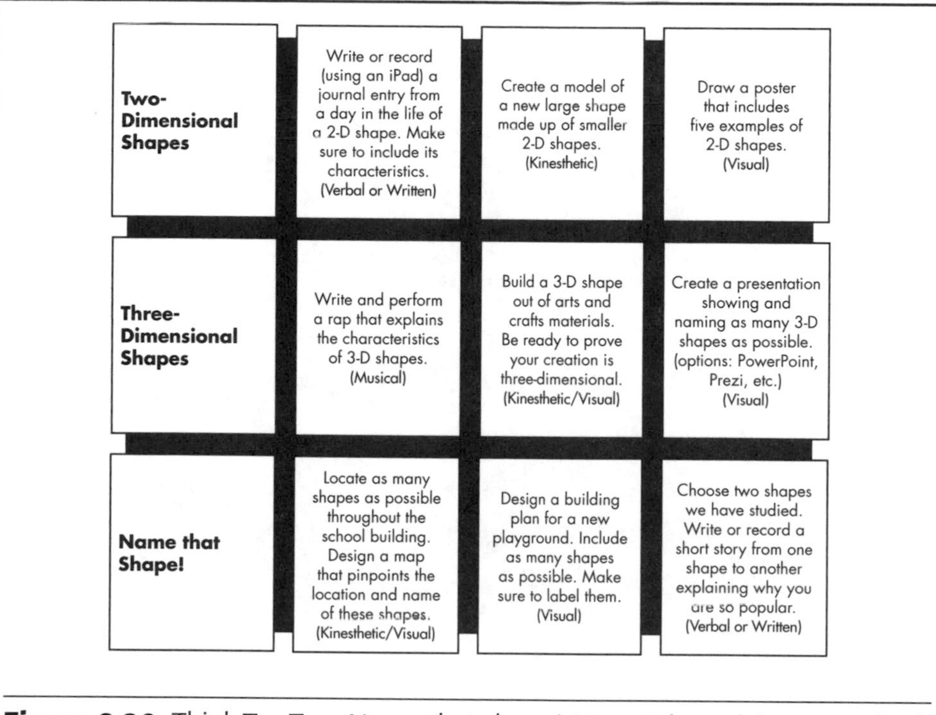

Two-Dimensional Shapes	Write or record (using an iPad) a journal entry from a day in the life of a 2-D shape. Make sure to include its characteristics. (Verbal or Written)	Create a model of a new large shape made up of smaller 2-D shapes. (Kinesthetic)	Draw a poster that includes five examples of 2-D shapes. (Visual)
Three-Dimensional Shapes	Write and perform a rap that explains the characteristics of 3-D shapes. (Musical)	Build a 3-D shape out of arts and crafts materials. Be ready to prove your creation is three-dimensional. (Kinesthetic/Visual)	Create a presentation showing and naming as many 3-D shapes as possible. (options: PowerPoint, Prezi, etc.) (Visual)
Name that Shape!	Locate as many shapes as possible throughout the school building. Design a map that pinpoints the location and name of these shapes. (Kinesthetic/Visual)	Design a building plan for a new playground. Include as many shapes as possible. Make sure to label them. (Visual)	Choose two shapes we have studied. Write or record a short story from one shape to another explaining why you are so popular. (Verbal or Written)

Figure 8.20. Think-Tac-Toe: Name that shape! *Note.* Adapted from *Teacher's Survival Guide: Differentiating Instruction in the Elementary Classroom* (p. 110), by J. L. Roberts and T. F. Inman, 2013, Waco, TX: Prufrock Press. Copyright ©2013 by Prufrock Press. Adapted with permission.

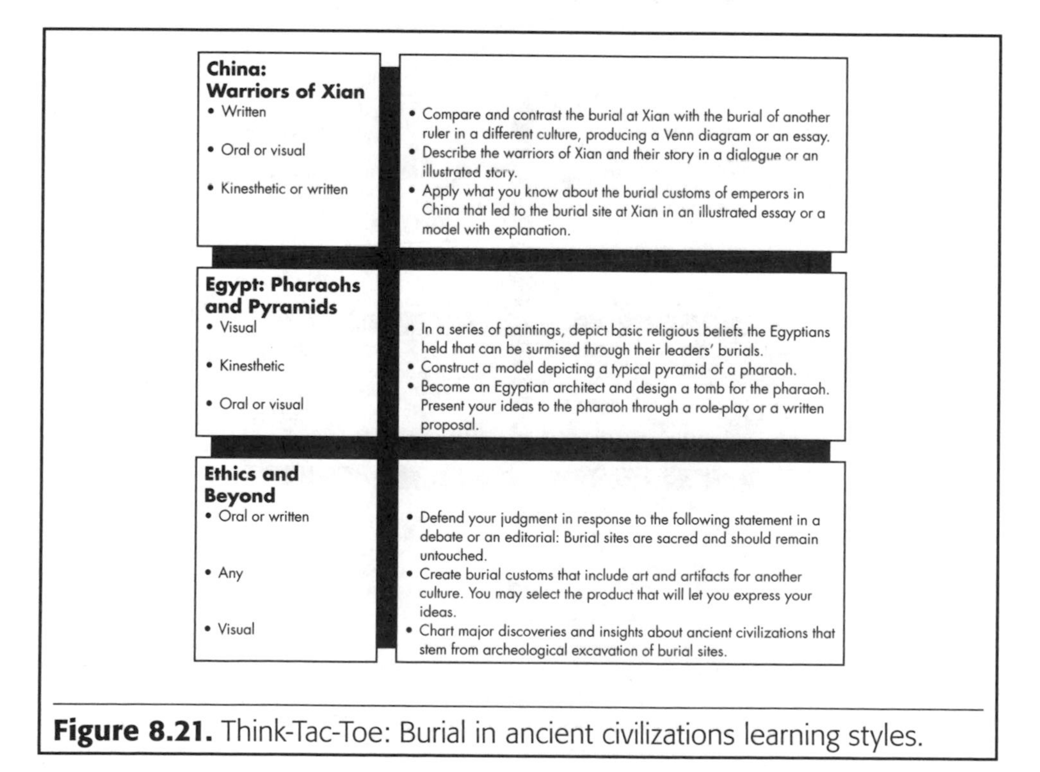

China: Warriors of Xian • Written • Oral or visual • Kinesthetic or written	• Compare and contrast the burial at Xian with the burial of another ruler in a different culture, producing a Venn diagram or an essay. • Describe the warriors of Xian and their story in a dialogue or an illustrated story. • Apply what you know about the burial customs of emperors in China that led to the burial site at Xian in an illustrated essay or a model with explanation.
Egypt: Pharaohs and Pyramids • Visual • Kinesthetic • Oral or visual	• In a series of paintings, depict basic religious beliefs the Egyptians held that can be surmised through their leaders' burials. • Construct a model depicting a typical pyramid of a pharaoh. • Become an Egyptian architect and design a tomb for the pharaoh. Present your ideas to the pharaoh through a role-play or a written proposal.
Ethics and Beyond • Oral or written • Any • Visual	• Defend your judgment in response to the following statement in a debate or an editorial: Burial sites are sacred and should remain untouched. • Create burial customs that include art and artifacts for another culture. You may select the product that will let you express your ideas. • Chart major discoveries and insights about ancient civilizations that stem from archeological excavation of burial sites.

Figure 8.21. Think-Tac-Toe: Burial in ancient civilizations learning styles.

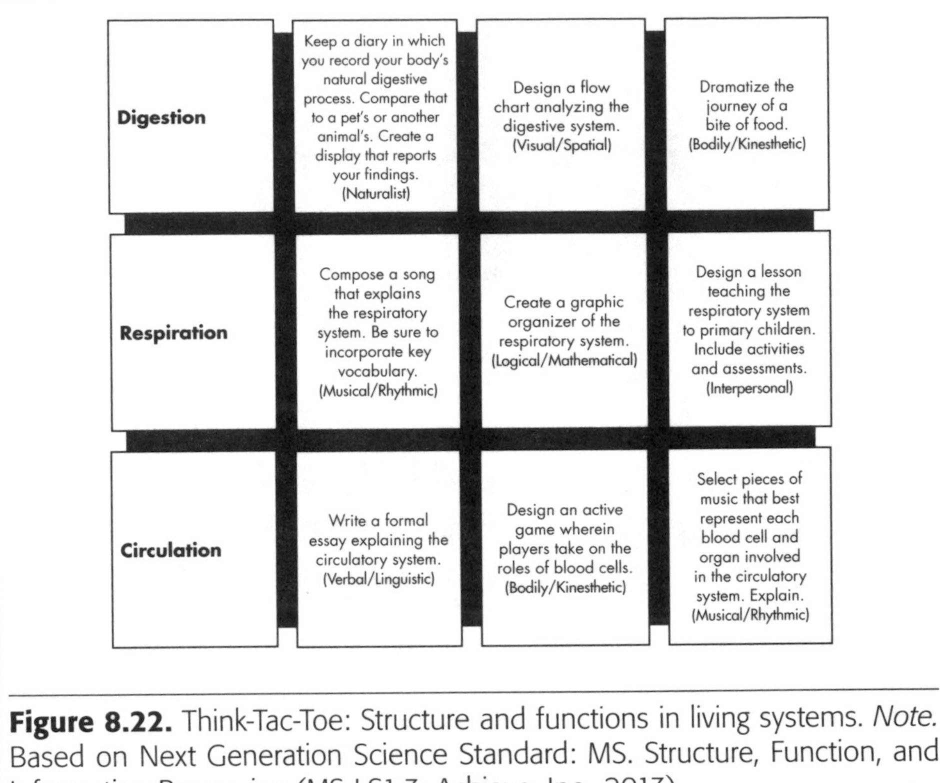

Figure 8.22. Think-Tac-Toe: Structure and functions in living systems. *Note.* Based on Next Generation Science Standard: MS. Structure, Function, and Information Processing (MS-LS1-3; Achieve, Inc., 2013).

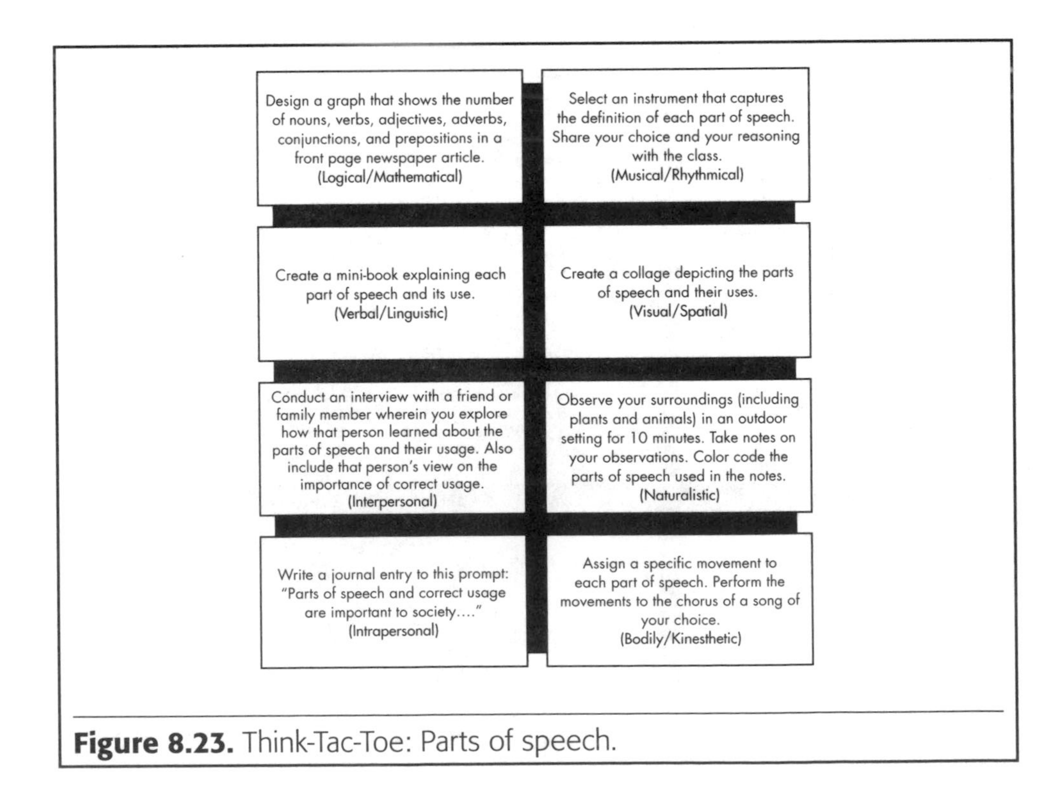

Figure 8.23. Think-Tac-Toe: Parts of speech.

HOW DO I DIFFERENTIATE WITH THINK-TAC-TOES?

EXPERIMENT WITH A FAVORITE LESSON

An excellent way to begin differentiating is to choose a favorite unit and then imagine the possibilities. Take the main concepts of the unit, a handy resource with lots of products listed, and an open mind, and then reconfigure that unit into a Think-Tac-Toe. The results just might surprise you.

Renee Watkins, a high school mathematics teacher, did just that with a lesson entitled "AIDS and Exponential Growth Experiment." Suitable for both math and science classrooms, her original lesson is shown in Figure 8.24.

In revamping her lesson to be a differentiated one, Renee kept the same experiment format but retrofitted the activities into a Think-Tac-Toe (see Figure 8.25). Renee shared her thoughts about her revamped unit in a personal correspondence:

> I love the AIDS exponential project because it is so real world, but the reality is that every student doesn't relate to it in the same way. When I first began to do this experiment, there was a push for all classes to do writing, so I required all of my students to write about the spread of AIDS in the United States and its connection to our experiment. I even gave them the U.S. AIDS data and required everyone to graph and find an equation for the data in the same way—but not anymore. With a little more knowledge and a lot more experience, I have learned that by giving students choices on the connections they can make, it will be much more interesting and challenging for them. Students have made connections to Hepatitis B and other communicable diseases, gossiping, population growth in India, and population growth in our school district. They now do a better job of hypothesizing about the causes of the exponential spread and how to stop it or be prepared for it. Because they have choice now in their topic of writing, their papers have more depth and better reasoning.

To emphasize versatility and open thinking, Renee also took the activity section of this lesson and turned it into a Bloom Chart (see Figure 8.26).

THE EXPERIMENT

SETUP

Perform the following experiment as a class. The experiment will occur in five stages. Set up 5 empty test tubes for each participant to represent the results at the end of each stage (Stage 0 through Stage 4). Each student will have 1 cup that is less than ½ full of water with the exception of one student who will have a cup less than ½ full of saturated NaHCO3 (baking soda in water). Sodium hydroxide (NaOH) also may be used. The student with the cup of saturated baking soda represents the "HIV positive" individual.

STAGE 0

At the beginning of the experiment, each student is given a dropper. At this time, using their dropper, students put a small sample from their cup into the stage 0 test tube corresponding to their cup number.

STAGE 1

Students will have 10 seconds to "mix" the contents of their cups. This represents the spread of HIV. The way that "mixing" will occur would be for student A to pour all the contents of his/her cup into student B's cup, and then student B to pour ½ of the contents of his/her cup (now full) back into student A's cup. Students may mix as many times as they wish or not at all in the 10 seconds. At the end of 10 seconds, each student should use his/her dropper to put a small amount from his/her cup into his/her stage 1 test tube.

STAGES 2 THROUGH 4

Repeat stage 1, mixing the contents of the cups for 10 more seconds at each stage. At the end of a stage, each student will use his/her dropper to put a small amount from his/her cup into the appropriate test tube, representing the results at the end of that stage.

WHO STARTED IT?

Put a drop of an indicator (phenophaline or liquid remaining after boiling a red cabbage leaf for approximately 1 hour) in the test tubes at each stage and count the number of "HIV positive" cases, represented by the contents of the cup changing colors. Phenophaline will change the color to pink and the liquid from boiled cabbage will change the color to green if infected and blue/purple if not.

THE ANALYSIS ACTIVITIES

1. A. Using a graphing utility, graph the number of people in the room that were "HIV positive" at each stage of our experiment and make observations.
   B. Using regression on a graphing utility, determine an equation that best fits the data and make observations.
2. A. Based on your equation of best fit for the experiment, predict the number of people in the school who could be "HIV positive" if our experiment had been continued to 7 stages, then 10 stages.
   B. Analyze the accuracy of your prediction.
3. A. Using the actual number of reported AIDS cases provided by your teacher, graph and find an equation of best fit (using algebra or regression) for the actual data.
   B. Compare the actual data results to those of our experiment. Make predictions about our future based on your calculations.

Figure 8.24. AIDS and exponential growth experiment. *Note.* Used with permission by Renee Watkins, high school teacher.

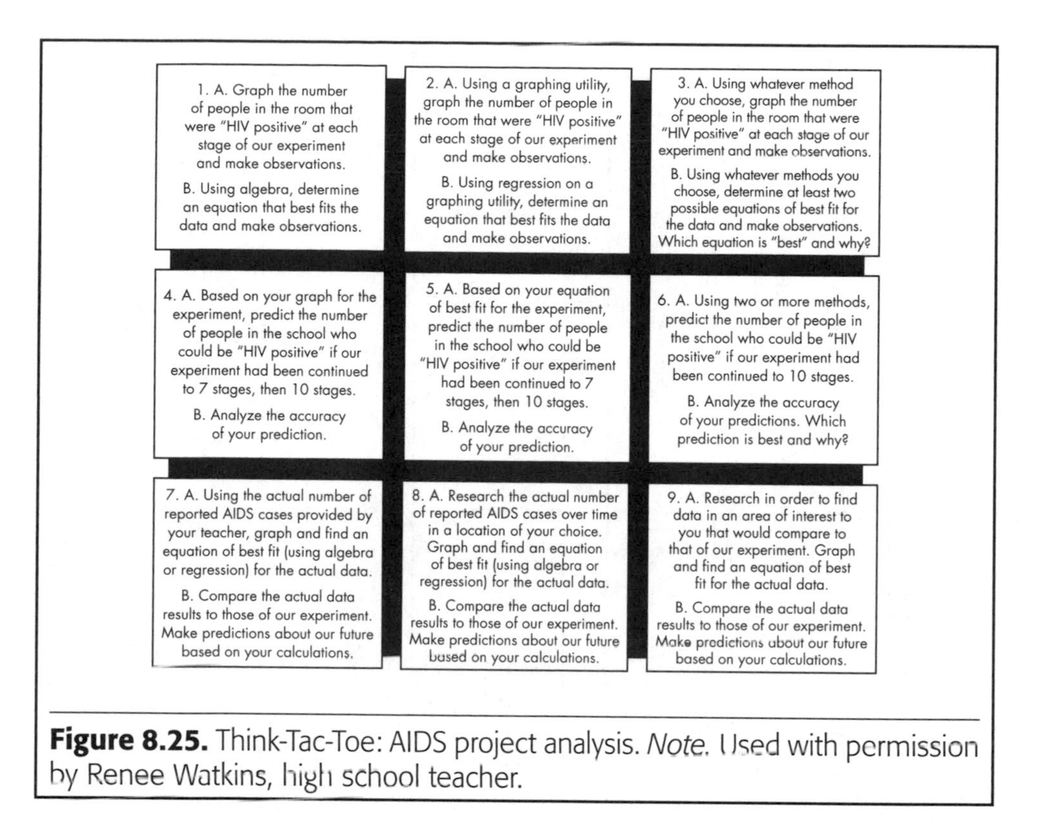

Figure 8.25. Think-Tac-Toe: AIDS project analysis. *Note.* Used with permission by Renee Watkins, high school teacher.

CREATING THINK-TAC-TOES FOR THE CLASSROOM

Ask yourself: What concepts do I want everyone to know and understand when they walk out the door? This is the first question to ask when planning a differentiated lesson or unit. If it will be used as a semester review, what key concepts or topics need be included about world geography or sixth-grade art? If a Think-Tac-Toe is to accompany a unit as a project, what concept(s) do you want students to analyze? Is it characteristics and examples of the parts of speech? Or, perhaps it's fractions, percents, and decimals and their real-world applications.

Whatever concepts you choose, be intentional and purposeful in the selection. After all, the *what* is what's critical here, not necessarily the *how*. Be sure to design it so that students can have multiple rows from which to choose. Remember that the rows are designed for *your* purposes, and your intent may range from students analyzing three different periods in music to students exploring the four main religions in the world.

Another very critical aspect to consider is how you are using the Think-Tac-Toe. The best way to ensure challenge for all is to tier with them. Remember, to tier effectively with a Think-Tac-Toe, you must develop two, one more challenging

	PROCESS	CONTENT	PRODUCT
CREATE	*Predict*	*AIDS Experiment and Data*	*Call to Action*
	Predict the number of AIDS cases for a future year (your choice) based on data and calculations. What are the implications of your predictions? Create a Call to Action for a Senate subcommittee exploring the AIDS epidemic.		
EVALUATE	*Judge*	*AIDS Experiment and Data*	*Technical Report*
	Judge whether or not data for the AIDS experiment and reported AIDS cases are truly exponential, giving reasons as to why or why not in an article for a scientific journal.		
ANALYZE	*Compare*	*AIDS Experiment and Data*	*Graph and Equations*
	Compare the data for the AIDS experiment with that for reported AIDS cases over time using graphs and equations.		
APPLY	*Graph*	*AIDS Experiment and Data*	*Graph with Explanation*
	Graph the equation of a line or curve of best fit for the AIDS experiment data. Make observations.		
UNDERSTAND	*Express*	*AIDS Experiment and Data*	*Graph*
	Express the data from the AIDS experiment in an appropriate graph. Make observations.		
REMEMBER	*Describe*	*AIDS Experiment and Data*	*Poster or Demonstration*
	Describe how the AIDS experiment chemically demonstrated the spread of disease with a poster or a demonstration.		

Figure 8.26. Bloom Chart: AIDS project. *Note.* Used with permission by Renee Watkins, high school teacher.

than the other, so that all students will be thinking at appropriately high levels. It's more important to be minds-on than hands-on. Of course, the preassessment determines who gets what and why.

You can also differentiate according to interests or learning profile. In this case, it's not so important that you create two Think-Tac-Toes; it is important, however, that you make sure choices have challenge. Perhaps your goal is to stretch students beyond their comfort zones when it comes to their learning profile, so you deliberately design the Think-Tac-Toe into kinesthetic, oral, technological, visual, and written rows to ensure that your students will complete at least two products that are not in their preferred mode of learning. Maybe you imbed multiple MI product options among learning experiences to appeal to students' preferred ways of learning. Maybe everyone is participating in a novels unit, and you allow them to choose a novel of interest at their appropriate reading level. A general novel Think-Tac-Toe encourages students to explore the main components of a novel of their choice.

In short, you're the one in control here. You must thoughtfully and intentionally design your rows to meet your goals for what the students will learn. The students, then, have choice, but it's controlled choice from carefully selected options.

INCORPORATE IMPORTANT CONCEPTS INTO THREE (OR MORE) ROWS

Remember to be intentional! Whether your rows are titled *character, theme,* and *setting,* or *political causes, social causes,* and *economic causes,* they must embody the critical attributes of the concept. As mentioned in the previous section, the rows also may be designed with another goal in mind (e.g., learning profile). You determine how many rows to include in the Think-Tac-Toe. Just make sure that they fit your purposes. A Think-Tac-Toe template has been included in Appendix G to help you get started.

DESIGN TASKS WITH VARIED PRODUCTS

This may be one of the most challenging parts of developing a Think-Tac-Toe, simply because most of us educators have difficulty breaking free of our content comfort zone; we may be too tied to our content to consider alternative products. For example, an English teacher may well provide options: short story, free verse poem, opinion piece, analytical essay, vignette—you get the picture. But, how does this address the mathematician in class? The artist? The computer guru? If we only offer options that fit naturally with our discipline, then we are more concerned with *how* they're showing us they've learned than *what* they've learned. Every science student must know how to conduct an experiment and write a lab report, just as all Advanced Placement history students must know how to write a document-based question. Of course, in various disciplines, there must be lessons devoted to teaching students how to create products specific to that discipline. If that is your purpose, the Think-Tac-Toe is not the best strategy to use. This strategy, remember, focuses on *what* they've learned more than *how* they will show you what they've learned.

How do you come up with products that address different needs? Surround yourself with rich resources that not only give ideas for products, but oftentimes provide rubrics or criteria guides for them. (Chapter 10 will be fully devoted to this topic of assessment.) Sure bets include the following resources:

Roberts, J. L., & Inman, T. F. (2015). *Assessing differentiated student products: A protocol for development and evaluation* (2nd Ed.). Waco, TX: Prufrock Press.

The Developing and Assessing Products (DAP) Tool (see Chapter 10) is fully explored in Roberts and Inman's (2015) follow-up book, *Assessing Differentiated Student Products: A Protocol for Development and Evaluation* (2nd Ed.). Numerous DAP Tools divided into kinesthetic, oral, technological, visual, and written products abound. With the innovative performance scale and tiered approach to differentiate assessment, the DAP Tool can make variety of products a "given" in any classroom.

Curry, J., & Samara, J. (1991). *Product guide kit: The curriculum project.* Austin, TX: Curriculum Project. (Visit the website at http://www.curriculumproject.com.)

This kit discusses oral, kinesthetic, written, and visual products. Curry and Samara have created four product folders designed for grades K–2, 3–5, 6–8, and 9–12. Each contains critical attributes of a particular product so that a teacher can offer a product choice with confidence. They have also designed Standard Writer® 2 Software for simple rubric development.

Karnes, F., & Stephens, K. (2009). *The ultimate guide for student product development and evaluation* (2nd ed.). Waco, TX: Prufrock Press.

Karnes and Stephens explore dozens of products and include vital information such as the definition, the title of the expert who might develop a particular product, types of the product, words to know, 21st-century skills, helpful hints, exemplary producers, community resources, books, websites, and quotes to inspire. They even provide a product criteria grid to make assessing the product as simple as possible. Now that English teacher (who doesn't quilt) doesn't have to worry about putting a quilt (pp. 135–137) down as a product option to demonstrate the theme of *To Kill a Mockingbird*. She can assess it on its merits (e.g., shows considerable attention to construction, demonstrates precise sewing and cutting skills, and every item in the quilt clearly relates to the selected theme/concept).

Product Pouch and Prima Product Booklets by Engine-Uity. (Visit the website at http://www.engine-uity.com.)

Both the *Prima Product Book* (grades K–3) and the *Product Pouches* (Grades 3–8) list dozens and dozens of possible products. A short student-friendly description is included for each product.

HOLD EVERYONE RESPONSIBLE FOR IMPORTANT CONCEPTS

All students will be responsible for the important concepts in a unit, although it will be tiered based on readiness levels or through varying interests or learning profiles. Once you've designed the options, allow students to choose. Because your options were purposeful and intentional, the concepts you are addressing will be differentiated. How will they be differentiated? That depends upon how you designed the Think-Tac-Toes. If you developed two different grids, giving the more challenging one to students who are ready for it, then you're tiering based on readiness or ability. If you ensure that options address the multiple intelligences or the different learning modalities, then you are differentiating according to how students prefer to learn. If you base the options on a student interest survey, then you're meeting their needs that way. All children will be responsible for the critical concepts you've selected. They may be exploring those concepts in different ways, through varying forms, and on multiple levels, but they are all responsible for learning the same concepts.

ALLOW STUDENTS TO CHOOSE ONE FROM EACH ROW/CONCEPT

Encourage students to stretch themselves (choose only two in their preferred MI, for example) when they make their choices. If you have designed your Think-Tac-Toe(s) well, then differentiation will occur regardless of the choices students make. Encourage exploration as well as alternate products. If someone really wants to create a diorama instead of a poster to depict a rainforest biome, please encourage the student to do so. Remember, the goal is for students to understand the characteristics of a rainforest biome. How they demonstrate that understanding should be open (at least some of the time).

DISTRIBUTE RUBRICS OR SCORING GUIDES AND ALLOW FOR VARIATIONS

Rubrics or scoring guides (see the DAP Tools described in Chapter 10) must accompany the Think-Tac-Toe when first given. It is critical for students to understand the basis for their assessment. An entire chapter will be devoted to this later, but for now realize that just as there are incredible sources for products, so are there incredible sources for rubrics.

If a student does approach you with an alternative product, be sure to address how it will be assessed. Encourage her to develop her own rubric. Show her *The Ultimate Guide for Student Product Development and Evaluation* (2nd ed.; Karnes & Stephens, 2009) or let her skim through the *Product Guide Kit* (Curry & Samara, 1991). Or, once you've read Chapter 10, introduce her to DAP Tools. The more ownership she takes in the product, the better the results.

ASSESS THE PRODUCTS

At the end of the week, or the month, or whatever timeline you've given them, it's time to collect the products along with the rubrics. Many teachers may be overwhelmed at having to assess three (or more) products when in the past they may have just graded a multiple-choice test. What are your options?

- Grade all three products.
- Randomly select one product to assess.
- Have students select their favorite product to turn in, and have them explain why it's their favorite. Of course, this only works once. The next time you use a Think-Tac-Toe, tell them that in addition to turning in their favorite product, you'll randomly select another one to grade as well. Not to doubt human nature, but this ensures that more than one product is completed well the next time!

Whenever possible, make the product visible to others—don't just put a grade on it and return it to the student. Have students perform for their classmates. If their product has an audience in the community, help them create opportunities to present it to interested adults. Display the products in the library or in the hallways. Print them in a newsletter. Post them on your classroom's website. Host an open house. Take them to the next school board meeting. Remember, we are celebrating the differences in our students.

IMPORTANT TAKE-AWAYS

- Always have a reason for providing certain learning options to certain students.
- Tiering with Think-Tac-Toes requires two: one with more challenging options and one with less challenging options. The match of Think-Tac-Toe to student is critical.
- The match of Think-Tac-Toe to student must be based on preassessment.

- Think-Tac-Toes can be used when a student has mastered the majority of content to be taught.
- Think-Tac-Toes can differentiate interest and learning profiles as well.
- Be sure to have strong rubrics to accompany all Think-Tac-Toes.
- Consider time and resources necessary for each learning experience on a Think-Tac-Toe.
- All learning experiences in a Think-Tac-Toe must not simply be hands-on; they must be minds-on.

CHAPTER 9

Managing the Differentiated Classroom

> The greatest sign of success for a teacher is to be able to say, "The children are now working as if I did not exist." —Maria Montessori

Typically when people look at classroom management issues, they're focusing on ways to manage the students and their behavior (or misbehavior). This chapter, however, explores managing the learning that occurs in a differentiated classroom. When students are given appropriate choices and when learning experiences are matched to their strengths, interests, or levels of readiness, far fewer cases of managing (mis)behavior exist. Engaged, interested students stay on task. It's that simple.

As a professional educator, you have conscientiously established a healthy climate for differentiation. You have intentionally (there's that word again) created a culture that develops and supports diversity, maintains high expectations, and generates openness. (See Chapter 3 if you need a refresher.) You plan your lessons and units using the key questions that lead to differentiation:

1. *Planning Question*—What do I want all students to know, understand, and be able to do?
2. *Preassessment Question*—Who already knows, understands, and/or can use the content or demonstrate the skills? Who needs additional support in order to know, understand, and/or demonstrate the skills?
3. *Differentiation Question*—What can I do for him, her, or them so they can make continuous progress and extend their learning?

Moreover, you intentionally incorporate tiering (through Bloom Charts, Think-Tac-Toes, and/or Venn diagrams) that fosters continuous learning for your students.

But, how do you group your students for learning? What are the possibilities? What sorts of procedures and routines do you establish to help ensure that the classroom runs well? How do you manage the time factor—both your time and the time students need to learn? These are all questions that must be addressed to establish an effectively differentiated classroom.

MANAGING STUDENT GROUPING

The word *intentional* has been repeated multiple times throughout this book. Hopefully that will not diminish the importance of the word in this next sentence but rather emphasize its meaning. It is critical that you as the educational professional be intentional about your understanding of grouping and your implementation of it. You need to know what is best practice and what isn't. You may be surprised at what you learn in this section.

Although debated in some circles, grouping can be key to continuous progress for kids—*if* the grouping is intentionally managed. You must have sound reasoning for grouping students, whether it will be in cooperative groups or groups based on readiness or interest. Whether your intent is optimal learning or social development, definitively decide *why* you want learners together or working alone and then consider *how* you want them grouped.

According to research, grouping is key for students with gifts and talents. Rogers (2006) did a meta-analysis of the studies on grouping gifted learners, and the research is very telling:

> In general, almost any form of grouping provides an academic or achievement gain to gifted learners with fairly positive social and emotional gains, as well. Grouping tends to be the "least restrictive environment" for gifted learners, and the most effective and efficient means for schools to provide more challenging coursework, giving these children access to advanced content and providing them with a peer group. (p. 4)

Intentional grouping coupled with differentiated learning experiences can provide opportunities for cognitive, social, and emotional growth for all learners, including those with gifts and talents. But you must be knowledgeable of the types of grouping and realize that their purposes and outcomes differ.

INEFFECTIVE GROUPING STRATEGIES: TRACKING AND MIXED-ABILITY GROUPS

First we begin with what *not* to do. Too often well-meaning educators mistakenly group students without knowing best practice. They need to know about the next two strategies, so they can avoid them.

TRACKING

Tracking (also known as grouping for life!) is the damaging practice of pegging kids early in their academic careers and forcing them to stay on one very narrow path (e.g., the "you're-never-going-to-amount-to-anything" track, the "you're-good-in-math-so-that-must-mean-you're-good-at-everything" path, or the "you-tested-as-average-in-third-grade-so-that-means-you'll-always-be-average" class selection).

Once upon a time I bet you proclaimed that you wanted to be a ballerina or a firefighter, or maybe an astronaut or a garbage collector when you grew up. What if your parents took that literally and only allowed you to experience life in relation to that 3-year-old's vision of the future? What if your schooling, your friends, your toys, and your books only encompassed that goal of becoming a ________? Imagine the limitations, the unrealistic expectations (either too high or too low), and the lack of possibilities!

The point is that all of us change, mature, develop new interests, and hone abilities. If we as educators label learners as noncollege track when they're in middle school, we stifle potential growth and opportunity. If we limit Advanced Placement classes to students who are gifted and talented, we thwart risk taking and hinder complex thinking.

Tracking places learners in one track from the time they begin school until they leave it. It encourages long-term academic planning with short-term indicators. Tracking is not best practice—it's not even good or mediocre practice.

MIXED-ABILITY GROUPING

There is a mistaken belief that placing a low-ability learner with a middle-ability learner and high-ability learner will result in all three equally working hard at the task and all three learning new things—even without doling out individual responsibilities (i.e., an incorrect adaptation of cooperative learning). Or perhaps the mistake takes place in the teacher's motive for creating this type of grouping: at least each "group" will complete the task. Many times, however, it isn't the group doing the work.

Typically, groups structured in this way prove frustrating for almost all involved. One student feels overwhelmed with content and may not feel she can contribute. She could easily check out of the learning altogether and even end up a behavioral issue. Another may feel that the burden is on him to ensure that the group gets an A, so he does all the work himself. Robinson (1990) argues these students, typically high achievers or those with gifts and talents, feel "exploited" in such situations. The third student may be trapped between the two, wanting to take an active role in the learning but a bit unsure of her ability compared to the others. She could very well make sure the pencils are sharpened and provide materials to the one "doing it all"—which does not equate with her actually learning the content. If roles are carefully defined (and, better yet, determined by some sort of preassessment), and, if all are held accountable, then you will be looking at a more effective cooperative learning group.

EFFECTIVE GROUPING STRATEGIES

TEACHER-CREATED GROUPS

This section explores the groups over which you the educator have control. Whether your class is heterogeneously or homogenously grouped, one grade level or multiple grade levels, you have the power to match content, process, product, and/or assessment to student strengths, interests, and levels of readiness.

Flexible grouping. Flexible grouping is the process of varying why and how students are grouped; the key is altering the grouping criteria so that learners are matched with a variety of young people for a variety of reasons. Robinson, Shore, and Enersen (2007) examined the research on grouping and found that "flexible grouping of students within elementary classrooms promotes achievement, especially in mathematics and reading. The achievement effects are positive for high-ability students, as well as average and low-achieving students" (p. 123). When done correctly, it's a win-win for everyone.

Flexible grouping for instructional purposes. Grouping for instructional purposes includes a variety of approaches (remember that *variety* is the key word here). If you always base your groups on any one factor (whether that be interest or learning profile), you limit the students' exposure to working with others. You also could inadvertently nurture a negative self-worth in those students who might always be placed in the lowest achieving group. And please remember these groups don't have to be physical groups. The students could be "grouped" together in that certain people have the same learning experience, yet the students work on the assignments individually.

So, how can you group learners for instructional purposes? Consider all of those inventories mentioned in Chapter 3.

Interests. An interest inventory allows you to match topics in a unit to the students most interested in those topics. Regardless of ability level or learning profile, those learners will work together exploring an aspect of the lesson they find worthy. Melinda Ridel, a primary teacher, shared her experience of grouping students based on interest in a personal correspondence:

> A unit on sea animals begins with reading a nonfiction story on jellyfish, followed by having students brainstorm a list of sea animals. After the brainstorming session, they write down their first and second choices of which sea animal they would like to research. Groups are formed based on their choices. Students research in the library and create a report with an illustration. Activities in this unit include reading about the animal, creating a web, writing, and using technology.

Reflecting on the specific strategies discussed in this book, a teacher could use a Venn diagram in small groups to differentiate based on interest. For example, a social studies class is studying leadership in World War II. Students could pick among any of the world leaders at that time to compare and contrast: Roosevelt, Truman, Churchill, Stalin, Hitler, Mussolini, etc. The entire class would discuss leadership decisions and styles, yet each small group of students would be contributing information about the person or people of its choice. In addition, if the teacher wanted to differentiate process at the same time, each student could be analyzing the leadership on varying tiers of complexity—with anywhere from one to four ovals. (Of course, Venn diagrams can be used individually, too, not just in small groups. This example just focuses on the use of it in group work.)

Learning profiles. Students also can be grouped according to the learning style or multiple intelligence component of their learning profiles. In this case, all students may learn about the same concept, but they will do so based on their preferred ways of learning. Gifted resource teacher Donna Stith has grouped her students based on learning styles:

> Some third-grade students in our school struggled with mastering multiplication facts even though many were in the Primary Talent Pool for our students who show high ability. We preassessed and grouped students based on those who had limited success, starting with 6 x 6 and working our way to 9 x 9. Based on a learning style inventory, those students who were visual or auditory learners were introduced to a math program that told stories and gave pictures for students to make connections. Students only received about 15 minutes of teacher-led instruction once a week wherein the math stories were told. They were asked to retell the story to a classmate, but this was not monitored. After 2 weeks, posttests (via games

> and other methods) showed 90% success rate for these students who did not succeed using traditional drill and practice. This just reinforced the idea that differentiation based on a child's learning style equals success. And, it was a great boost for those students' self-esteem.

Once you've preassessed kids as to their multiple intelligence preferences to learning, you can create alternate assignments that stem from those intelligences. Yes, that means you could have eight groups in your classroom exploring the solar system in eight different ways. Stephanie Paynter, a third-grade teacher, has preassessed her students using this method:

> During the first few weeks of school, I feel that it is important to learn about how each student learns best. One of the ways that I do this is by giving the students and parents a multiple intelligence survey to fill out about their learning strengths and weaknesses. I want my students to be exposed to all different types of genres in literature. They use a READO board that is played similar to a Bingo game. In each square, there is a different genre and after they have read books within the genres found on a row, they win a prize. In order for them to get credit for reading the book, they must complete a project. These are based on which multiple intelligence fits their learning style best. Within each category, the students have about five choices from which to pick. Giving them options promotes independent learning and usually produces higher quality work. The projects are graded by the use of a rubric that correlates to the descriptors of that learning style.

Of the strategies explored in this book, perhaps the Think-Tac-Toe is the most natural fit for differentiating with groups based on learning profile. Group work with Think-Tac-Toes is an option wherein small groups select learning experiences to work on together. A Think-Tac-Toe can be created that addresses all eight multiple intelligences, for example, for a unit on biomes. Students are grouped by multiple intelligences with each group selecting the learning experiences that match their preferred ways of learning.

Ability, readiness, or level of achievement. Are those terms really synonymous? Technically no, but the idea is that each person brings different levels of understanding and experience to the classroom. As a professional educator, you determine what those differences are through preassessment, and then you intentionally group kids together. You may have three groups learning about fractions: those at grade level, those below, and those above. Maybe you have students in your elementary math class who have mastered the multiplication tables, those close to being there, and those who need more drill and practice.

They definitely don't all need the same math assignment. Stephanie Paynter incorporates this approach, as well:

> Another approach that I try to use when differentiating for students is grouping based on ability. I want the students to learn the same content standards, but at varying degrees. I try to use literature circles to help differentiate content for my students. First, I preassess their skill level and reading level for each new unit that I teach. Then, I group the children according to how their skills and reading levels match with each other. Usually there are between four and six students in each group. They are given different articles, short stories, poems, and the like that correspond to fit their needs. Each group has different activities that teach and assess the content standard. I try to use rubrics that vary in the degree of expectation levels for each group. At the end of the unit, the students are given a posttest that corresponds to the difficulty level of what they have been doing throughout the unit. At the start of the next unit, the students are again preassessed, and most of the time the groups change and diversify.

Kim Wolfram, a gifted resource teacher, has worked with teachers to help them preassess and group their students:

> In a rural school, a second-year sixth-grade teacher asked me for help. She said she knew that some of her gifted students were bored in her math class, but she didn't know what to do for them. We decided to give the students a pretest at the beginning of the next chapter. There were four students who scored 85% or higher on the pretest. When the teacher and I first started working together, she was concerned about the students missing skills if she let them work on enrichment activities. I suggested giving them another assessment if she felt it was needed for documentation. She decided that was not necessary and started to plan enrichment activities using the same concepts and skills in the chapter. I check with this teacher periodically, and she reports that the students are much happier and managing the grouping is becoming much easier.

Regardless of the reason for instructional grouping, remember that each member of that group needs to be equally challenged and each must be held accountable.

Each of the three strategies discussed in this book is a strong match for group differentiation based on levels of readiness. For example, two Think-Tac-Toes, one with challenging learning tasks about the periodic table and one with more challenging learning tasks about the same concept, could be distributed to groups of students, making sure that each group is composed of similar-ability students and that the Think-Tac-Toe given to the group would be appropriately challenging. Likewise, a Bloom Chart could contain six learning experiences focused on the periodic table, spanning from the least complex way of processing information (remembering) to the most complex way (creating). Those tasks would be divided between the three highest and three lowest levels with each group receiving the appropriate list of choices to learn about the periodic table. A Venn diagram could also be used to tier the learning process for groups of students. Small groups would have one to four ovals to compare and contrast aspects of the periodic table. Remember that differentiating for readiness encourages continuous progress for all students, regardless of their level of readiness or ability.

Flexible grouping for other purposes. Sometimes we have other goals in mind for students in addition to the content being learned, such as assessing the social dynamics of the class or motivating students socially. Grouping students for these reasons is no less worthy than grouping for instructional purposes, but realize that differentiated learning experiences may be more difficult to plan. For example, you are much more likely to develop lessons that extend learning if you group learners according to readiness level than you would if they chose their own groups or counted off in fours. This type of grouping typically dictates the students who will work together, but all groups will probably work on the same lesson. Let's go back to that intent word again: What is your intent in grouping the kids? What are your goals? Once you discover the answers, group away.

Gender. Perhaps we want to encourage our middle school girls to be themselves, to show their intelligences without fear of losing potential boyfriends. Grouping kids according to gender could alleviate that tension and possible social restrictions that inhibit learning. Lori Frint, a curriculum coordinator, shares her experience with grouping by gender.

> After attending training on "How the Brain Works," our sixth-grade teachers decided to try gender grouping for math, social studies, and science to see if it made a difference in student learning. Teachers prepared activities and lessons for girls that allowed more opportunities for socialization and talking during class, while providing more hands-on and construction activities for boys. The results? The girls' classes thrived. Teachers stated, "Girls were less inhibited and spoke out much more than in a mixed-gender classroom. They seemed to thrive." The boys preferred hands-on activities and when given opportunities to build or construct, they went right to it. They loved map-making activities in social studies, whereas the girls weren't as interested in that. One interesting find was that teachers assumed boys would show off less because girls were not in the room, but they actually seemed to show off for one another

just as much. They also seemed to be in constant competition with one another. The noise level was very high even when they were engrossed in an activity.

Self-selection. Sometimes having the kids choose their own groups is a motivating, exciting option for kids, but it also can be humiliating. Be mindful of those students who may not be selected, and have a plan in place before you give this option.

Random grouping. Random grouping can mix things up and perhaps provide novel group membership. Counting off by threes, using birthday months, and polling the color of shirts are all ways to group randomly. Just be sure to have a reason for this random grouping because other grouping measures can be so much more powerful.

Cooperative learning groups. Within cooperative learning groups, each student has a specific task so that the success of the group is dependent upon each member completing his or her task well. According to Johnson and Johnson (1999), cooperative learning groups must embody five criteria to be successful:

- *Positive interdependence*: Members understand that they must learn together to accomplish the goal; they need each other for support, explanations, and guidance.
- *Individual accountability*: The performance of each group member is assessed against a standard, and members are held responsible for their contribution to achieving goals.
- *Promotive interaction*: Students interact face-to-face and close together, not across the room.
- *Group processing*: Groups reflect on their collaborative efforts and decide on ways to improve effectiveness.
- *Development of small-group interpersonal skills*: These skills, such as giving constructive feedback, reaching consensus, and involving every member, are necessary for effective group functioning. They must be taught and practiced before the groups tackle a learning task. (as cited in InTime, n.d., para.3)

Cooperative learning can be an incredible vehicle for learning social responsibility and interpersonal skills. Different theories exist regarding cooperative learning, some of which require mixed-ability grouping (Johnson & Johnson, 1999), but mixed ability is not inherent in the definition. Remember that the grouping strategy used must be a match with the educational intent determined by the teacher. For example, if your goal is for students to learn that each group member is invaluable and necessary for success, then cooperative learning with mixed abilities works beautifully. However, if your goal is for all students to learn new math concepts based on their individual abilities, then cooperative learning with mixed abilities isn't the best match. Cooperative learning with similar ability groups would be a more appropriate option.

Students with gifts and talents, in particular, may be frustrated with cooperative learning, especially when those groups are of mixed ability in a heterogeneous class (Robinson, 1990). The National Association for Gifted Children (1996) issued a policy statement regarding cooperative learning and gifted children and youth:

> NAGC believes that cooperative learning should be viewed within a range of instructional strategies that may enhance some learning objectives for some gifted students some of the time but should not be used as a panacea to replace differentiated services addressing the educational needs of gifted students. (p. 1)

Coleman (2005) described successful ways to implement cooperative learning in a class with gifted students. She argued that cooperative learning activities must include "flexibility, choice, and challenge" (p. 527), such as problem-based learning and the jigsaw method.

Given the collaborative background of this method, how do you use it when differentiating? If each group is doing the same activity, then it is not differentiation. That bears repeating: Even when students are seated together in small clusters, unless the learning experiences differ for the clusters or for the students in the cluster, it is not differentiation. Therefore, if your goal is to differentiate instruction and build cooperative skills, you would need to preassess the students to determine the specific role (such as leader or recorder) that would best address the strengths or interests of the students. The students are placed into the cooperative learning groups and assigned the roles that best match them. Then all groups would have the same learning task that must be accomplished through group collaboration and cooperation. The differentiation occurs in role assignment. Remember to group the students with gifts and talents in the same cooperative learning group because "there is no support for mixed-ability cooperative learning providing any type of benefit for gifted learners" (Rogers, 2006, p. 19).

SCHOOL-CREATED GROUPS

Readiness/ability or performance grouped classes. The decision to offer classes on various levels (such as juniors in high school having the option of taking English III, English III Honors, or even Advanced Placement English Language and Composition) occurs before the school year begins. These classes may be readiness- or ability-based—that is, students are assigned to classes based on their scores on placement measures, achievement tests, IQ tests, etc. Based on these measures, students are placed in classes wherein class objectives are commensurate with student readiness or ability; grouping and regrouping occur inside the classroom. These classes can also be performance grouped—that is, they are filled with students whose past performance has indicated certain levels of achievement. Often, in middle and high school, classes are offered on various levels so that teachers have students whose readiness levels or past performances match the class offering. The same grouping can be done on the elementary level. Young readers of the same ability could be placed in the same classroom to facilitate learning. Grouping and regrouping would still be necessary in any of these examples.

Take a middle school math option, for instance. Although algebra is typically viewed as an advanced math class for eighth graders, there may be a class-sized group of seventh graders ready for it. So, math class offerings for that particular seventh-grade year might include fundamental seventh-grade math, seventh-grade math, pre-algebra, and algebra. Students would take the math class that best matched their skill or readiness levels or their past performance in math class. For example, the algebra class may comprise students who have been formally identified as gifted and talented in mathematics along with students who have demonstrated high achievement in math even though they are not identified as gifted in math. Then, based on the topic, students could be flexibly grouped inside the class.

Kulik (1992) analyzed the research on grouping. Problems arise when all students have the same work regardless of how they're grouped. Some of his results follow:

> Programs that entail only minor adjustment of course content for ability groups usually have little or no effect on student achievement. In some grouping programs, for example, school administrators assign students by test scores and school records to high, middle, and low classes, and they expect all groups to follow the same basic curriculum. The traditional name for this approach is *XYZ grouping.* Pupils in middle and lower classes in XYZ programs learn the same amount as equivalent pupils do in mixed classes. Students in the top classes in XYZ programs outperform equivalent pupils from mixed classes by about one month on a grade-equivalent scale. Self-esteem of lower aptitude students rises slightly and self-esteem of higher aptitude students drops slightly in XYZ classes. (Abstract)

The key, then, is making adjustments within the students' work, regardless of the grouping arrangement.

Purposeful placement of students in classes with well-articulated curricula greatly affects student learning. The founder of the Value-Added Research and Assessment Center, William Sanders (1998) argues that "huge variations exist among districts, schools, and classrooms in providing academic growth opportunities for students" (p. 27). He believes that the variability can in part be lessened by administrators "provid[ing] measurement of the academic progress by each student" (p. 27)—in short, educators must be able to document continuous progress for each student. If a learner is ready for algebra in the seventh grade, she should have the opportunity to take a class designed to teach students algebra. Within that class, though, students will differ in their strengths, interests, and levels of readiness; differentiation should occur to ensure continuous progress for each of those young mathematicians.

Cluster groups. Cluster grouping is an incredibly powerful (and completely inexpensive) grouping method that encourages young people with gifts and talents to thrive academically and allows new academic leaders to emerge. It takes place before young people ever walk into the classroom. Perhaps the greatest challenge lies in creative scheduling.

Rogers (2006) explains cluster grouping:

> Top 5–8 academically gifted students are placed with one teacher at a grade level and proportionate amount of that teacher's class time is spent in direct differentiation for this group. Remainder of class is normal mix of ability levels. Or, the top 5–8 math students are placed in one classroom and a concomitant reading/language arts cluster classroom is provided at each grade level. (p. 34)

Math and reading are natural choices for clustering, but all content areas are fair game. The results for cluster grouping can be profound—clustered students can gain well over a year's growth in a year's time, with studies showing as much as an additional three-fifths year's growth (Rogers, 2006). Teachers are much more likely to differentiate for a group of five students working off grade level than for only one student working off grade level. In fact, cluster grouping is a wonderful way to meet both the cognitive and social-emotional needs of gifted and talented young people.

But, what happens to the other students when the top students are no longer there? Have they lost their role models? The answer is no. Schunk (1987) found that students of low and average ability do not model themselves after gifted students: "In general, the more alike observers are to models, the greater is the probability that similar actions by observers are socially appropriate and will produce comparable results" (p. 151). From goal setting to behaviors, students model themselves after others whose accomplishments may be attainable, whose behaviors and habits may be imitable. In fact, students of low or average ability seem to thrive when the top students are taken out of the equation; new leaders emerge and achievement occurs (Gentry, 1996; Winebrenner & Devlin, 1996).

Students could also be clustered across classrooms. For example, an elementary school has common reading time for its campus. This encourages the teachers to take their top readers—even if that's one or two per class—and cluster them together with one teacher during common reading time. Students then receive direct reading instruction and practice reading at their individual reading levels.

KEYS TO SUCCESSFUL GROUPING

- *Always* have a strong reason for grouping kids. Base it on preassessments, inventories, or other anecdotal data (if being grouped for a noninstructional reason). Keep to the goal of continuous progress for all.
- Once kids are placed in different groups for instructional purposes, all groups should have different learning experiences matched to their learning profile, strengths, interests, or readiness levels.
- The task should be equally challenging to everyone in the group, and each student should be held accountable for the task.
- Grouping does not have to be a physical concept. Everyone can still be sitting in rows but working on assignments that correlate to the preassessment or inventory.
- Vary the way you group kids. Don't always use learning modalities because the same kids will end up with each other each time. Be flexible.
- Some kids work better alone. Give students that opportunity if grouping causes great stress. Perhaps students will work individually on a task and then share results in a small-group setting. Remember the openness component to a differentiated classroom.

MANAGING THE CLASSROOM

Thinking back to the chapter on culture (Chapter 3), we explored the concept that a differentiated classroom is one that utilizes procedures and routines fully in order to maximize instruction. Just as grouping is intentional and differentiating is intentional, the procedures and routines must be intentional as well. Ideally, these will be practiced frequently early in the year so that students internalize them. When routines and procedures become second nature, valuable learning time in the classroom is not wasted while students try to figure out where to go and what to do. Although certainly not exhaustive, the following ideas will help you get a strong start.

GETTING INTO GROUPS

Ideally, you will be grouping and regrouping students throughout the semester. Depending on the physical structure of your classroom, this involves moving desks and/or tables and chairs. Organization simplifies this process. Visuals are key. For example, create posters that visually display the various grouping arrangements you typically use in class. You may design one poster to reflect reading or math group placement. Another could show the layout for groups based on multiple intelligences. Other posters could display the arrangement for groups of threes or pairs. Color-coding the posters helps as well. For example, the groups-of-three poster may be done in blue. In addition to reviewing the illustration of how the room looks, students could also look for small strips of blue tape on the floor, marking the spots where the desks or tables go. Yellow tape might match the reading groups poster and red for math groups. Each student knows his role in preparing the room for certain groups. The entire class has practiced moving desks and chairs for each variation, so when the time comes for a particular grouping, students are on automatic pilot.

Find easy ways to let students know which group they are in. This could be as simple as listing groups on the white board or chalk board. You could also color code student names on a poster that lists all students in the class. Whatever the method, be efficient with it. Valuable time is wasted when you call out each student's name and assign each verbally to a group.

MANAGING GROUPS

Directions. This may sound obvious, but do not give individual group instructions to the whole class. This causes confusion as some students tune in to the wrong group's directions and miss their own while other students are not paying attention to anything because they don't know what's meant for them. Direction giving can be a source of frustration to both students and teachers. Simplify the process. Put all individual group instructions in writing (or create an audio recording), making sure each group has its own directions for the learning task as soon as the group forms. There may very well be whole-class instructions first, such as an overview of the concept or discussion of the time frame for the learning experiences. However, when you are differentiating and each group has distinct learning tasks, each group needs its own instructions written down; in fact, seeing or hearing others' tasks may cause confusion or even encourage off-task discussions. Of course, you will need to rotate among the groups to make sure they understand what is being asked of them.

Assistance. Another possible source of frustration for teachers working with multiple groups is the mistaken belief that you have to be everywhere at once to answer questions. Again, simplify the process. For example, each group may have a red plastic cup and green plastic cup on their table or desks. A green cup on top signifies smooth sailing while a red cup indicates help is needed. Stop at those with red cups first. Similarly, a two-colored sign works well, or you could even borrow the idea of the Bubba Gump Shrimp Company's Alabama license plates that read *Run, Forrest, Run* and *Stop, Forrest, Stop*. Of course, the idea is to have some sort of visual indicator that students can use when they need assistance. This is better than students interrupting you when you're working with other groups or calling out. Ideally, students should be able to work on at least one part of the learning activity while waiting for your input. Remember, too, that the clearer the instructions, the better. Questions should stem from content, not from confusing directions.

Time. Another issue with group work deals with time. What happens to the group who finishes before the others? What happens to the group who seems like they'll never finish? By this point in the book, you know that differentiation means appropriately different work—not more work. So the group that completes the task before time is up should not receive additional tasks or questions. Anchor activities work beautifully here. Anchor activities are ongoing learning experiences that students can return to throughout the unit or even the year. Their purpose is multifold:

- they provide a strategy for teachers to deal with "ragged time" when students complete work at different times;
- they allow the teacher to work with individual students or groups;
- they provide ongoing activities that relate to the content of the unit;
- they allow the teacher to develop independent group work strategies in order to incorporate a mini lab of computers in classroom. (Curry School, 2011, p. 7)

They prove most effective "when expectations are clear and the tasks are taught and practiced prior to use" and "when students are held accountable for task behavior and/or task completion" (Curry School of Education, 2011, p. 5). Whether the anchor activity is a learning log, ACT preparation, silent reading about the concept, or an independent investigation, the message is that learning is continuous in the classroom. You should definitely establish a procedure for students to follow when they have completed a learning task.

MANAGING MATERIALS

Resources and materials. Multiple learning opportunities for your students often require multiple resources. For example, if you are differentiating based on readiness, you will probably provide an array of reading materials on various Lexile or reading levels for whatever concept or content you are teaching. You may also have a wide variety of math resources to accommodate students' learning profiles: manipulatives for students who prefer to learn bodily/kinesthetically, math books for those who learn best linguistically, graphic organizers for those who are visual-spatial learners, etc. Color coding is an excellent way to organize materials and resources. For example, green could be the designated hue for all science-related materials. The scales and rock collections are stored in green bins. Science materials on various reading levels go on the green bookshelf. Green folders hold science work in progress while completed science assignments are placed in the green box on the table. The poster on the wall for science groups is even green. Of course, a high school science class may not have this same setup, but colors could be designated for the individual units of study. The idea is to organize materials and resources so students have easy access. Time is devoted to instruction and learning, not hunting for the right tools to use or answering the same questions about what goes where.

Don't forget the storage area for the generic rubrics. Whether it's a file drawer full of DAP Tools or rubrics stored on a flash drive, be sure to have a central location to house them so students can find them with ease. Also remember to label generously—label bins, boxes, shelves, folders—whatever is used to organize specific materials.

Homework. Students should know where to turn in completed assignments or homework. This could be as simple as a basket on your desk or as sophisticated as a set of color-coded files with each color representing a subject. The structure depends on you.

Makeup work. Just as students know the process for turning in completed work, they should also know the process for finding out what happened while they were absent. This includes everything from getting notes if needed to the time allotted for makeup work. A bulletin board works well here. Not only can you list instructions, but you can also include copies of handouts and other resources. Reminders about time frame and other specifics should be there as well. This station could be set up anywhere in the room. The goal is for students to know the routine, so they can do this independently.

Remember how important it is to establish these procedures and routines early in the school year. Then students must practice them. The more organized you are, the easier it is to manage a differentiated classroom. Many resources exist that provide guidance, such as http://www.diffcentral.com, which contains excellent tips and strategies for managing a differentiated classroom.

MANAGING TIME

Teachers often cite time constraints as one of the main reasons why they don't differentiate. They don't have time to preassess, much less create preassessments or read them. They don't have time to prepare multiple lessons on the same topic. They don't have time to develop enrichment or remedial tasks. They don't have time to grade different products. They don't have time to find resources. And, they don't have time to let students explore the content thoroughly—especially because their goal is to finish the entire textbook in order for the students to do well on the state and national assessments.

There are many philosophical issues presented in that last paragraph, but for the sake of staying on topic, let's focus on the management of time in a differentiated classroom. When you plan a unit of study, you allocate time for that unit, whether it's 3 weeks or 3 days. The time will be the same for everyone in the class regardless of how they're learning the material (unless you are differentiating the pace of instruction by letting those who need fewer repetitions or less time with material to master it move ahead—a very effective strategy for students with gifts and talents). The variance comes into play when you examine the individual or small-group learning experiences. Ideally, if you prepare differentiated or tiered experiences with one class time frame in mind, then all students will complete the learning task (regardless of what that task is) by the end of the period. The time frame is constant. Strategies emphasizing tiering or the differentiation of process, such as Venn diagrams (see Chapter 7), can be structured so that the tasks provide the appropriate level of challenge and ensure that all students finish in the same time frame.

Unit time and individual class time are constants, but managing time gets trickier with varied learning experiences because these can differ greatly. The more prepared you are, the better you can manage your time. For example, if the preassessments truly reflect the mastery level of the content or the readiness to learn a new concept, then you will be much better able to design challenging tasks so that all learners have continuous progress. If you harmoniously match the learning experience with the student, the student will not zip through the activities or be frustratingly stuck on the first part of the assignment forever. Your professional judgment—based on preassessment—can determine time needs accurately.

Each of the strategies presented in this book can be incorporated in myriad ways in the classroom. When a climate that encourages and supports a culture for effective differentiation is established at the beginning of the school year, students understand that all people learn in different ways, bring varying interests and experiences to the learning environment, and learn at different paces. They are taught to respect those differences and be open to the flexible use of time. Each way, though, requires a different approach to time.

Time for Bloom Charts. When Bloom Charts are used as an end assessment or as a project to accompany the unit, ample time is needed. Not only does this mean plenty of time for the project/product itself to be planned and created (perhaps a week in a 2-week unit), but class time to work also must be incorporated into the unit. Too few students have the resources (i.e., unscheduled time, money for supplies, and guidance from an adult) to complete the products strictly at home. Bloom Charts also can be used for a single lesson as long as the tasks are designed to be manageable in that amount of time. This may sound obvious, but sometimes educators are quick to include an engaging learning experience without realistically considering the time involved.

Time for Venn diagrams. Venn diagrams, primarily a vehicle for differentiating process and making the content more complex, should be designed to take the same amount of time for completion—roughly one class period. Preassessment is critical here to ensure the right matching of challenge level to student. Remember, too, that if some students finish their 1- or 2-oval Venn more quickly than expected, they can join forces to increase the level of difficulty and stimulate higher level thinking.

Time for Think-Tac-Toe. Think-Tac-Toe is very similar to the Bloom Chart in that it is primarily used as a way to enrich the entire unit or semester. Therefore, the same thoughts come into play. Allow time in class to work on the products. Provide access to supplies. Make sure the students know the assignment is coming when the unit is introduced, and then allocate enough time for them to thoughtfully complete the task. Realize that although the options themselves may demand varying amounts of time, large time frames are needed for the class as a whole.

PRISONERS OF TIME

Historically, we have not been very open to that flexible use of time. For example, all kids begin kindergarten at age 5 regardless of whether they've been reading for a year or have a learning problem that required early intervention. Age 18 is when people are granted the right to vote, whether they've followed politics since fourth grade or can't distinguish the Democrats from the Republicans. We seem to have established—at times rather arbitrarily—the dictate of time. *Prisoners of Time*, a report of the National Education Commission on Time and Learning (1994), candidly explores the constraints that time has had on our educational system:

> If experience, research, and common sense teach nothing else, they confirm the truism that people learn at different rates, and in different ways with different subjects. But we have put the cart before the horse: our

> schools and the people involved with them—students, parents, teachers, administrators, and staff—are captives of clock and calendar. The boundaries of student growth are defined by schedules for bells, buses, and vacations instead of standards for students and learning. (para. 4)

Even though we as educators may not have control over how many days we have in the classroom, we do have control over how we utilize the time we have with our students. We can use the time effectively to ensure that all students make continuous progress.

The exterior demands on time can be very damaging:

> The results are predictable. The school clock governs how families organize their lives, how administrators oversee their schools, and how teachers work their way through the curriculum. Above all, it governs how material is presented to students and the opportunity they have to comprehend and master it. (National Education Commission on Time and Learning, 1994, para. 6)

We must, as intentional educators concerned with continuous progress for all, take back time. The report continues:

> This state of affairs explains a universal phenomenon during the last quarter of the academic year: as time runs out on them, frustrated teachers face the task of cramming large portions of required material into a fraction of the time intended for it. As time runs out on the teacher, perceptive students are left to wonder about the integrity of an instructional system that behaves, year-in and year-out, as though the last chapters of their textbooks are not important. (National Education Commission on Time and Learning, 1994, para. 7)

One way to take back that time, to stress what is and isn't important, is through our long-term planning. We must choose our differentiated units carefully, looking for depth over breadth, so that optimum learning occurs during the time we have.

IMPORTANT TAKE-AWAYS

- Grouping must be intentional. You must have a valid reason for placing certain students together.
- Grouping alone does not ensure differentiation. Each group must have varying learning experiences based on the reason for the grouping: level of readiness, strengths, interest, etc.
- Establishing and practicing routines and procedures simplify the differentiation process and make a differentiated classroom manageable.
- Don't become a victim of time. Plan early and plan well.

CHAPTER
10

Taming the Assessment Beast

Differentiated instruction is rooted in assessment. —Carol A. Tomlinson

Differentiation without documentation is whimsical. Tiering without documentation is ungrounded. Teachers who randomly put learners into groups and then give them different assignments miss the point. That is *not* differentiation. Differentiation is *not* just doing something different. Differentiation is providing varying learning experiences for students for specific reasons, such as grouping based on the results of an interest inventory or a preassessment evaluating readiness or prior learning. The teacher provides learning experiences that match readiness and/or interests of the students in each group. Differentiation is intentional.

Assessment is the only real communication that lets students know if they are making progress—if they are learning or just marking time. This assessment comes in various forms. Preassessment tells the teacher and student what he knows before the unit has begun, formative assessment informs both teacher and student of progress toward the learning goals, and summative assessment provides information about performance at the end of the unit. Assessment documents why students are learning what they are and in the way they are. Assessment also provides additional data that allow you to communicate with parents about the continuous progress their child is making.

Just as grouping and regrouping are ongoing, so is effective assessment; it is not simply some test you give at the end of the unit so you have something to put in the gradebook before moving on to the next unit. Rather, you preassess to see who already knows what; you assess throughout the unit as you determine who is learning what, at what pace, and on what level of sophistication; and you assess at the end to see what progress individual students are making—then decide what comes next and for which students.

AUTHENTIC ASSESSMENT

Although traditional end assessments have a place in the classroom, they should by no means be used exclusively. Educators have begun to focus on authentic assessment in lieu of pen-and-paper tests that rely on multiple-choice and true/false questions. Entire books and graduate classes have been devoted to authentic assessment and performance assessment. For our purposes (i.e., How do I best match kids to content, process, and product so that continuous learning occurs?), we will look at multiple products as a venue for authentic assessment.

Various definitions have been offered for authentic assessment. The concept is not new, but it has become a well-known term in the 21st century.

> Any goals that suggest the integration of sophisticated, complex, and in-depth understanding; creative productivity; the investigation of authentic problems; the use of alternative means of expression; or performance that emulates or represents that of professionals must be assessed using performance and product assessments. (Callahan, 2006, p. 32)

> Engaging and worthy problems or questions of importance, in which students must use knowledge to fashion performances effectively and creatively. The tasks are either replicas of or analogous to the kinds of problems faced by adult citizens and consumers or professionals in the field. (Wiggins, 1993, p. 229)

> Performance assessments call upon the examinee to demonstrate specific skills and competencies, that is, to apply the skills and knowledge they have mastered. (Stiggins, 1987, p. 34)

Notice the connection between content and realistic application of the content. Real-world products encourage and require high-level thinking, including creative thinking about the content. We all know that Fortune 500 companies aren't looking for dioramas in their board meetings any more than they're looking for true/false and multiple-choice-formatted presentations. Teachers must start somewhere and break away from traditional pen-and-paper assessments (or typical non-pen-and-paper assessments such as dioramas) as the only means of assessment. Granted, most standardized tests and some college- and career-ready indicators are pen-and-paper assessments, but educators and students must acknowledge and prepare for a wide variety of products that exist in the world of work.

PRODUCTS

The whole point of differentiation is to engage each student in making continuous progress. Products are primary vehicles to do just that. Matching products to the students' interests, levels of readiness, and/or strengths can boost engagement in learning. After all, increasing interest in what is being learned is key to creating a classroom in which everyone is learning. Products make learning real. Appropriate use of a range of products facilitates differentiating to ensure that each student is making continuous progress.

Several of the strategies in this book focus on products as authentic assessment. Remember that the products show you, the teacher, what your students have learned. Hopefully, those products are designed to be shared with other audiences as well—audiences with individuals who are interested in the content of the product as well as the product itself. Content, then, and presentation of that content (e.g., book jacket, podcast, collage) are critical for you to evaluate the learning. However, many students have not been exposed to the nuances or the important characteristics of the presentation of the content—the unique qualities that make a skit a skit or a mural a mural. For example, the fact that they have seen sculptures (or even created them) does not necessarily mean that they understand the criteria inherent in outstanding sculptures. Therefore, learning about the products themselves may indeed coincide with learning about the content, especially when the student is first given the opportunity to create that particular product. Teachers also need to learn about products. If we are to assess pieces of technical writing, a dance, or a monologue, we need to understand what the critical components of each of those products are and what indicates excellence.

Hanna and Dettmer (2004) described product assessment and the challenge that assessing products can present:

> In product assessment, the examinee is directed to create a specific product (e.g., essay, fired pot, research paper, math proof, charcoal sketch, or tuned-up engine). The product is assessed after it is completed. Some products are created under tightly controlled conditions, whereas others are produced in the variable settings of everyday life. The assessment of products can be analytic, objective and detailed or it can be impressionistic and global. (p. 195)

Whether analytic or global, the assessment of products must be intentional. The products must be realistic representations of the learning that has occurred (i.e., the content), and the product itself should ideally mirror that same product in the real world. So, careful assessment of products is desirable.

RUBRICS/SCORING GUIDES

Once you commit to a differentiated classroom that encourages student choice within limits, you run into two main problem areas regarding choice in product. The first is providing rich options of products (this chapter and Chapter 8 suggest options for enriching product selection). The second involves assessing all of those products. You're probably mumbling to yourself: "How do I find time to grade all those things? And, when I find time, how do I grade them? Do I use rubrics? If so, how do I create all those rubrics?" and maybe even a few other comments unsuitable for printing. Let's find some answers.

- *How do I find time to grade the products?* Simplify the grading process by first making sure that all students know what's expected in their product. If you use the same vocabulary and general criteria for all products, then it's even easier. A well-developed scoring guide or rubric that contains those expectations in language everyone is familiar with lessens the actual grading time. (Don't worry, we'll show you how!)
- *When I find time, how do I grade them? Do I use rubrics?* You can use rubrics, scoring guides, or product assessments—all terms used interchangeably. Of course, we prefer our version: Developing and Assessing Product Tool (DAP Tool), which will be discussed in further detail in this chapter. We suggest the DAP Tool because it is a protocol that can be used with all products, eliminating the need to create multiple rubrics.
- *If so, how do I create those rubrics?* This could easily be a multiple-choice question with the answer being "E. All of the above." You can create your own rubrics from scratch—always a possibility but very time consuming. Rubrics also abound in such resources as *Solving the Assessment Puzzle Piece by Piece* (Coil & Merritt, 2001).Websites are also a rich resource—even for the technologically challenged. Typing in the word *rubric* on Google resulted in more than five million hits. Most educators have heard of Rubistar, a free service that not only posts dozens of rubrics but allows for easy creation of rubrics, as well (see http://rubistar.4teachers.org). One of our favorites is Kathy Schrock's Guide to Everything: Assessment and Rubrics (see http://www.schrockguide.net/assessment-and-rubrics.html). She lists dozens of links to websites and articles focusing on rubrics—some free and some by subscription. Some are general, while others are specific to content or grade level. The site is a goldmine of information and possibility.

DEVELOPING AND ASSESSING PRODUCT TOOL (DAP TOOL)

The DAP Tool was initially introduced in the first edition of this book; due to interest, a separate book followed that solely focused on this protocol for developing and assessing products (Roberts & Inman, 2009, 2015). The DAP Tool makes using products to differentiate learning experiences easy because it provides consistency in guiding the development of products (a wide range of products) and in assessing them. The components of the DAP Tool provide that consistency whether you are teaching primary, intermediate, middle, or high school students or whether your content area is science, the arts, language arts, social students, practical living, or mathematics. The DAP Tool is a protocol that can be used by teachers at all levels and in all content areas.

It's important to see what a complete DAP Tool looks like before exploring the individual components and nuances of the protocol. Figure 10.1 provides the complete DAP Tool for a poster. Take a moment to look at it in its entirety to see it for what it is: a tool for students to use to guide them in developing a poster and a tool for educators to use to assess it.

DAP COMPONENTS

Remember when we mentioned simplifying assessment by using the same vocabulary and general criteria for each assessment? Well, here we go!

Content. Content (i.e., what you want the student to learn) is certainly the most important component of any product. After all, the product is primarily a vehicle to demonstrate what the student has learned. The meat of the product, the content, must be accurate, have depth and complexity, and be organized. In order to preserve your sanity, the language must be general enough so that the product can be applied in all content areas. The student is responsible for being content specific. For example, the general content requirements (i.e., accuracy, depth of understanding, and organization of content) for a monologue if the student were depicting a plant cell would parallel the general content requirements for a monologue if the student were depicting a character in a novella. Of course, the specific content would differ greatly (unless the character in the novella thinks he's a plant cell!). The content component is based on these three questions:

- Is the content correct and complete?
- Has the content been thought about in a way that goes beyond a surface understanding?
- Is the content put together in such a way that people understand it?

Regardless of the concepts studied, the accuracy, complexity, and organization of information are the cornerstones of content mastery.

POSTER Tier 1—DAP TOOL

CONTENT								
	» Is the content correct?	0	1	2	3	4	5	6
	» Has the content been thought about in a way that goes beyond a surface understanding?	0	1	2	3	4	5	6
	» Is the content put together in such a way that people understand it?	0	1	2	3	4	5	6
PRESENTATION								
TEXT	» Is the title easy to see, clear, and well placed? Do labels clearly explain the graphics?	0	1	2	3	4	5	6
GRAPHICS	» Are the graphics (e.g., illustrations, photos) important and appropriate to the topic?	0	1	2	3	4	5	6
LAYOUT	» Are the images carefully selected and emphasized? Is the labeling linked to the graphic? Is it pleasing to the eye? Is the spacing deliberate to draw attention to main parts of the poster?	0	1	2	3	4	5	6
CORRECTNESS	» Is the poster mostly free from usage, punctuation, capitalization, and spelling errors? If sources are used, are they cited correctly?	0	1	2	3	4	5	6
CREATIVITY								
	» Is the content seen in a new way?	0	1	2	3	4	5	6
	» Is the presentation done in a new way?	0	1	2	3	4	5	6
REFLECTION								
CONTENT	» What connections can you make between what you have learned by completing this project and previous learning?	0	1	2	3	4	5	6
PRODUCT	» In what ways could you improve your product when completing this product with a different assignment?	0	1	2	3	4	5	6
LEARNING	» How did the amount of effort affect your learning about the content and creating the product?	0	1	2	3	4	5	6

Comments:

Meaning of Performance Scale:
6—PROFESSIONAL LEVEL: level expected from a professional in the content area
5—ADVANCED LEVEL: level exceeds expectations of the standard
4—PROFICIENT LEVEL: level expected for meeting the standard
3—PROGRESSING LEVEL: level demonstrates movement toward the standard
2—NOVICE LEVEL: level demonstrates initial awareness and knowledge of standard
1—NONPERFORMING LEVEL: level indicates no effort made to meet standard
0—NONPARTICIPATING LEVEL: level indicates nothing turned in

Figure 10.1. Poster Tier 1 DAP Tool.

Presentation. This component will be more unique in wording than the other three components because the descriptors will be specific to the product itself. For instance, you'll see terms like *graphics* and *layout* in a pamphlet rubric but no mention of *clear voice projection* or *eye contact*, terms that would be included in the rubric for a speech. When developing multilevel rubrics for the same product, language becomes much more sophisticated. The main question for this area follows:

- Are product-specific components included in the presentation?

The presentation component and its detailed descriptors will guide the student in the actual creation of the product. Here, the student takes the accurate, well-thought-out, and organized information and shapes it into the product, then the teacher assesses the worth of the product. The presentation component is important but no more so than the content. Sometimes a teacher will be so impressed with the product itself that she neglects to assess the actual content. Assessing the product without assessing the content is dangerous in that it encourages students to produce a flashy product with a weak content understanding.

Creativity. The *creativity* component is the spark of originality that an individual student puts into the product that makes his writing, speech, or pamphlet different from those done by other individuals. It is the creative spark that personalizes the product.

Creativity, that personal insight that inspires the student, surfaces in both the content (distinct viewpoint) and presentation (unique approach). It's originality. It's what distinguishes one diorama of a rainforest biome from another diorama on the same topic. The following two questions form the basis of the creativity component:

- Is the content seen in a new way?
- Is the presentation done in a new way?

It is in this component that the student blends the accurate and organized content and the specific requirements of the product with him- or herself, and the teacher assesses originality or innovation in both approach to content and to product.

Reflection. *Reflection*, highly personal in nature, is the process of examining what was learned in the process of creating that specific product with regard to the content, product, and learning itself. This component of the DAP Tool involves metacognitive skills that will empower the student to become a lifelong learner. The following questions—with support for their answers below—form the basis of the reflection component:

- Content: What connections can you make between what you have learned by completing this project and previous learning? What questions has this content raised for you? What aspect of the content do you want to learn more about?
- Product: In what ways could you improve your product when completing this product with a different assignment?
- Learning: How did the amount of effort affect your learning about the content and creating the product?

This high-level thinking serves as impetus for future learning. Reflection should stretch thinking, encouraging the student to make continuous progress—to learn new things on an ongoing basis. A reflection should be written and should accompany every product created.

Not only does reflection allow the student to think logically about her learning, but it also allows you to assess her learning. Was this product too challenging? Too simple? Did the presentation cause problems? How? Answers to these questions serve as a vital information tool for future learning.

In short, each DAP Tool, regardless of product, must have these same four components: Content, Presentation, Creativity, and Reflection. The only component to be specialized each time is the presentation piece. As students become familiar with the language of the assessments and the expectations inherent in them, the whole assessment process is simplified for everyone, teacher and student alike. The teacher has the protocol to use for all products, and the student learns the components of the protocol and applies them repeatedly with a variety of products in multiple content areas across grades.

Differentiating through assessment is necessary for students to make continuous progress with regard to the content being studied and the product selected to demonstrate what was learned. Creativity is an essential element of outstanding products, and reflection promotes lifelong learning. Establishing these four components of the DAP Tool provides focus for students as they develop a variety of products in a wide range of subject areas. The DAP Tool allows assessment to be specific in relation to the content, presentation, creativity, and reflection. Specific feedback guides the student so she knows what she needs to work on with the next product. Most important, the DAP Tool is the protocol that teachers can use to facilitate all students making continuous progress.

Schlechty (2002) described the importance of a "clear and compelling product" in his book *Working on the Work*:

> When products, performances, or exhibitions are part of the instructional design, students understand the standards by which these products, performances, or exhibitions will be evaluated. They are committed to

> these standards and see the real prospect of meeting the stated standard if they work diligently at the tasks assigned and are encouraged. (p. 26)

The DAP Tool not only makes these standards by which the products will be evaluated clear, but it also emphasizes the importance of standards in the performance scale.

A PERFORMANCE SCALE FOR THE DAP TOOL THAT GOES BEYOND PROFICIENCY

Not only are the components consistent for the DAP Tool, the levels for assessing performance are consistent as well. The performance scale has seven levels (see Figure 10.2). Let's start with the top level, the one that removes the learning ceiling.

- Level 6 is called *professional.* The professional designation specifies the level of performance expected from a professional in a career that uses that specific product. This level seldom if ever will be reached by a student; however, the purpose of including the professional level is to set a high target for the student to strive to reach that is way beyond the level of proficient.
- Level 5 is named *advanced.* The advanced designation indicates that the student's work exceeds the standard set as proficient. This level is so important because it provides a target beyond the norm that will be recognized in products that go beyond age-level expectations.
- Level 4 is *proficient.* This level designates a standard that students are expected to meet. State and national standards set the standard for the proficient level.
- Level 3 is called the *progressing* level. Student work at this level indicates movement toward the proficient level while not yet reaching the standard.
- Level 2 is named the *novice* level. This level indicates that the student has initial awareness and knowledge of the standard.
- Level 1 is designated *nonperforming.* The student turned a product in, but little effort was directed toward meeting the standard. A student could be assessed at the nonperforming level on any of the four components of the DAP Tool—Content, Presentation, Creativity, and Reflection (or for any of the subcategories under those four primary designations).
- Level 0 is the lowest point on the performance scale, *nonparticipating.* A student who receives the zero level is not submitting any product.

This seven-level scale is placed across from each question or description of performance for each component (i.e., Content, Presentation, Creativity, and Reflection) of the DAP Tool. Figure 10.3 is a sample of the Content component.

Meaning of Performance Scale:
6—PROFESSIONAL LEVEL: level expected from a professional in the content area
5—ADVANCED LEVEL: level exceeds expectations of the standard
4—PROFICIENT LEVEL: level expected for meeting the standard
3—PROGRESSING LEVEL: level demonstrates movement toward the standard
2—NOVICE LEVEL: level demonstrates initial awareness and knowledge of standard
1—NONPERFORMING LEVEL: level indicates no effort made to meet standard
0—NONPARTICIPATING LEVEL: level indicates nothing turned in

Figure 10.2. DAP Tool performance scale.

This placement is to make it convenient for you to assess the performance of each student on each component of each product. Remember to keep the standard by which you will judge the performance on the seven-level scale front and center in your mind.

THREE TIERS TO DIFFERENTIATE

For each product, there are three variations or tiers of the DAP Tool; these three tiers vary in sophistication and expectation. The tiers provide a ready means of differentiating your expectations for students based on their current performance level. Once again, it is your match between performance and your level of expectations that will provide appropriate differentiation. Remember that this is the assessment piece for differentiation; you can differentiate content, process, product, and assessment. (However, if you are not ready to differentiate assessment, remember that you can use the DAP Tool as a rubric. Period.)

Kindergartners, as well as seniors in high school, have the ability to create posters. Should the scoring guide be the same for both? Isn't a poster a poster? Although the criteria may be the same in the rubrics (or increased in number for the older student or the student who is ready to use a more advanced set of criteria in the preparation of the product), the level of sophistication should vary greatly. A 17-year-old's poster should be far more sophisticated than the 5-year-old's. One single DAP Tool designed for a poster can't be used for both students (unless, of course, the senior has never created a poster before and needs to use a Tier 1.)

That sophistication of product isn't limited to varying grades; within one class, students differ greatly. More specific wording at different levels of sophistication guides the young person as she works on the product, and it also provides the guidelines for you to assess the product when it is completed. Because of your preassessment, you know that expectations need to be different for some students. This is where multiple DAP Tools for the same product come into play. The main variation will be upping the expectations and the level of sophistication in wording. Moreover, the tiers can also be used across grades. Whenever someone

CONTENT								
» Is the content correct?	0	1	2	3	4	5	6
» Has the content been thought about in a way that goes beyond a surface understanding?	0	1	2	3	4	5	6
» Is the content put together in such a way that people understand it?	0	1	2	3	4	5	6

Figure 10.3. Tier 1 content.

POSTER—DAP TOOL Content

TIER ONE CONTENT							
» Is the content correct?	0	1	2	3	4	5	6
» Has the content been thought about in a way that goes beyond a surface understanding?	0	1	2	3	4	5	6
» Is the content put together in such a way that people understand it?	0	1	2	3	4	5	6
TIER TWO CONTENT							
» Content is accurate and complete.	0	1	2	3	4	5	6
» Content has depth and complexity of thought.	0	1	2	3	4	5	6
» Content is organized.	0	1	2	3	4	5	6
TIER THREE CONTENT							
» Content is accurate and thorough in detail.	0	1	2	3	4	5	6
» Product shows complex understanding and manipulation of content.	0	1	2	3	4	5	6
» Product shows deep probing of content.	0	1	2	3	4	5	6
» Organization is best suited to the product.	0	1	2	3	4	5	6

Figure 10.4. Poster DAP Tool: Content component.

has never created the product before—whether he is a senior or kindergartner—a Tier 1 for that product could be the most appropriate one to use.

Take a close look at the DAP Tool for a poster's content component only (see Figure 10.4). Figure 10.3 shows how each tier focuses on the three main criteria (accuracy, complexity, and organization). Note, though, how each differs in wording and subtly increases the level of expectation. Information can be put together so that people understand it; it also can be organized so that it best suits the product. The level of expectation increases dramatically as one moves from Tier 1 to Tier 3.

Now examine the presentation components for a poster (see Figure 10.5). Each tier focuses on text, graphics, and layout—all pertinent components of any

POSTER—DAP TOOL Presentation

TIER ONE PRESENTATION								
TEXT	» Is the title easy to see, clear, and well placed? Do labels clearly explain the graphics?	0	1	2	3	4	5	6
GRAPHICS	» Are the graphics (e.g., illustrations, photos) important and appropriate to the topic?	0	1	2	3	4	5	6
LAYOUT	» Are the images carefully selected and emphasized? Is the labeling linked to the graphic? Is it pleasing to the eye? Is the spacing deliberate to draw attention to main parts of the poster?	0	1	2	3	4	5	6
CORRECTNESS	» Is the poster mostly free from usage, punctuation, capitalization, and spelling errors? If sources are used, are they cited correctly?	0	1	2	3	4	5	6
TIER TWO PRESENTATION								
TEXT	» Title enhances the poster's purpose and is well placed. Text highlights most important concepts.	0	1	2	3	4	5	6
GRAPHICS	» Graphics (e.g., illustrations, photos) add information and are relevant for the topic.	0	1	2	3	4	5	6
LAYOUT	» Layout design clearly emphasizes graphics in an organized and attractive manner. Text is placed to clearly describe/explain all graphic images. Spacing is carefully planned with consideration of space not used.	0	1	2	3	4	5	6
CORRECTNESS	» The poster is free from usage, punctuation, capitalization, and spelling errors. Sources, when used, are thoroughly cited.	0	1	2	3	4	5	6
TIER THREE PRESENTATION								
TEXT	» Title, clearly reflecting purpose, is strategically placed. Text highlights most important concepts in clear, concise manner.	0	1	2	3	4	5	6
GRAPHICS	» Graphics (e.g., illustrations, photos) enhance meaning and are best suited for the purpose.	0	1	2	3	4	5	6
LAYOUT	» Successful composition of graphic images and design concepts communicates the purpose. Text is strategically placed to enhance the message of the poster. Negative space is used to highlight key points.	0	1	2	3	4	5	6
CORRECTNESS	» The poster is error free, with correct usage, punctuation, capitalization, and spelling used. All sources are cited correctly with the citation placed appropriately.	0	1	2	3	4	5	6

Figure 10.5. Poster DAP Tool: Presentation component.

POSTER—DAP TOOL Creativity

TIER ONE CREATIVITY								
» Is the content seen in a new way?	0	1	2	3	4	5	6
» Is the presentation done in a new way?	0	1	2	3	4	5	6
TIER TWO CREATIVITY								
» Originality is expressed in relation to the content.	0	1	2	3	4	5	6
» Originality is expressed in relation to the presentation.	0	1	2	3	4	5	6
TIER THREE CREATIVITY								
» Innovation is evident in relation to the content.	0	1	2	3	4	5	6
» Innovation is evident in relation to the presentation.	0	1	2	3	4	5	6

Figure 10.6. Poster DAP Tool: Creativity component.

pamphlet—yet they do so on different levels. For example, a title can be clear (which may be challenging for some students), it may enhance the pamphlet, or it could reflect purpose. The task becomes more complex and sophisticated as the tiers increase. As part of differentiation, you intentionally decide which DAP Tool tier to use with each student. It's just one more way of addressing students' needs. Remember, you don't have to create the tiers, as that has been done for you.

The third component, creativity, also may be assessed on varying tiers of sophistication as *looking at content and presentation in new ways* morphs into *originality being expressed,* then *innovation being evident in content and presentation.* Looking at a product in a new way is much less demanding than being innovative when creating it (see Figure 10.6).

Reflection, that critical component wherein students analyze their own learning, also becomes more complex as the levels increase (see Figure 10.7). Note that all students are asked to reflect upon their learning of the content itself, the creation of the product, and their role as a learner—just on varying levels of complexity. (Appendix H contains three forms that students can use to develop this reflection component fully and thoughtfully.)

Those four components combine to create a one-page tool that has three variations or tiers of complexity. Figure 10.1 near the beginning of the chapter shows the DAP Tool for a poster, which is designed for students who work at beginning or lower levels. The Tier 2 DAP Tool for a poster features language and expectations that are a little more sophisticated (see Figure 10.8). Finally, the third tier has even greater expectations (see Figure 10.9).

As you are exploring ways to address your students' strengths, interests, and levels of readiness, don't neglect the fact that they can be held accountable based on those strengths, interests, and levels of readiness. The DAP Tool, with its three tiers for each product, gives you greater control over the level of expectation.

POSTER—DAP TOOL Reflection

TIER ONE REFLECTION								
CONTENT	» What connections can you make between what you have learned by completing this project and previous learning?	0	1	2	3	4	5	6
PRODUCT	» In what ways could you improve your product when completing this product with a different assignment?	0	1	2	3	4	5	6
LEARNING	» How did the amount of effort affect your learning about the content and creating the product?	0	1	2	3	4	5	6
TIER TWO REFLECTION								
CONTENT	» Reflections include connections to previous learning and questions raised for future learning.	0	1	2	3	4	5	6
PRODUCT	» Reflections include improvements made over other times the product was created as well as suggestions for improvements when creating the same product in a future learning experience.	0	1	2	3	4	5	6
LEARNING	» Reflections include analysis of self as a learner, including effort, work habits, and thought processes.	0	1	2	3	4	5	6
TIER THREE REFLECTION								
CONTENT	» Reflections analyze and evaluate connections to previous learning and project insightful future connections.	0	1	2	3	4	5	6
PRODUCT	» Reflections analyze and evaluate the product components in light of past and future creations of the same product.	0	1	2	3	4	5	6
LEARNING	» Reflections include analysis of self as a learner and project how changes to the process would increase capacity as a learner.	0	1	2	3	4	5	6

Figure 10.7. Poster DAP Tool: Reflection component.

Additional examples of DAP Tools for cartoons, models, pamphlets, PowerPoint presentations, speeches, and technical reports have been included in Appendix H. Note how the sophistication levels increase as one moves from a Tier 1 DAP Tool to a Tier 3. Students creating a product with Tier 1 expectations should be working on a very different level from students creating a product with Tier 2 or 3 expectations. That's all a part of differentiation.

If differentiation of assessment seems overwhelming, remember that DAP Tools can simply be used as rubrics. A teacher can easily differentiate products by allowing students the choice of product then providing high-quality rubrics to assess those products. When the students receive the rubric at the beginning

POSTER Tier 2—DAP TOOL

CONTENT								
	» Content is accurate and complete.	0	1	2	3	4	5	6
	» Content has depth and complexity of thought.	0	1	2	3	4	5	6
	» Content is organized.	0	1	2	3	4	5	6
PRESENTATION								
TEXT	» Title enhances the poster's purpose and is well placed. Text highlights most important concepts.	0	1	2	3	4	5	6
GRAPHICS	» Graphics (e.g., illustrations, photos) add information and are relevant for the topic.	0	1	2	3	4	5	6
LAYOUT	» Layout design clearly emphasizes graphics in an organized and attractive manner. Text is placed to clearly describe/explain all graphic images. Spacing is carefully planned with consideration of space not used.	0	1	2	3	4	5	6
CORRECTNESS	» The poster is free from usage, punctuation, capitalization, and spelling errors. Sources, when used, are thoroughly cited.	0	1	2	3	4	5	6
CREATIVITY								
	» Originality is expressed in relation to the content.	0	1	2	3	4	5	6
	» Originality is expressed in relation to the presentation.	0	1	2	3	4	5	6
REFLECTION								
CONTENT	» Reflections include connections to previous learning and questions raised for future learning.	0	1	2	3	4	5	6
PRODUCT	» Reflections include improvements made over other times the product was created as well as suggestions for improvements when creating the same product in a future learning experience.	0	1	2	3	4	5	6
LEARNING	» Reflections include analysis of self as learner, including effort, work habits, and thought processes.	0	1	2	3	4	5	6

Comments:

____

____

____

Meaning of Performance Scale:
6—PROFESSIONAL LEVEL: level expected from a professional in the content area
5—ADVANCED LEVEL: level exceeds expectations of the standard
4—PROFICIENT LEVEL: level expected for meeting the standard
3—PROGRESSING LEVEL: level demonstrates movement toward the standard
2—NOVICE LEVEL: level demonstrates initial awareness and knowledge of standard
1—NONPERFORMING LEVEL: level indicates no effort made to meet standard
0—NONPARTICIPATING LEVEL: level indicates nothing turned in

Figure 10.8. Poster Tier 2 DAP Tool.

POSTER Tier 3—DAP TOOL

CONTENT								
	» Content is accurate and thorough in detail.	0	1	2	3	4	5	6
	» Product shows complex understanding and manipulation of content.	0	1	2	3	4	5	6
	» Product shows deep probing of content.	0	1	2	3	4	5	6
	» Organization is best suited to the product.	0	1	2	3	4	5	6
PRESENTATION								
TEXT	» Title, clearly reflecting purpose, is strategically placed. Text highlights most important concepts in clear, concise manner.	0	1	2	3	4	5	6
GRAPHICS	» Graphics (illustrations, photos) enhance meaning and are best suited for the purpose.	0	1	2	3	4	5	6
LAYOUT	» Successful composition of graphic images and design concepts communicates the purpose. Text is strategically placed to enhance the message of the poster. Negative space is used to highlight key points.	0	1	2	3	4	5	6
CORRECTNESS	» The poster is error free, with correct usage, punctuation, capitalization, and spelling used. All sources are cited correctly with the citation placed appropriately.	0	1	2	3	4	5	6
CREATIVITY								
	» Innovation is evident in relation to the content.	0	1	2	3	4	5	6
	» Innovation is evident in relation to the presentation.	0	1	2	3	4	5	6
REFLECTION								
CONTENT	» Reflections analyze and evaluate connections to previous learning and project insightful future connections.	0	1	2	3	4	5	6
PRODUCT	» Reflections analyze and evaluate the product components in light of past and future creations of the same product.	0	1	2	3	4	5	6
LEARNING	» Reflections include analysis of self as a learner and project how changes to the process would increase capacity as a learner.	0	1	2	3	4	5	6

Comments:

____

____

____

Meaning of Performance Scale:
6—PROFESSIONAL LEVEL: level expected from a professional in the content area
5—ADVANCED LEVEL: level exceeds expectations of the standard
4—PROFICIENT LEVEL: level expected for meeting the standard
3—PROGRESSING LEVEL: level demonstrates movement toward the standard
2—NOVICE LEVEL: level demonstrates initial awareness and knowledge of standard
1—NONPERFORMING LEVEL: level indicates no effort made to meet standard
0—NONPARTICIPATING LEVEL: level indicates nothing turned in

Figure 10.9. Poster Tier 3 DAP Tool.

of the assignment, they can use the rubrics to guide the development of their products. DAP Tools simplify the process.

GRADING WITH DAP TOOLS

This tool can be used in myriad ways depending on need and intent—that is why it is called a tool. Some may use the DAP Tool as an assessment *for* learning while others may use it as an assessment *of* learning (Chappuis, Stiggins, Arter, & Chappuis, 2005). When used as an assessment for learning, the DAP Tool can be used holistically, providing in-depth feedback to students regarding all four components. When used formatively in this manner, then no specific grade would necessarily be transferred to the grade book. When used as an assessment of learning in a more summative manner, a grade is typically recorded. It would be a mistake, however, to simply tally the numbers on the DAP Tool, find a percentage, and record a grade—especially if you are counting a 6 as the highest score (which, remember, you may never circle or highlight on a single DAP tool descriptor in your lifetime.) The grade should ideally reflect the learning of the student. Arter and Chappuis (2006) believe that logic should prevail over percentages: "Percentages don't accurately represent level of learning as measured by a rubric" (p. 116). Go to Arter and Chappuis (2006) for a detailed explanation of changing rubrics into grades, and see Roberts and Inman (2015) for a discussion of multiple ways to transfer a DAP Tool to the grading book.

CONCLUDING THOUGHTS

In order for your students to experience continuous progress in their learning, think about assessment in these terms:

- assessment needs to be authentic and linked to the real world,
- instruction should be a response to assessment,
- assessment should be ongoing throughout a unit—it's not just an ending to the unit,
- one way to differentiate instruction is to vary the levels of expectations when assessing student work (using the DAP Tool ensures ease and clarity), and
- don't limit students' learning by setting the learning ceiling at proficiency or grade-level learning.

Why is it important to preassess and have ongoing assessment? Why is it better for students when they have authentic learning tasks? The answer is simple: Students are preparing to be successful as they continue learning at the next level, whether that be the next grade, the next school, or postsecondary opportunities. Better still, the young people are experiencing learning at levels that will encourage them to be lifelong learners.

IMPORTANT TAKE-AWAYS

- Effective assessment is ongoing assessment that modifies instruction and helps facilitate continuous progress for the student.
- The development and assessment of products must be intentional. The products must be realistic representations of the learning that has occurred (i.e., the content), and the product itself should ideally mirror that same product in the adult, professional world.
- Rubrics or scoring guides must hold students to real-world standards so that products are authentic.
- DAP Tools, a protocol for student development of products and teacher or self-assessment of the product, guides students in product development, facilitates differentiation, simplifies assessment, and removes learning ceilings.
- DAP Tools can be used at all grade levels and in all content areas.
- DAP Tools focus on the same four components for all products—Content, Presentation, Creativity, and Reflection.
- The seven-level performance scale ranges from nonparticipating to professional.
- The DAP Tool has three tiers, providing a ready way to differentiate the assessment of products.
- The DAP Tool provides a consistent means of feedback to students in order to improve their performance on the next product.
- Performance scales should not put a lid on learning or potential achievement.
- The tiering of assessment is a viable differentiation option.

CHAPTER 11

Building Support for Differentiation

Hard But Not Impossible to Do Alone

> The mantra needs to be "working harder makes us smarter." The key is to acknowledge ability while recognizing that effort went into its development. —Del Siegle

Have you ever attended a party and known no one there? You try to strike up a conversation, first with one person and then another, but you can't quite find a topic of mutual interest. One person is talking about the latest local scandal while another elaborates on the art of growing hothouse orchids—topics about which you know nothing and are of no interest to you. You bring up national politics, and they look at you as if you have bean dip on your cheek. It seems ironic to feel isolated in the midst of a crowd, but when we're fascinated by something no one else is, it's lonely. Before long you are wishing that you could leave and move to an activity of your choosing—even if it's just the bean dip.

Teaching can be an isolating profession due to the nature of the beast. But, when you're alone in your philosophy (e.g., your commitment to differentiation), you may be even more removed from your colleagues. You may feel isolated as you look for a colleague who also is interested in trying new strategies in order to ensure that students make continuous progress. Perhaps you have been differentiating learning experiences for some time and would like to find a fellow teacher who could help you move to the next level. Perhaps you could support him as he also modifies his planning to expect to differentiate rather than respond to differences—a distinct difference as discussed in the National Middle School Association's monthly e-newsletter: "One of the positive characteristics of the movement toward more fully differentiated instruction is the focus it places on being proactive in response to student differences rather than (or in addition to) being reactive to those differences" (Strickland, 2005, p. 1). Perhaps this pairing with your colleague could lead to small groups of teachers learning to differentiate and sharing their work, and then, before you know it, . . . well, we can dream!

Of course, the dream or ideal situation is to have the entire faculty at a school interested in differentiation and to have a principal who understands that differentiation is essential if learners in the school are to make continuous progress. When this happens, differentiation is built into the accountability system in the school, and all teachers are held responsible for differentiating the curriculum.

How do we get our school engaged and interested? Three suggestions come to mind to encourage a faculty to embark on a journey of differentiation. The first is to use a faculty meeting to engage in the How Do You Learn It? Activity (as described in Chapter 3). The discussion following that activity can help all educators see how the "one-size-fits-all-students" way of implementing units won't begin to support all students making continuous progress. The debriefing is more important than the activity itself. The second activity is to have your colleagues examine the school's mission, vision, and/or philosophy statements. What words are embedded in those important documents that require teachers to differentiate in order to ensure that all children and young people are making continuous progress? You (and your colleagues) may be surprised to see differentiation concepts throughout these statements. Then, talk about what would have to be in place for continuous progress to become the mantra of the school. It should be an exciting discussion. A last suggestion would be a book study on this book. Appendix I is a study guide developed by the Spring Branch ISD of the Houston Area Cooperative on the Gifted and Talented (2001) for a book study they conducted.

But, what if the school isn't ready to embark on that journey? What happens if the faculty as a whole is not interested in differentiation and the principal isn't quite there either? Don't despair. We've already mentioned all those reasons that people don't or won't differentiate (ranging from lack of time to lack of training). Just because you're alone doesn't mean that you're not right. You know that it is essential for students to learn what they don't already know at levels that are appropriately challenging.

So, what do you do? Before you put in for that transfer, try to find just one colleague who sees the merit in differentiation—someone with whom you can talk, brainstorm, and develop ideas. That person doesn't have to be at your same school, but it helps. You can plan together. You can encourage each other. You can provide feedback on plans and implementation. Coaches are great at providing feedback so that young people develop their talents or, in the words of this book, make continuous progress. You can coach each other as you develop and hone differentiation skills.

Also, don't just try one strategy one time. All skills develop with practice and become more comfortable as you practice them. The more times you implement a strategy, the more comfortable it feels. You know what works—and you know what doesn't. Ask for honest feedback from your students. The reflection part of the DAP Tool can be one avenue for gathering information.

It isn't possible to go from little or no differentiation to differentiating all the time. You won't be able to differentiate every lesson every day (and still expect to maintain your sanity!). That is a giant step that none of us can take. Start with differentiating one lesson or one unit, and then plan for the next one. Being intentional continues to be important: Why are you teaching this particular concept to this particular student in this particular way?

Once you begin (i.e., consistently asking yourself the planning, preassessing, and differentiation questions before each unit; experimenting with strategies until you're comfortable with them; and faithfully being intentional in your teaching), you can provide information in various ways to pique the interest of your fellow teachers. Share experiences that work well. Sharing can be anything from an informal conversation in the hall to a presentation at a board meeting. Make sure that people have access to the information supporting differentiation. For example, if you are a middle school teacher or principal, is the joint position statement between NMSA and NAGC (2004) available and known to teachers and counselors at your school? Provide short articles on differentiation for teachers' mailboxes. Sometimes a short e-mail sent to all faculty members can accomplish wonders. Suggest professional development that focuses on higher levels of thinking or on product development. Both of those topics lay the foundation for differentiation without necessarily focusing on the subject. Perhaps one of the greatest testimonials will be the contented look on your face, your eagerness to come to work every day, and the minimal number of office referrals from your classroom.

No doubt, the ideal situation would be to have every teacher at your school differentiating instruction to address the abilities, interests, and needs of all students. However, if all teachers don't seem to be interested, your classroom will be wonderful for your students if you put differentiation strategies into play as often as possible. Making continuous progress is vitally important. How else will students learn to become the best learners they can be?

Remember Alice as she wandered through Wonderland. The Cheshire Cat told her that any road would get her to her destination if she hadn't decided where she was going. If you read this book from start to finish, you know your destination—having your students learn what they don't already know. You also know that reaching that destination involves addressing these three important questions:

1. *Planning Question*—What do I want students to know, understand, and be able to do?
2. *Preassessing Question*—Who already knows, understands, and/or can use the content or demonstrate the skill? Who needs additional support in order to know, understand, and/or demonstrate the skills?
3. *Differentiation Question*—What can I do for him, her, or them so they can make continuous progress and extend their learning?

These three directional questions will guide you to the road of continuous progress for your students.

Have you ever given a party where different groups of people were invited and not everyone knew each other? If so, I bet when the Pistons fan entered the room, you steered him toward another basketball fan and introduced them to each other. Checking the glazed expression of your guest who has been cornered by your orchid-growing enthusiast cousin, you deftly intervened to ask the guest to help you in the kitchen for a moment (you knew that he loved cooking!). You probably noticed the government professor hanging out by the bean dip alone and quickly brought her over to meet the state representative. (Speaking of bean dip, you considered the fact that some of your guests may be allergic to beans or just don't appreciate them, so you also provided a tasty alternative.) If you want all your guests to come away satisfied, you must address their individual needs, interests, and abilities. After all, they're the reason you're throwing a party!

References

Achieve, Inc. (2013). *Next Generation Science Standards.* Washington, DC: Author.

Adams, C. M., & Pierce, R. L. (2006). *Differentiating instruction: A practical guide to tiered lessons in the elementary school.* Waco, TX: Prufrock Press.

Anderson, L. W., Krathwohl, D. R. (Eds.). (2001). *A taxonomy for learning, teaching, and assessing: A revision of Bloom's taxonomy of educational objectives* (Abridged ed.). New York: Longman.

Armstrong, T. (2000). *Multiple intelligences in the classroom* (2nd ed.). Alexandria, VA: Association for Supervision and Curriculum Development.

Arter, J. A., & Chappuis, J. (2006). *Creating and recognizing quality rubrics.* Boston, MA: Pearson Education.

Barell, J. (2008). Did you ask a good question today? In B. Z. Presseisen (Ed.), *Teaching for intelligence* (2nd ed.) (101–110). Thousand Oaks, CA: Corwin.

Beasley, J. (2009, July). *Establishing classroom routines that support the differentiated classroom.* Presentation at the Association for Supervision and Curriculum Development Conference, Houston, TX.

Bloom, B. S. (Ed.). (1956). *Taxonomy of educational objectives: The classification of educational goals. Handbook I: Cognitive domain.* New York: Longman.

Buzan, T. (1983). *Use both sides of your brain* (Rev. ed.). New York: Dutton.

Callahan, C. M. (2006). Assessment in the classroom: The key to good instruction. In F. A. Karnes & K. R. Stephens (Eds.), *The practical strategies series in gifted education.* Waco, TX: Prufrock Press.

Carroll, L. (2000). *Alice's adventures in wonderland.* New York: Signet Classic/New American Library. (Original work published 1865)

Cash, R. M. (2011). *Advancing differentiation: Thinking and learning for the 21st century.* Minneapolis, MN: Free Spirit.

Chappius, S., Stiggins, R. J., Arter, J., & Chappius, J. (2005). *Assessment for learning: An action guide for school leaders.* Portland, OR: Educational Testing Service.

Clark, B. (2013). *Growing up gifted: Developing the potential of children at home and at school* (8th ed.). Boston, MA: Pearson.

Coil, C. (2004). *Standards-based activities and assessments for the differentiated classroom.* Marion, IL: Pieces of Learning.

Coil, C., & Merritt, D. (2001). *Solving the assessment puzzle piece by piece.* Marion, IL: Pieces of Learning.

Colangelo, N., Assouline, S. G., & Gross, M. U. M. (2004). *A nation deceived: How schools hold back America's brightest students.* Iowa City: University of Iowa, The Connie Belin & Jacqueline N. Blank International Center for Gifted Education and Development.

Coleman, M. R. (2005). Cooperative learning and gifted learners. In. F. A. Karnes & S. M. Bean (Eds.), *Methods and materials for teaching the gifted* (519–539). Waco, TX: Prufrock Press.

Committee on Prospering in the Global Economy of the 21st Century. (2005). *Rising above the gathering storm: Energizing and employing America for a brighter economic future.* Washington, D. C.: National Academies Press. Retrieved from http://www.nap.edu/catalog/11463.html

Consortium of National Arts Education Associations. (1994). *National standards for arts education: What every young American should know and be able to do in the arts.* Reston, VA: Music Educators National Conference.

Council for the Accreditation of Educator Preparation. (2013). *CAEP accreditation standards.* Washington, DC: Author.

Council of Chief State School Officers, & National Governors Association Center for Best Practices. (2010). *Common Core State Standards: Mathematics.* Washington, DC: Author.

Council of Chief State School Officers' Interstate Teacher Assessment and Support Consortium (2011). *Model core teaching standards: A resource for state dialogue.* Washington, DC: Author.

Curry, J., & Samara, J. (1991). *Product guide kit.* Austin, TX: Curriculum Project.

Curry School of Education, University of Virginia. (2011). *Anchor activities.* Retrieved from http://curry.virginia.edu/uploads/resourceLibrary/nagc_anchor_activities.pdf

Dweck, C. S. (2006). *Mindset: The new psychology of success.* New York, NY: Random House.

Engine-Uity. (2006). *Algebraic functions: Guided secondary source research for grades 9–12.* Phoenix, AZ: Author.

Engine-Uity. (2014). *Physical science: An Engine-Uity learning center about inanimate matter and energy for grades 4–6.* Phoenix, AZ: Author.

Fay, J., & Funk, D. (1995). *Teaching with love and logic: Taking control of the classroom.* Golden, CO: Love and Logic Press.

Fleming, N. (2012).*VARK.* Retrieved from http://www.vark-learn.com/english/page.asp? p=questionnaire

Gardner, H. (1983). *Frames of mind: The theory of multiple intelligences.* New York, NY: Basic.

Gentry, M. (1996, Spring). *Total cluster grouping: An investigation of achievement and identification of elementary school students.* NRC/GT Newsletter, 1–2, 4.

Gentry, M., Steenbergen-Hu, S., & Choi, B. (2011). Student-identified exemplary teachers: Insights from talented teachers. *Gifted Child Quarterly, 55*(2), 111–125.

Hanna, G. S., & Dettmer, P. A. (2004). *Assessment for effective teaching: Using context-adaptive planning.* Boston, MA: Pearson.

Hattie, J. (2014). *Visible learning: A synthesis of over 800 meta-analysis relating to achievement.* Thousand Oaks, CA: Corwin.

Heacox, D. (2002). *Differentiating instruction in the regular classroom.* Minneapolis, MN: Free Spirit.

Heacox, D. (2009). *Making differentiation a habit: How to ensure success in academically diverse classrooms.* Minneapolis, MN: Free Spirit.

Hersey, P., & Blanchard, K. H. (1978). *The family game: A situational approach to effective parenting.* Reading, MA: Addison-Wesley.

Houston Area Cooperative on the Gifted and Talented. (2001). *Study Guide.* Houston, TX: Author.

Institute of Education Sciences. (2014). *Mathematics achievement of fourth- and eighth-graders in 2011.* Retrieved from https://nces.ed.gov/TIMSS/results11_math11.asp

InTime. (n.d.). *Cooperative learning overview: Definition.* Retrieved from http://www.intime.uni.edu/coop_learning

Johnson, D. W., & Johnson, R. T. (1999). *Learning together and alone: Cooperative, competitive, and individualistic learning.* Boston: Allyn & Bacon.

Kanevsky, L. S. (2003). Tiering with Venn diagrams. *Gifted Education Communicator, 34*(2), 42–44.

Karnes, F. A., & Stephens, K. R. (2000). *The ultimate guide for student product development and evaluation.* Waco, TX: Prufrock Press.

Karnes, F., & Stephens, K. (2009). *The ultimate guide for student product development and evaluation* (2nd ed.). Waco, TX: Prufrock Press.

Kentucky Department of Education. (2000). *School level performance descriptors and glossary for Kentucky's standards and indicators for school improvement.* Frankfort, KY: Author.

Kettle, K. E., Renzulli, J. S., & Rizza, M. G. (n.d.). *My way . . . an expression style inventory.* Retrieved from http://www.gifted.uconn.edu/sem/pdf/myway.pdf

Kingore, B. (2006, Winter). Tiered instruction: Beginning the process. Retrieved from http://www.bertiekingore.com/tieredinstruction.htm

Kuhner, J. (2008). *In a nutshell: High achieving students in the era of NCLB.* Washington, DC: Thomas B. Fordham Institute. Retrieved from http://www.

nagc.org/uploadedFiles/ News_Room/NAGC_Advocacy_in_the_News/In%20a%20Nutshell%20%28fordham%29.pdf

Kulik, J. A. (1992). *An analysis of the research on ability grouping: Historical and contemporary perspectives* (RBDM 9204). Storrs: University of Connecticut, The National Research Center on the Gifted and Talented.

Loveless, T., Farkas, S., & Duffett, A. (2008). *High-achieving students in the era of NCLB.* Washington, DC: Thomas B. Fordham Institute.

McCoach, D. B., & Siegle, D. (2013). Underachievers. In J. A. Plucker & C. M. Callahan (Eds.), *Critical issues and practices in gifted education: What the research says* (2nd ed.) (pp. 691–706). Waco, TX: Prufrock Press.

McCrary, P. (2002, Fall). Kentucky teacher of the year speaks out about meeting the needs of high ability students. *KAGE Update: The Newsletter of the Kentucky Association for Gifted Education, 1,* 3.

National Academy of Sciences, Institute of Medicine, & National Academy of Engineering. (2010). *Rising above the gathering storm, revisited: Rapidly approaching category 5.* Washington, DC: National Academies Press. Retrieved from http://www.nap.edu/catalog.php?record_id=12999

National Association for Gifted Children. (1996). *Position paper on cooperative learning for gifted students.* Washington, DC: Authors.

National Education Commission on Time and Learning. (1994). *Prisoners of time.* Retrieved from http://www.ed.gov/pubs/PrisonersOfTime/Prisoners.html

National Middle School Association, & National Association for Gifted Children. (2004). *Meeting the needs of high-ability and high-potential learners in the middle grades: A joint position statement of the National Middle School Association and the National Association for Gifted Children.* Retrieved from http://nmsa.org/AboutNMSA/PositionStatements/GiftedChildren/tabid/119/Default.aspx

No Child Left Behind Act, 20 U. S. C. 6301. (2001).

Organisation for Economic Co-operation and Development (OECD). (2013). *Program for international student assessment (PISA) mathematics literacy: Average scores.* Retrieved from http://nces.ed.gov/surveys/pisa/pisa2012/pisa2012highlights_3a.asp

Reis, S. M., Westberg, K. L., Kulikowich, J., Caillard, F., Hébert, T., Plucker, J., et al. (1993). *Why not let high ability students start school in January? The curriculum compacting study* (Research Monograph No. 93106). Storrs: University of Connecticut, The National Research Center on the Gifted and Talented.

Ricci, M. C. (2013). *Mindsets in the classroom: Building a culture of success and student achievement in schools.* Waco, TX: Prufrock Press.

Roberts, J. L. (2010). Preassessment: The linchpin for defensible differentiation. *The Challenge, 24,* 10.

Roberts, J. L., & Boggess, J. R. (2011). *Teacher's survival guide: Gifted education.* Waco, TX: Prufrock Press.

Roberts, J. L., & Boggess, J. R. (2012). *Differentiating instruction with centers in the gifted classroom.* Waco, TX: Prufrock Press.

Roberts, J. L., & Inman, T. F. (2009). *Assessing differentiated student products: A protocol for development and evaluation.* Waco, TX: Prufrock Press.

Roberts, J. L., & Inman, T. F. (2013). *Teacher's survival guide: Differentiating instruction in the elementary classroom.* Waco, TX: Prufrock Press.

Roberts, J. L., & Inman, T. F. (2015). *Assessing differentiated student products: A protocol for development and evaluation* (2nd ed.). Waco, TX: Prufrock Press.

Roberts, J. L., & Roberts, R. A. (2009). Writing units that remove the learning ceiling. In F. A. Karnes & S. M. Bean (Eds.), *Methods and materials for teaching the gifted* (3rd ed., pp. 189–221). Waco, TX: Prufrock Press.

Robinson, A. (1990). Cooperation or exploitation? The argument against cooperative learning for talented students. *Journal for the Education of the Gifted,* 14, 9–27, 31–36.

Robinson, A., Shore, B. M., & Enersen, D. L. (2007). *Best practices in gifted education: An evidence-based guide.* Waco, TX: Prufrock Press.

Rogers, K. (2006). *A menu of options for grouping gifted students.* Waco, TX: Prufrock Press.

Samara, J., & Curry, J. (Eds.). (1994). *Developing units for primary students.* Bowling Green, KY: KAGE Publications.

Sanders, W. L. (1998, December). Value-added assessment: A method for measuring the effects of the system, school and teacher on the rate of student academic progress. *The School Administrator,* 24–27.

Schemo, D. J. (2004, March 2). Schools, facing tight budgets, leave gifted programs behind. *New York Times,* pp. A1, A16.

Schlechty, P. C. (2002). *Working on the work: An action plan for teachers, principals, and superintendents.* San Francisco, CA: Jossey-Bass.

Schunk, D. H. (1987). Peer models and children's behavioral change. *Review of Educational Research, 57,* 149–174.

Silver, H. F., Strong. R. W., & Perini, M. J. (2001). *Tools for promoting active, in-depth learning* (2nd ed.). Ho-Ho-Kus, NJ: Thoughtful Education Press.

Smutny, J. F., Walker, S. Y., & Meckstroth, E. A. (1997). *Teaching young gifted children in the regular classroom: Identifying, nurturing, and challenging ages 4–9.* Minneapolis, MN: Free Spirit.

Stanley, J. C. (2000). Helping students learn only what they don't already know. *Psychology, Public Policy, and Law, 6,* 216–222.

Stiggins, R. J. (1987). The design and development of performance assessments. *Educational Measurement: Issues and Practice, 6,* 33–42.

Stiggins, R. J. (2002, June 6). Assessment crisis: The absence of assessment for learning. *Phi Delta Kappan*. Retrieved from http://electronicportfolios.org/afl/Stiggins-AssessmentCrisis.pdf

Strickland, C. A. (2005, April). *Differentiation or differentiation? National Middle School Association Middle E-Connections*. Retrieved from http://www.nmsa.org

Teele, S. (1997). *The Teele inventory for multiple intelligences*. Retrieved from http://www.sueteele.com

tier [Def.1]. (n.d.). In Merriam-Webster's online dictionary. Retrieved from http://www.merriam-webster.com/dictionary/tier

Tomlinson, C. A. (1999). *The differentiated classroom: Responding to the needs of all learners*. Alexandria, VA: Association for Supervision and Curriculum Development.

Tomlinson, C. A. (2002, November 6). Proficiency is not enough. *Education Week, 22*, 36, 38.

Tomlinson, C. A. (2003). *Fulfilling the promise of the differentiated classroom: Strategies and tools for responsive teaching*. Alexandria, VA: Association for Supervision and Curriculum Development.

Tomlinson, C. A., & Imbeau, M. (2010). *Leading and managing a differentiated classroom*. Alexandria, VA: Association for Supervision and Curriculum Development.

Tomlinson, C. A., & McTighe, J. (2006). *Integrating differentiated instruction and understanding by design*. Alexandria, VA: Association for Supervision and Curriculum Development.

Torrance, E. P. (1963). *Education and the creative potential*. Minneapolis: University of Minnesota Press.

Venn, J. (1881). *Symbolic logic* (2nd ed.). New York, NY: Chelsea.

Vygotsky, L. S. (1978). *Mind in society: The development of higher psychological processes*. Boston, MA: Harvard University Press.

Westberg, K. L., Archambault, F. A., Jr., Dobyns, S. M., & Salvin, T. J. (1993). The classroom practices observation study. *Journal for the Education of the Gifted, 16*, 120–146.

Westberg, K. L., & Daoust, M. E. (2003, Fall). The results of the replication of the classroom practices survey replication in two states. *The National Research Center on the Gifted and Talented Newsletter*, 3–8.

Westphal, L. E. (2007). *Differentiating instruction with menus: Social studies, grades 3–5*. Waco, TX: Prufrock Press.

Westphal, L. E. (2009). *Differentiating instruction with menus: Language arts, grades 6–8*. Waco, TX: Prufrock Press.

Westphal, L. E. (2011). *Differentiating instruction with menus: Math, grades K–2*. Waco, TX: Prufrock Press.

Wiggins, G. P. (1993). *Assessing student performance.* San Francisco: Jossey-Bass.

Winebrenner, S. (1992). *Teaching gifted kids in the regular classroom.* Minneapolis, MN: Free Spirit.

Winebrenner, S. (2001). *Teaching gifted kids in the regular classroom.* Minneapolis, MN: Free Spirit.

Winebrenner, S., & Devlin, B. (1996, August). *Cluster grouping of gifted students: How to provide full-time services on a part-time budget.* Reston, VA: Clearinghouse on Disabilities and Gifted Education. (ERIC Digest No. EDO-EC-95-1)

APPENDIX A

What a Child Doesn't Learn . . .

By Tracy Inman

Sometimes simple questions provoke profound answers. These questions solicit your immediate responses, and those responses multiply when several people are involved in the discussion, expanding on each other's thoughts. Some of these questions will also stick with you, and you will find yourself coming up with additional answers hours, even days, after the discussion. This one will:

> If during the first 5 or 6 years of school, a child earns good grades and high praise without having to make much effort, what are all the things he doesn't learn that most children learn by third grade?

This question has been discussed with groups of parents, in gatherings of educators, with students in summer programming, in meetings of superintendents and administrators, and in statewide symposia with key decision makers. The immediate answers are almost always the same. Those responses develop throughout the discussion, and participants leave a bit overwhelmed by the ramifications of the answers. It turns out that what a student doesn't learn can adversely affect him his entire life!

Take a moment to answer this question yourself, or have your child's educators and administrators answer it. What isn't learned? As you skim over your answers, you may be surprised at the sheer volume. But look closer and you may be astounded by the depth and weight of those answers—and the impact they make on a child's life.

WHAT ISN'T LEARNED?

WORK ETHIC

Books such as *That Used to Be Us: How America Fell Behind in the World It Invented and How We Can Come Back* (Friedman & Mandelbaum, 2012) remind us how readily Asian countries are bypassing us technologically, educationally, and economically. One main reason for this, according to Friedman and Mandelbaum, is their work ethic. They know that education and sacrifice are the paths for reaching a middle-class lifestyle. They look at education as a privilege—and it is.

Everyone in America has the right to an education. Sometimes it seems, though, that our young people would argue that everyone has the right to a PlayStation®4 with unlimited playing time, a cell phone by fifth grade, and a car by 16. They may also argue they are entitled to an allowance and that days off from school are for relaxation and play and not chores. Experts argue that this will be the first generation whose standard of living will not surpass (or even match) their parents' socio-economic level. This is an entitled generation—or so they think.

How a person thinks about his talent and ability has an impact on his actions. Cognitive psychologist Carol Dweck (2007) argues that there are two types of mindset: fixed and growth. Unfortunately many mistakenly believe they are born with a fixed mindset, a certain level of talent and ability that cannot be altered. Rather, people should embrace the growth mindset, a belief that ability, talent, and intelligence are malleable—that they can change through hard work and effort. "Without effort, a student's achievement suffers, if not sooner than later. Thus, it is important for the student to value and believe in effort as a vehicle for academic success" (Dweck, 2012, p. 11). Our children must understand that without effort, success is fleeting.

Ben Franklin once said, "Genius without education is like silver in the mine." We could alter that a bit for the 21st-century American young person: "Genius without work ethic is like silver in the mine." No matter how bright, our children will not succeed personally or professionally without a strong work ethic. Working hard at intellectually stimulating tasks early in their lives helps to develop that ethic.

This first response is definitely lengthier than the others. That is because work ethic is the cornerstone to success.

RESPONSIBILITY

Responsibility is conscience driven. We make the choices we do because they are the right things to do. Dishes must be washed in order to be ready for the next meal. The research paper must be done well and on time if we want that top grade. Punctuality helps us keep our jobs, so even though we choose to stay up until 3:00 am to finish a novel, when the alarm sounds a very short 2 hours later, we're up. Each day's responsibilities must be met to be a productive family member, employee, and citizen.

Early in life, we should learn the orchestrating role responsibility plays in our lives. And we also should realistically learn the outcomes when responsibilities are not met. It's all about cause and effect. If children do not live up to their responsibilities and if natural consequences are not enforced, we are not equipping children with this vital virtue.

COPING WITH FAILURE

To be perfectly frank, failure for a gifted child is neither an F nor a D. Sometimes it is a B—and sometimes even a mid-A! For gifted children (and for most of us), failure is not meeting the self-imposed expectations. Realistically, though, our greatest lessons in life often stem from falling flat on our faces. Through failure, we learn how to pick ourselves up and continue. We learn perseverance and resilience. We learn that we're not always right and that we don't need to be, that we may discover more through our failures than we ever imagined we could through our accomplishments! Dweck (2007) remarked: "Success is about being your best self, not about being better than others; failure is an opportunity, not a condemnation; effort is the key to success" (p. 44).

When we face obstacles early on, we discover how to separate our identities from the task itself—that means the failure of meeting the goal or accomplishing the task does not equal failure of us as people. Young people, especially those who are gifted and talented, must learn to take academic risks. They must learn to celebrate the outcome and be able to learn from the failure!

SELF-WORTH STEMMING FROM THE ACCOMPLISHMENT OF A CHALLENGING TASK

We have all faced obstacles that seemed overwhelming, tasks that seemed too challenging. Giving up was never an option, so we worked and struggled and toiled until finally we overcame that obstacle or completed the task. The intrinsic rewards far outweighed the praise or even the pay earned at the end. We felt good about ourselves, our work ethic, our management skills, our persistence, and our ability. And even if the tangible outcome wasn't the promotion or "A" we wanted, that was secondary to the inner sense of accomplishment and pride we felt.

When students never work hard at challenging tasks, they can't experience those intrinsic rewards. Naturally, then, they focus on the extrinsic rewards. Unfortunately, being in an age of high stakes accountability only reinforces extrinsic motivation for students as they earn pizza parties for improved scores and best effort on statewide testing in the spring. Likewise, by giving them good grades for little effort that merits no intrinsic value, we're depriving them of this life-driving tool.

TIME-MANAGEMENT SKILLS

Adults constantly juggle roles: parent, spouse, child, person, employee/employer, volunteer, neighbor, friend, etc. With each role come demands on our time and energy. Often these demands conflict with each other, requiring us to budget our time carefully. Through experience, we have gained time-management skills by keeping track of the responsibilities of each role, estimating the time needed to meet that responsibility, and then following through. We adjust and readjust based on our experiences.

We know how difficult we make our lives when we procrastinate; likewise we know the sweetness of free time that comes from managing our time well. Young people who don't have to put effort into their work to earn high grades won't understand the time needed in order to develop a high-quality product necessary in more demanding classes, much less the time needed to do a job that would be acceptable in the work environment. Instead of gradually learning these lessons in schools, they may very well have crash (and burn) courses in the real world.

GOAL SETTING

We can't reach goals if we never set them, nor can we reach goals if they are unrealistic. We also can't reach goals if we don't have a strategy in place that incrementally encourages us to meet that end goal. Students must have practice in goal setting and goal achievement. Those skills will impact their personal lives, their professional lives, their social lives, and even their spiritual lives.

STUDY SKILLS

Time management, goal setting, self-discipline—all of these are embedded in study skills. When children don't need to study (because they already know the information or they have the ability to absorb it as they listen in class), they never learn vital study skills. So when they are presented with challenging material, whether that be in their first honors class or, even worse, in college, they simply don't know how to study! How do you attack a lengthy reading assignment? How do you take notes in an organized fashion? How do you prepare for an exam that covers the entire semester's material? Yes, study skills can be learned, but like most things in life, the earlier we acquire those skills, the better.

DECISION-MAKING AND PROBLEM-SOLVING SKILLS

Weighing pros and cons. Predicting outcomes of possible choices. Systematically breaking down issues according to importance. Ranking possibilities and importance of criteria. All of these skills come into play when making a decision. All of these skills come into play when problem solving. If children don't ever have experience with this early on in their learning, then when it is time to make decisions about learning and life, when it is time to solve professional and personal problems, they are ill-equipped to do so.

SACRIFICE

Yes, I would rather curl up with a wonderful read than dig into my taxes. But if my taxes aren't complete by April 15, I am in trouble. Period. I would rather catch the latest Academy Award-winning film than bulldoze the dirty clothes into the laundry room and lose myself for the rest of the day. But wrinkled, dirty clothes don't go very well with a professional image nor do they encourage lunch mates. As responsible adults, we well understand sacrifice. Sometimes we sacrifice our free time for our responsibilities. Sometimes we sacrifice what we want to do because others wish to do something else. We fully understand that we must "pay our dues" in life.

But if young people procrastinate on assignments because they really want to finish the Xbox One game or text their friends and their shoddy work earns A's, they're not learning about real life. Excellence requires sacrifice. The IRS won't care that the reason your taxes were late (and incorrect in a couple of places) was because you'd rather spend time reading a novel. Your potential employer doesn't even want to hear the excuse of choosing to watch a movie over preparing your clothing for the interview. Life's not always about fun or about what you want and when you want it. It's about sacrifice and work ethic. It's about working your hardest at challenging tasks.

These answers to the question *What does a child not learn?* is only partial, and yours may well include values that this one didn't. What's particularly frightening with this one is that these are some of the most important concepts for a successful life.

So what does a child not learn when he earns good grades and high praise without having to make much effort? Simply put, he doesn't learn the values and skills needed in order to be a productive, caring person who contributes positively to our world.

Note. This article is a revision of *What a Child Doesn't Learn* originally published in *The Challenge* (Winter, 2007), pp. 17–19.

REFERENCES

Dweck, C. S. (2007). *Mindset: The new psychology of success.* New York, NY: Ballantine Books.

Dweck, C. S. (2012). Mindsets and malleable minds: Implications for giftedness and talent. In R. F. Subotnik, A. Robinson, C. M. Callahan, & E. J. Gubbins (Eds.), *Malleable minds: Translating insights from psychology and neuroscience to gifted education* (pp. 7–18). Storrs: University of Connecticut, The National Research Center on the Gifted and Talented.

Friedman, T. L., & Mandelbaum, M. (2012). *That used to be us: How America fell behind in the world it invented and how we can come back.* New Work, NY: Picador.

APPENDIX B

My Way . . . An Expression Style Inventory

Products provide students and professionals with a way to express what they have learned to an audience. This survey will help determine the kinds of products **YOU** are **interested** in creating.

My Name is: ______________________________

Instructions:

Read each statement and circle the number that shows to what extent **YOU** are **interested** in creating that type of product. (Do not worry if you are unsure of how to make the product.)

		Not At All Interested	Of Little Interest	Moderately Interested	Interested	Very Interested
	Example: writing song lyrics	1	2	3	(4)	5
1.	writing stories	1	2	3	4	5
2.	discussing what I have learned	1	2	3	4	5
3.	painting a picture	1	2	3	4	5
4.	designing a computer software project	1	2	3	4	5
5.	filming & editing a video	1	2	3	4	5
6.	creating a company	1	2	3	4	5
7.	helping in the community	1	2	3	4	5
8.	acting in a play	1	2	3	4	5

My Way ...

An Expression Style Inventory

		Not At All Interested	Of Little Interest	Moderately Interested	Interested	Very Interested
9.	building an invention	1	2	3	4	5
10.	playing a musical instrument	1	2	3	4	5
11.	writing for a newspaper	1	2	3	4	5
12.	discussing ideas	1	2	3	4	5
13.	drawing pictures for a book	1	2	3	4	5
14.	designing an interactive computer project	1	2	3	4	5
15.	filming & editing a television show	1	2	3	4	5
16.	operating a business	1	2	3	4	5
17.	working to help others	1	2	3	4	5
18.	acting out an event	1	2	3	4	5
19.	building a project	1	2	3	4	5
20.	playing in a band	1	2	3	4	5
21.	writing for a magazine	1	2	3	4	5
22.	talking about my project	1	2	3	4	5
23.	making a clay sculpture of a character	1	2	3	4	5

		Not At All Interested	Of Little Interest	Moderately Interested	Interested	Very Interested
24.	designing information for the computer internet	1	2	3	4	5
25,	filming & editing a movie	1	2	3	4	5
26.	marketing a product	1	2	3	4	5
27.	helping others by supporting a social cause	1	2	3	4	5
28.	acting out a story	1	2	3	4	5
29.	repairing a machine	1	2	3	4	5
30.	composing music	1	2	3	4	5
31.	writing an essay	1	2	3	4	5
32.	discussing my research	1	2	3	4	5
33.	painting a mural	1	2	3	4	5
34.	designing a computer game	1	2	3	4	5
35.	recording & editing a radio show	1	2	3	4	5
36.	marketing an idea	1	2	3	4	5
37.	helping others by fundraising	1	2	3	4	5
38.	performing a skit	1	2	3	4	5
39.	constructing a working model	1	2	3	4	5
40.	performing music	1	2	3	4	5
41.	writing a report	1	2	3	4	5
42.	talking about my experiences	1	2	3	4	5

		Not At All Interested	Of Little Interest	Moderately Interested	Interested	Very Interested
43,	making a clay sculpture of a scene	1	2	3	4	5
44.	designing a multi-media computer show	1	2	3	4	5
45.	selecting slides & music for a slide show	1	2	3	4	5
46.	managing investments	1	2	3	4	5
47.	collecting clothing or food to help others	1	2	3	4	5
48.	role-playing a character	1	2	3	4	5
49.	assembling a kit	1	2	3	4	5
50.	playing in an orchestra	1	2	3	4	5

The End

My Way... A Profile

Instructions: **Write your score beside each number. Add each ROW to determine YOUR expression style profile.**

Products						Total
Written	1. ____	11. ____	21. ____	31. ____	41. ____	____
Oral	2. ____	12. ____	22. ____	32. ____	42. ____	____
Artistic	3. ____	13. ____	23. ____	33. ____	43. ____	____
Computer	4. ____	14. ____	24. ____	34. ____	44. ____	____
Audio/Visual	5. ____	15. ____	25. ____	35. ____	45. ____	____
Commercial	6. ____	16. ____	26. ____	36. ____	46. ____	____
Service	7. ____	17. ____	27. ____	37. ____	47. ____	____
Dramatization	8. ____	18. ____	28. ____	38. ____	48. ____	____
Manipulative	9. ____	19. ____	29. ____	39. ____	49. ____	____
Musical	10.____	20. ____	30. ____	40. ____	50. ____	____

APPENDIX C

Interest Inventory

Name: ________________________________

1. What do you do in the hours you are home from school?

2. What books do you enjoy most? Why?

3. What are your favorite TV shows? Why?

4. What are your favorite websites? Why?

5. Describe your favorite game and explain why it's your favorite.

6. In which recreational, social, or athletic activities are you involved? Which activities do you most enjoy?

7. What are your favorite subjects to study? Why?

8. What are your least favorite subjects to study? Why?

9. What would your ideal career be and why?

10. Do you have a collection? What do you collect? What got you interested in it?

11. What responsibilities do you have at home?

12. Do you have access to the Internet at home or at the public library? How many hours a day do you spend on the Internet?

13. Do you like to learn best in pairs, small groups, or alone?

14. Is there anything more you would like me to know about you?

APPENDIX D

Bloom Chart Template

BLOOM CHART TEMPLATE

	PROCESS	CONTENT	PRODUCT
CREATE			
EVALUATE			
ANALYZE			
APPLY			
UNDERSTAND			
REMEMBER			

APPENDIX E

Venn Diagrams

Venn (One Oval)

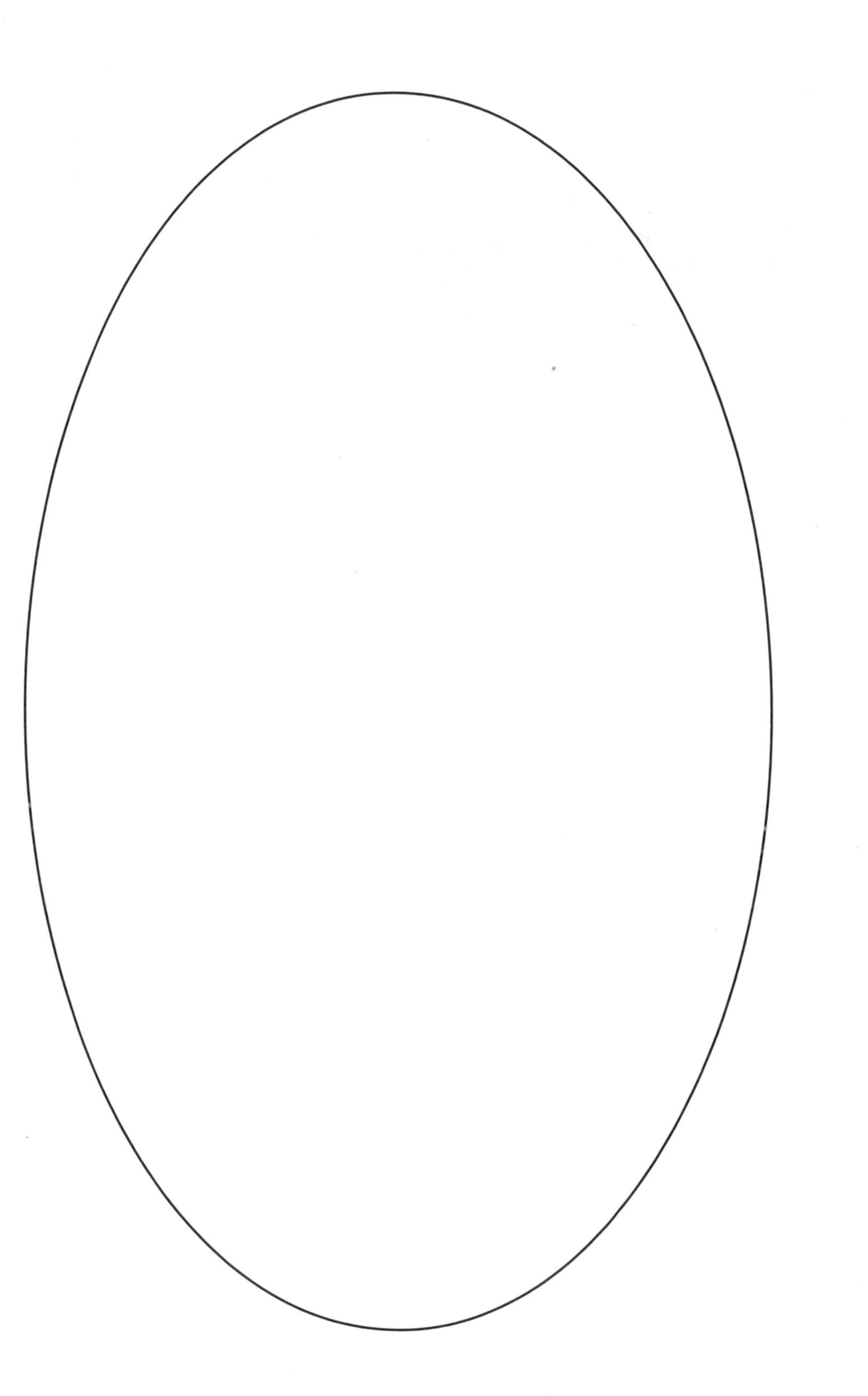

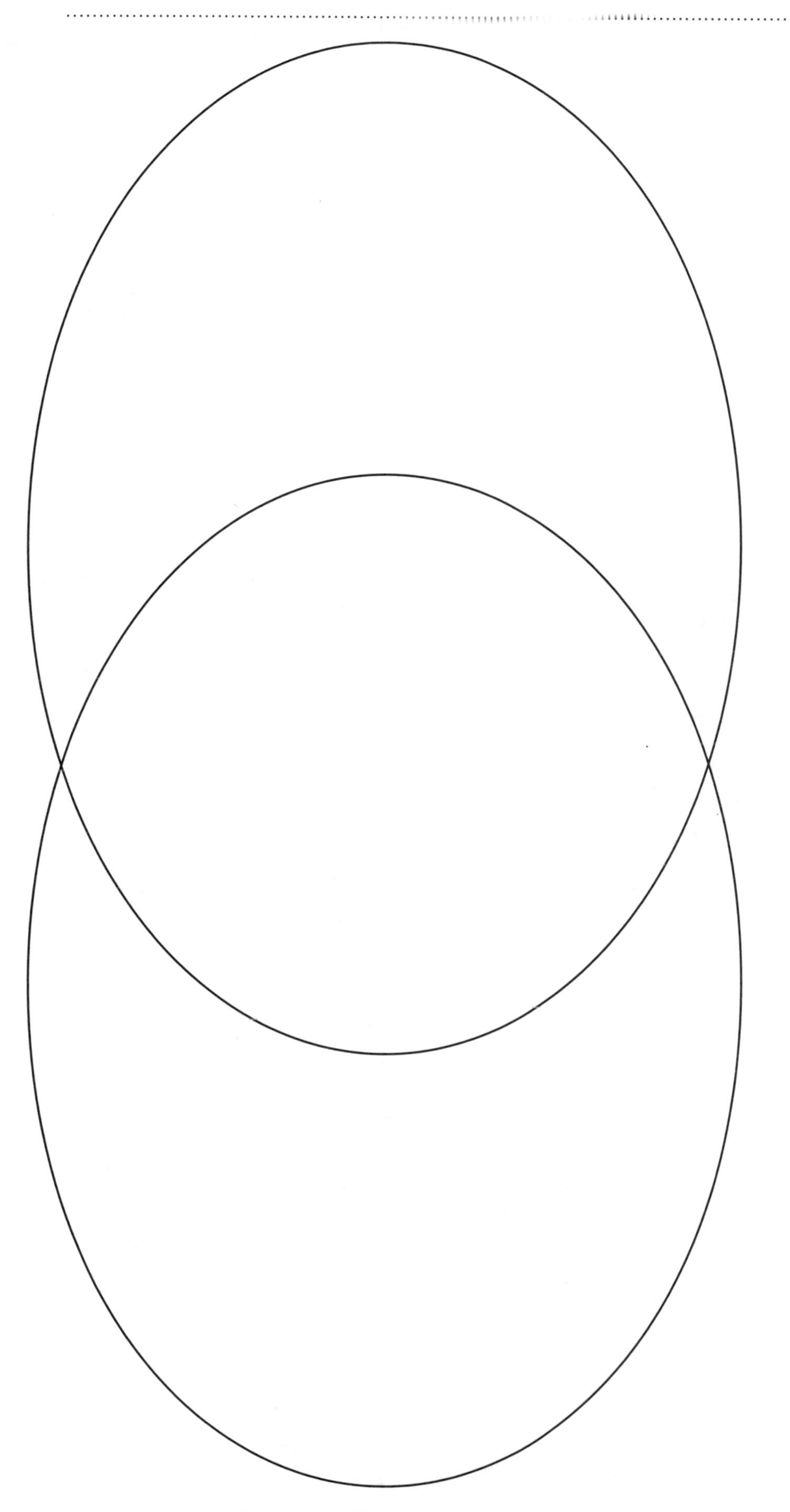

Venn (Two Ovals)

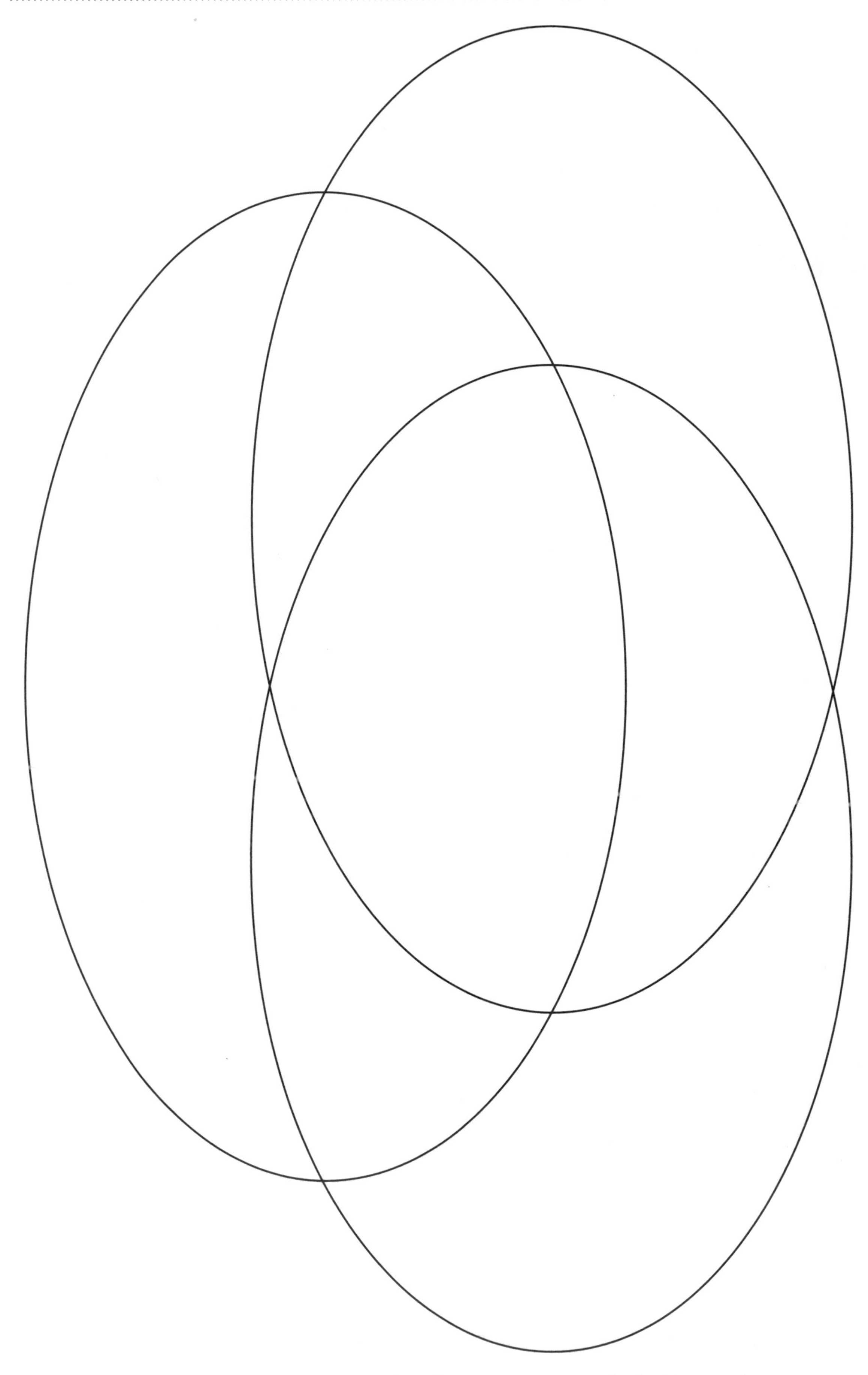

Venn (Three Ovals)

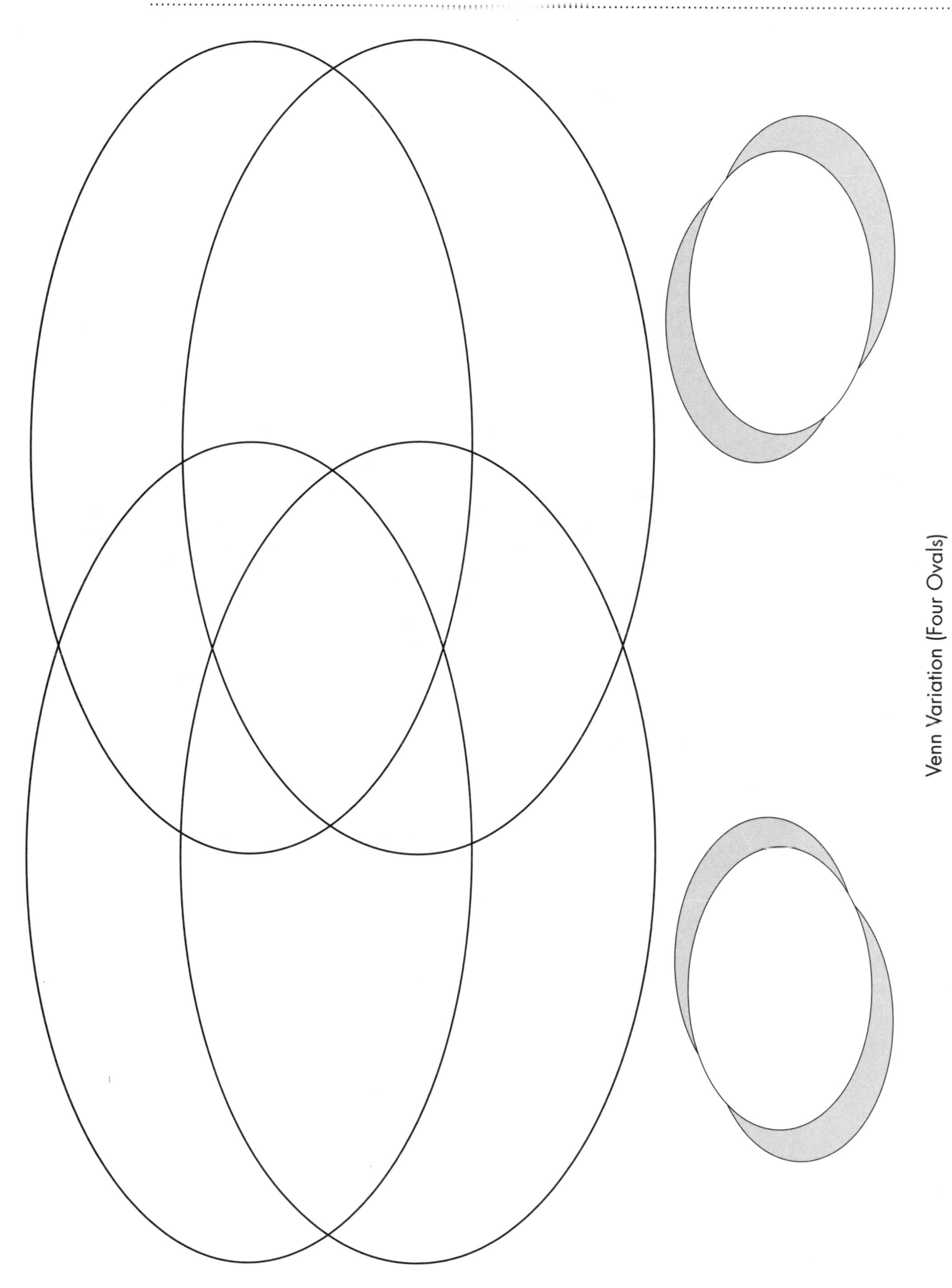

Venn Variation (Four Ovals)

Four-Item Flower Venn Template

16 Universal Set Numbered Template

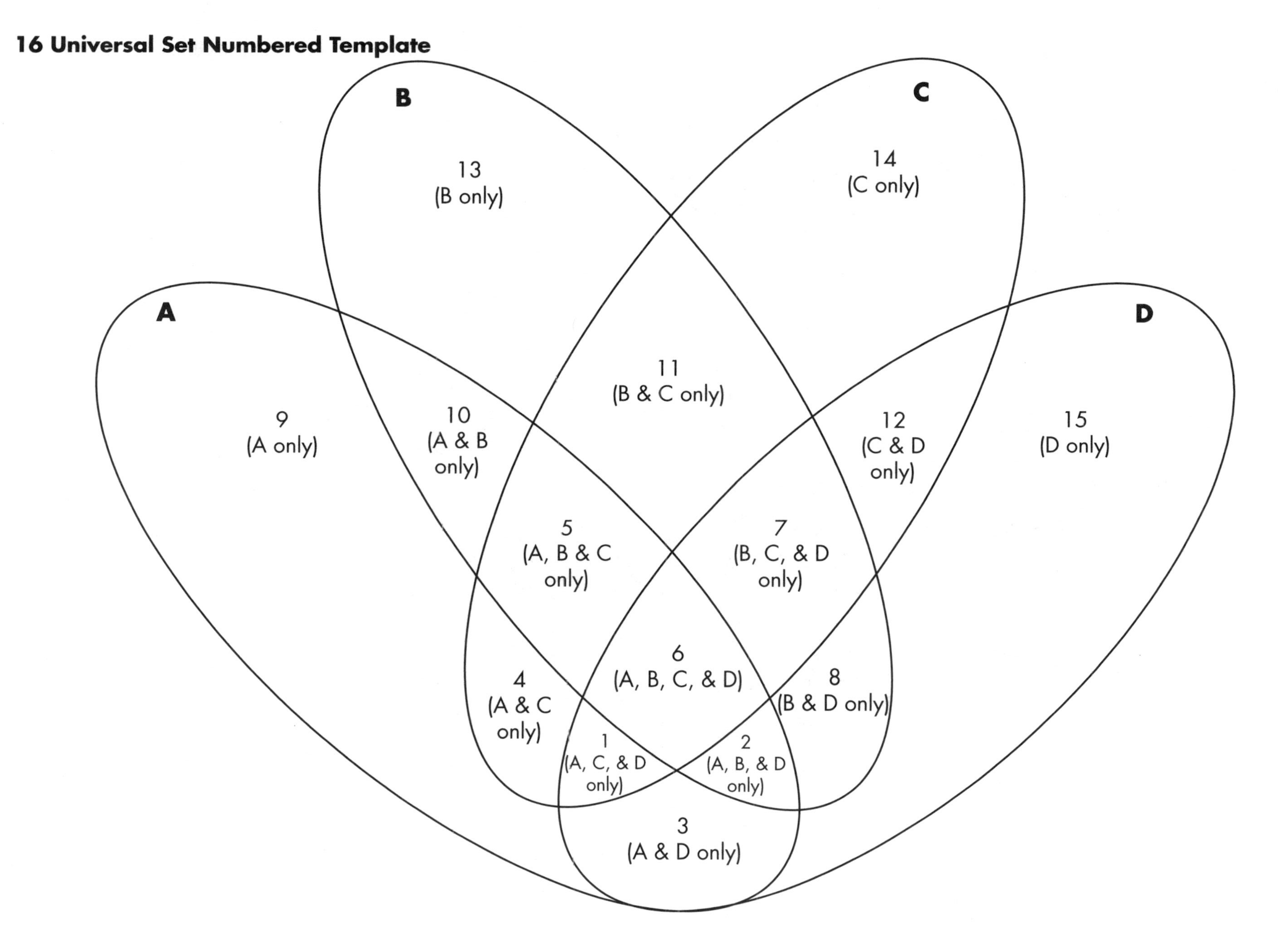

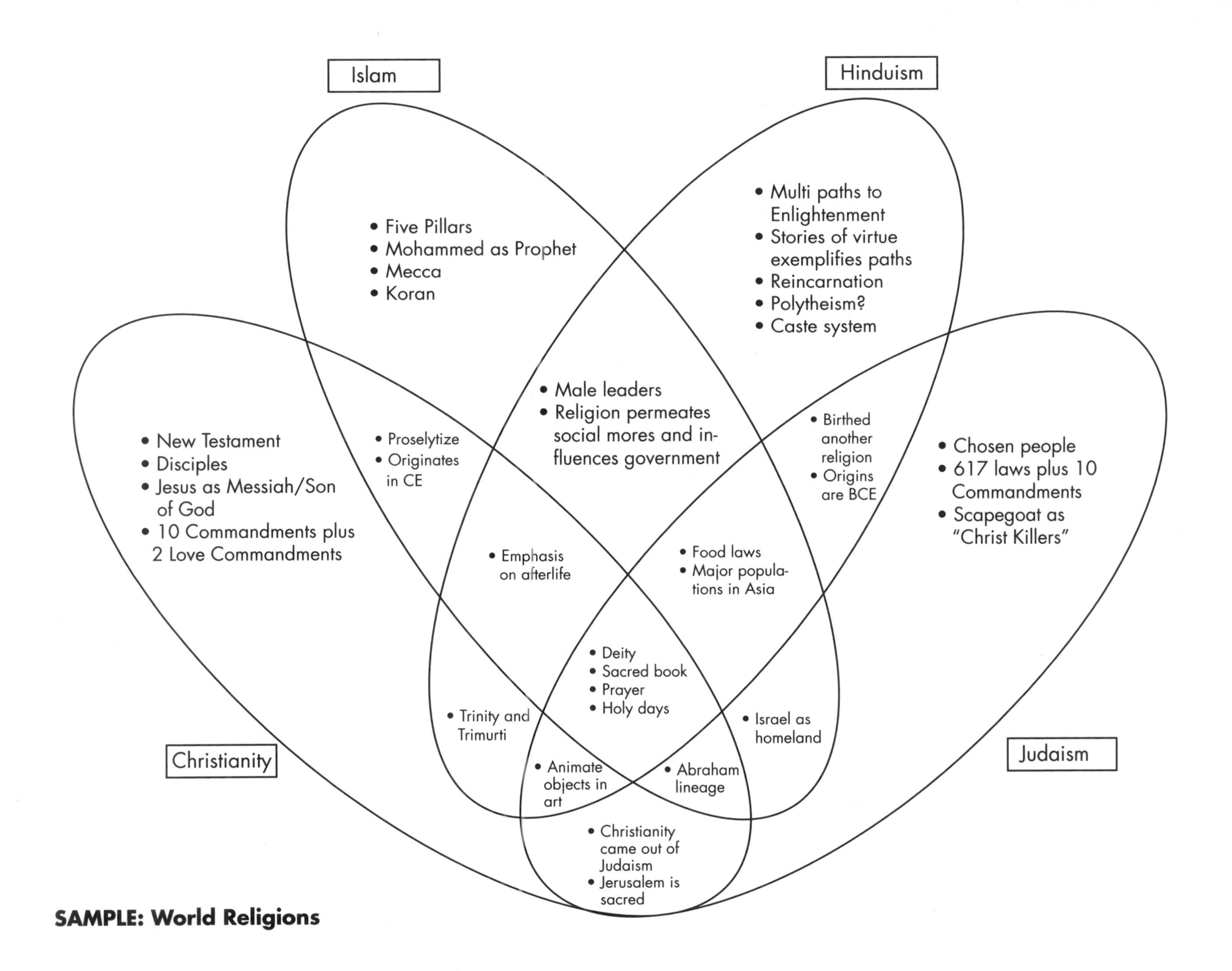

SAMPLE: World Religions

Letters and Boxes

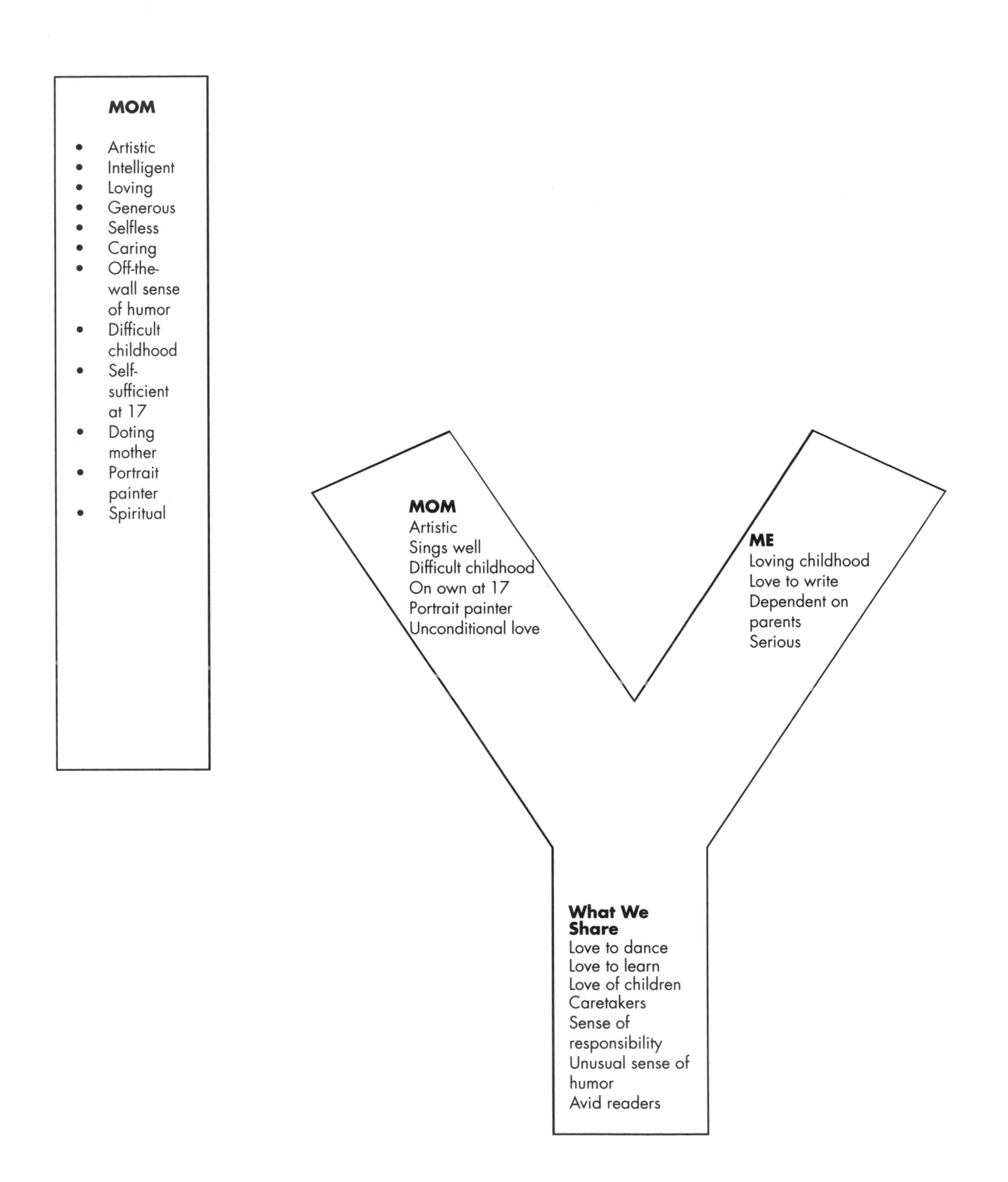
MOM
Artistic
Intelligent
Loving
Generous
Selfless
Caring
Off-the-wall sense of humor
Difficult childhood
Self-sufficient at 17
Doting mother
Portrait painter
Spiritual
MOM
Artistic
Sings well
Difficult childhood
On own at 17
Portrait painter
Unconditional love
ME
Loving childhood
Love to write
Dependent on parents
Serious
What We Share
Love to dance
Love to learn
Love of children
Caretakers
Sense of responsibility
Unusual sense of humor
Avid readers

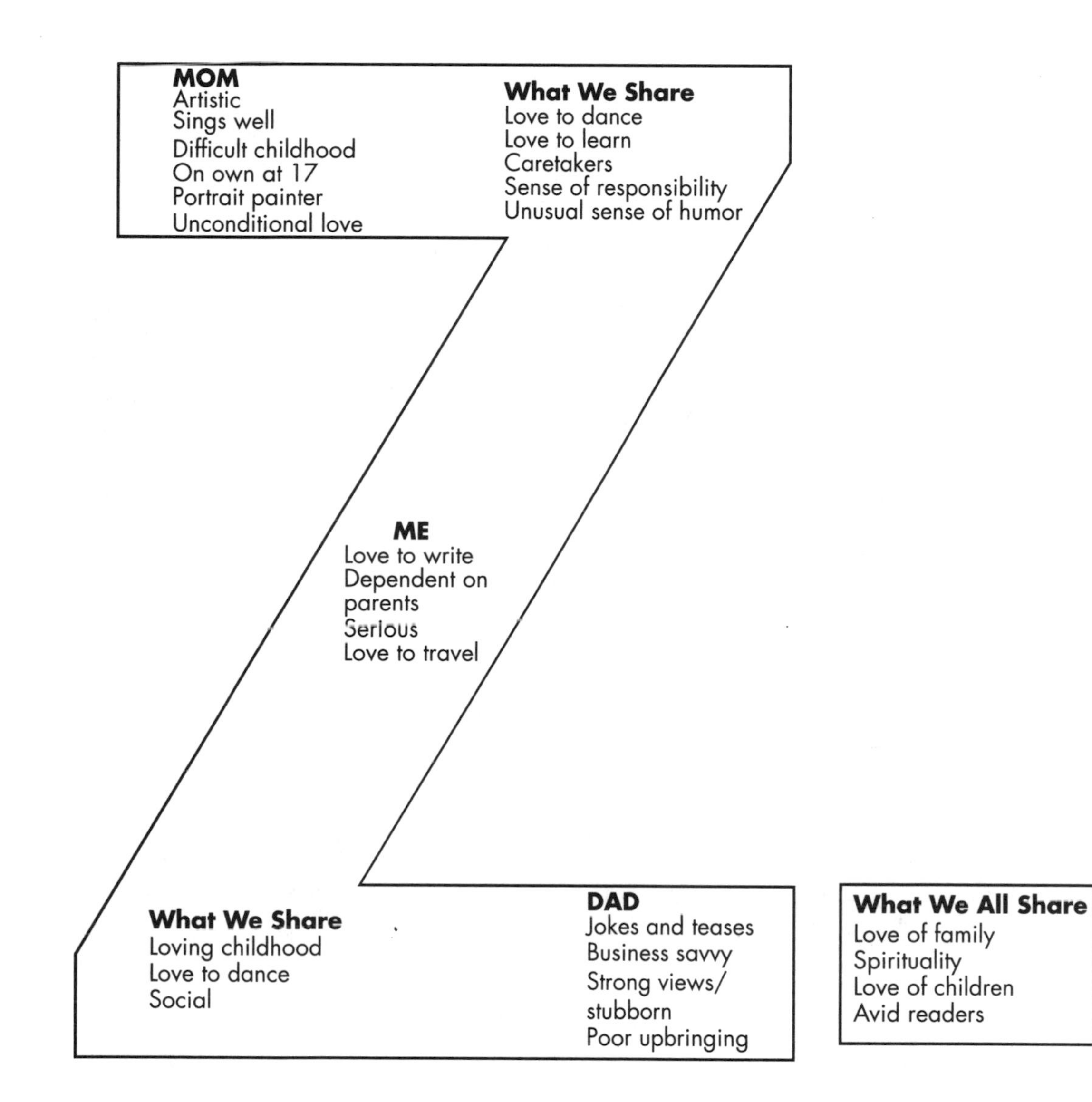
MOM
Artistic
Sings well
Difficult childhood
On own at 17
Portrait painter
Unconditional love
What We Share
Love to dance
Love to learn
Caretakers
Sense of responsibility
Unusual sense of humor
ME
Love to write
Dependent on parents
Serious
Love to travel
What We Share
Loving childhood
Love to dance
Social
DAD
Jokes and teases
Business savvy
Strong views/ stubborn
Poor upbringing
What We All Share
Love of family
Spirituality
Love of children
Avid readers

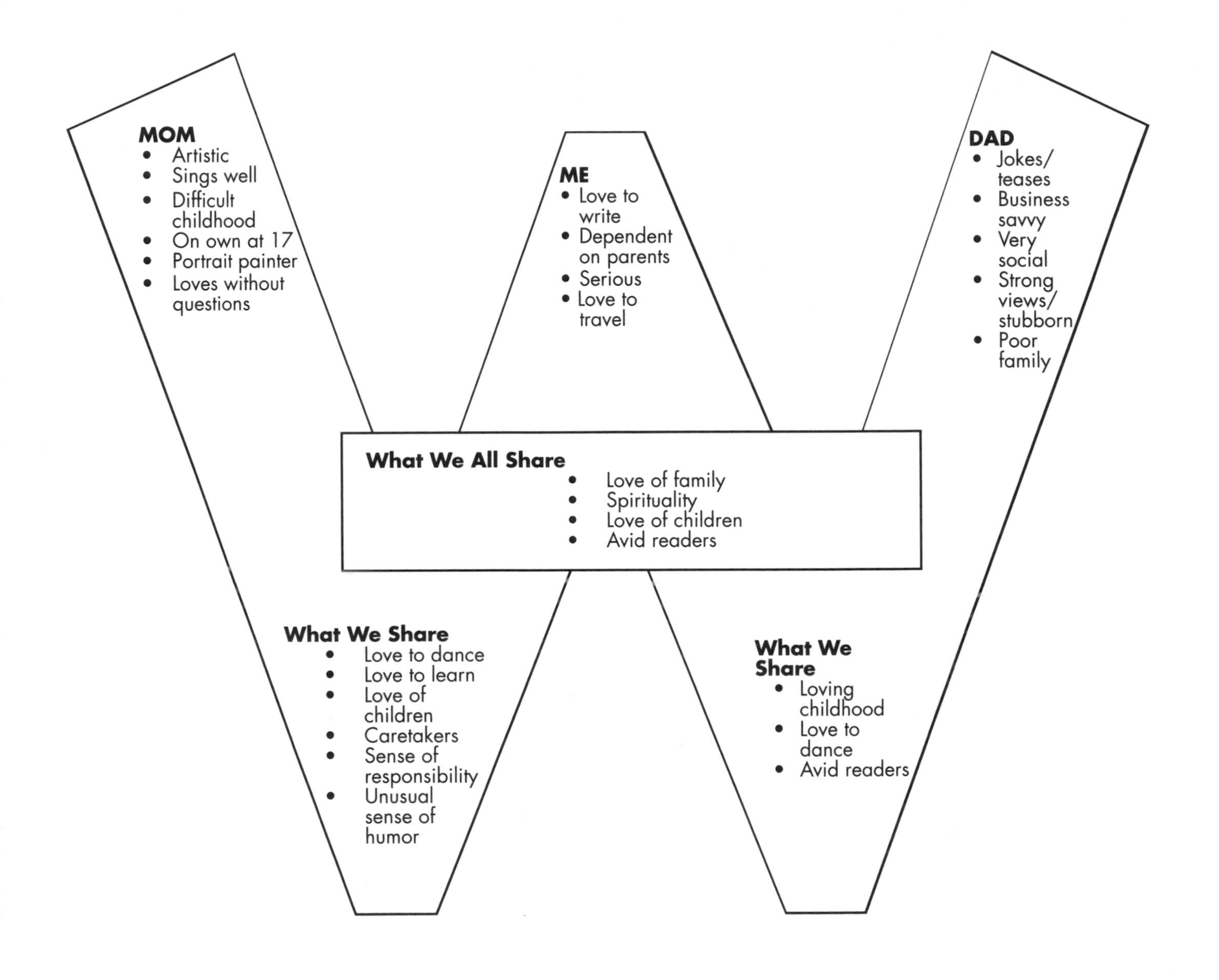
MOM
• Artistic
• Sings well
• Difficult childhood
• On own at 17
• Portrait painter
• Loves without questions
ME
• Love to write
• Dependent on parents
• Serious
• Love to travel
DAD
• Jokes/ teases
• Business savvy
• Very social
• Strong views/ stubborn
• Poor family
What We All Share
• Love of family
• Spirituality
• Love of children
• Avid readers
What We Share
• Love to dance
• Love to learn
• Love of children
• Caretakers
• Sense of responsibility
• Unusual sense of humor
What We Share
• Loving childhood
• Love to dance
• Avid readers

Box Chart (Two Concepts)

TOPIC A	TOPIC B

Note. From *Tools for Promoting Active, In-depth Learning* (2nd ed., p. 150), by H. F. Silver, R. W. Strong, and M. J. Perini, 2001, Ho-Ho-Kus, NJ: Thoughtful Education Press. Copyright ©2001 by Thoughtful Education Press. Adapted with permission.

Box Chart (Three Concepts)

TOPIC A	A and B Similarities	TOPIC B	B and C Similarities	TOPIC C	C and A Similarities
Similarities of A, B, and C					

Note. From *Tools for Promoting Active, In-depth Learning* (2nd ed., p. 150), by H. F. Silver, R. W. Strong, and M. J. Perini, 2001, Ho-Ho-Kus, NJ: Thoughtful Education Press. Copyright ©2001 by Thoughtful Education Press. Adapted with permission.

Box Chart (Four Concepts)

TOPIC A	A and B Similarities	TOPIC B	B and C Similarities	TOPIC C	C and D Similarities	TOPIC C	D and A Similarities
A and C Similarities		A, B and C Similarities		B, C, and D Similarities		B and D Similarities	
Similarities of A, B, C, and D							

Note. From *Tools for Promoting Active, In-depth Learning* (2nd ed., p. 150), by H. F. Silver, R. W. Strong, and M. J. Perini, 2001, Ho-Ho-Kus, NJ: Thoughtful Education Press. Copyright ©2001 by Thoughtful Education Press. Adapted with permission.

APPENDIX G

Think-Tac-Toe Template

THINK-TAC-TOE TEMPLATE

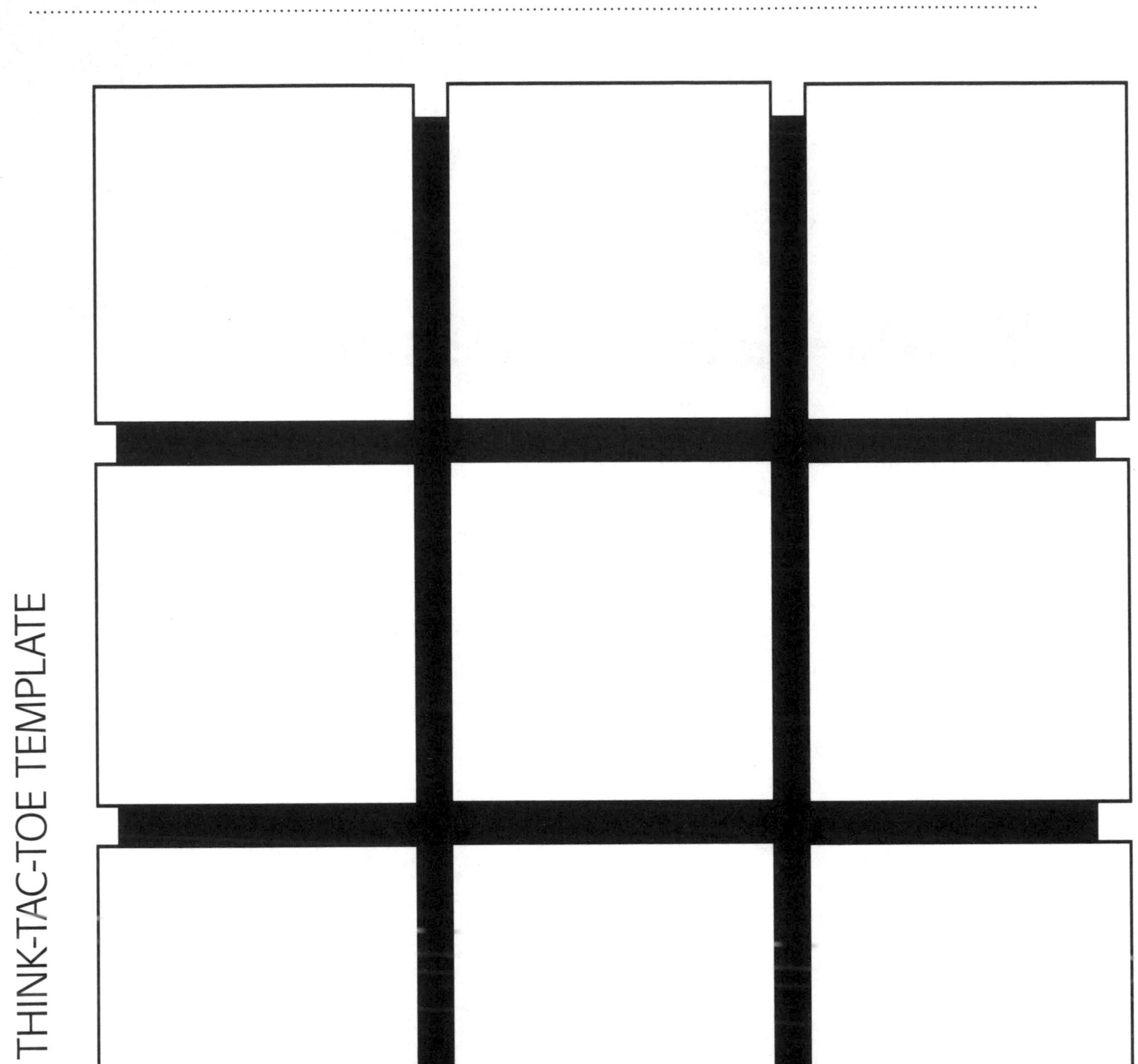

APPENDIX H

Developing and Assessing Product (DAP) Tools

CARTOON TIER 1—DAP TOOL

CONTENT								
	» Is the content correct?	0	1	2	3	4	5	6
	» Has the content been thought about in a way that goes beyond a surface understanding?	0	1	2	3	4	5	6
	» Is the content put together in such a way that people understand it?	0	1	2	3	4	5	6
PRESENTATION								
PURPOSE	» Does the illustration fulfill its intended purpose, for example, to amuse, to humor, to provoke thought, etc.?	0	1	2	3	4	5	6
ILLUSTRATIONS	» Are the illustrations clear and easy to understand? Do the illustrations help the reader appreciate the purpose?	0	1	2	3	4	5	6
LAYOUT	» Is the cartoon a single panel or does it have multiple panels? Is it the best number to get across the purpose?	0	1	2	3	4	5	6
TEXT (OPTIONAL)	» Is the title clear? If used, are the character balloons easy to read? Is the text clear and to the point? Does it complement the illustrations? Is the cartoon mostly free from usage, punctuation, capitalization, and spelling errors? If sources are used, are they cited correctly?	0	1	2	3	4	5	6
CREATIVITY								
	» Is the content seen in a new way?	0	1	2	3	4	5	6
	» Is the presentation done in a new way?	0	1	2	3	4	5	6
REFLECTION								
CONTENT	» What connections can you make between what you have learned by completing this project and previous learning?	0	1	2	3	4	5	6
PRODUCT	» In what ways could you improve your product when completing this product with a different assignment?	0	1	2	3	4	5	6
LEARNING	» How did the amount of effort affect your learning about the content and creating the product?	0	1	2	3	4	5	6

Comments:

____

____

____

Meaning of Performance Scale:
6—PROFESSIONAL LEVEL: level expected from a professional in the content area
5—ADVANCED LEVEL: level exceeds expectations of the standard
4—PROFICIENT LEVEL: level expected for meeting the standard
3—PROGRESSING LEVEL: level demonstrates movement toward the standard
2—NOVICE LEVEL: level demonstrates initial awareness and knowledge of standard
1—NONPERFORMING LEVEL: level indicates no effort made to meet standard
0—NONPARTICIPATING LEVEL: level indicates nothing turned in

CARTOON TIER 2—DAP TOOL

CONTENT								
	» Content is accurate and complete.	0	1	2	3	4	5	6
	» Content has depth and complexity of thought.	0	1	2	3	4	5	6
	» Content is organized.	0	1	2	3	4	5	6
PRESENTATION								
PURPOSE	» The cartoon is designed for a specific audience as evidenced in text, illustration, and layout. The intended audience will find humor or amusement in the cartoon.	0	1	2	3	4	5	6
ILLUSTRATIONS	» The illustrations enhance or embody the purpose. It aids reader understanding and increases enjoyment and understanding.	0	1	2	3	4	5	6
LAYOUT	» Whether single- or multipaneled, the layout enhances the enjoyment and understanding of the cartoon.	0	1	2	3	4	5	6
TEXT (OPTIONAL)	» Title enhances the cartoon. The text effectively complements the purpose. The text incorporates word play, allusions, or parody effectively. If used, character balloons are well incorporated. The cartoon is free from usage, punctuation, capitalization, and spelling errors. Sources, when used, are thoroughly cited.	0	1	2	3	4	5	6
CREATIVITY								
	» Originality is expressed in relation to the content.	0	1	2	3	4	5	6
	» Originality is expressed in relation to the presentation.	0	1	2	3	4	5	6
REFLECTION								
CONTENT	» Reflections include connections to previous learning and questions raised for future learning.	0	1	2	3	4	5	6
PRODUCT	» Reflections include improvements made over other times the product was created as well as suggestions for improvements when creating the same product in a future learning experience.	0	1	2	3	4	5	6
LEARNING	» Reflections include analysis of self as a learner, including effort, work habits, and thought processes.	0	1	2	3	4	5	6

Comments:

Meaning of Performance Scale:
6—PROFESSIONAL LEVEL: level expected from a professional in the content area
5—ADVANCED LEVEL: level exceeds expectations of the standard
4—PROFICIENT LEVEL: level expected for meeting the standard
3—PROGRESSING LEVEL: level demonstrates movement toward the standard
2—NOVICE LEVEL: level demonstrates initial awareness and knowledge of standard
1—NONPERFORMING LEVEL: level indicates no effort made to meet standard
0—NONPARTICIPATING LEVEL: level indicates nothing turned in

CARTOON TIER 3—DAP TOOL

CONTENT									
	» Content is accurate and thorough in detail.	0	1	2	3	4	5	6
	» Product shows complex understanding and manipulation of content.	0	1	2	3	4	5	6
	» Product shows deep probing of content.	0	1	2	3	4	5	6
	» Organization is best suited to the product.	0	1	2	3	4	5	6
PRESENTATION								
PURPOSE	» The cartoon is deliberately created for a specific audience. The text, illustration, and layout all fully support the specific viewpoint of the cartoonist with regard to a current event, person, or situation. Reader's rights are respected and honored.	0	1	2	3	4	5	6
ILLUSTRATIONS	» Purpose, inherent in the illustration, plays an integral role in reader appreciation. The craftsmanship is of high quality.	0	1	2	3	4	5	6
LAYOUT	» The number of panels purposely supports and furthers the cartoon's meaning.	0	1	2	3	4	5	6
TEXT (OPTIONAL)	» Title reflects the purpose of the cartoon. The text fully complements and enhances the purpose. The text artfully incorporates word play, allusions, or parody to reflect the purpose. If used, character balloons enhance the overall meaning of the cartoon. The cartoon is error free, with correct usage, punctuation, capitalization, and spelling used. All sources are cited correctly with the citation placed appropriately.	0	1	2	3	4	5	6
CREATIVITY								
	» Innovation is evident in relation to the content.	0	1	2	3	4	5	6
	» Innovation is evident in relation to the presentation.	0	1	2	3	4	5	6
REFLECTION								
CONTENT	» Reflections analyze and evaluate connections to previous learning and project insightful future connections.	0	1	2	3	4	5	6
PRODUCT	» Reflections analyze and evaluate the product components in light of past and future creations of the same product.	0	1	2	3	4	5	6
LEARNING	» Reflections include analysis of self as a learner and project how changes to the process would increase capacity as a learner.							

Comments:

____

____

____

Meaning of Performance Scale:
6—PROFESSIONAL LEVEL: level expected from a professional in the content area
5—ADVANCED LEVEL: level exceeds expectations of the standard
4—PROFICIENT LEVEL: level expected for meeting the standard
3—PROGRESSING LEVEL: level demonstrates movement toward the standard
2—NOVICE LEVEL: level demonstrates initial awareness and knowledge of standard
1—NONPERFORMING LEVEL: level indicates no effort made to meet standard
0—NONPARTICIPATING LEVEL: level indicates nothing turned in

MODEL TIER 1—DAP TOOL

CONTENT								
	» Is the content correct?	0	1	2	3	4	5	6
	» Has the content been thought about in a way that goes beyond a surface understanding?	0	1	2	3	4	5	6
	» Is the content put together in such a way that people understand it?	0	1	2	3	4	5	6
PRESENTATION								
REPRESENTATION	» Does the model clearly look like what it represents?	0	1	2	3	4	5	6
CONSTRUCTION	» Does the construction make the model stable? Are the materials appropriate for the construction?	0	1	2	3	4	5	6
LABELS	» Are the labels clear? Are the labels mostly free from usage, punctuation, capitalization, and spelling errors? If sources are used, are they cited correctly?	0	1	2	3	4	5	6
CREATIVITY								
	» Is the content seen in a new way?	0	1	2	3	4	5	6
	» Is the presentation done in a new way?	0	1	2	3	4	5	6
REFLECTION								
CONTENT	» What connections can you make between what you have learned by completing this project and previous learning?	0	1	2	3	4	5	6
PRODUCT	» In what ways could you improve your product when completing this product with a different assignment?	0	1	2	3	4	5	6
LEARNING	» How did the amount of effort affect your learning about the content and creating the product?	0	1	2	3	4	5	6

Comments:

____

____

____

Meaning of Performance Scale:
6—PROFESSIONAL LEVEL: level expected from a professional in the content area
5—ADVANCED LEVEL: level exceeds expectations of the standard
4—PROFICIENT LEVEL: level expected for meeting the standard
3—PROGRESSING LEVEL: level demonstrates movement toward the standard
2—NOVICE LEVEL: level demonstrates initial awareness and knowledge of standard
1—NONPERFORMING LEVEL: level indicates no effort made to meet standard
0—NONPARTICIPATING LEVEL: level indicates nothing turned in

MODEL TIER 2—DAP TOOL

CONTENT								
	» Content is accurate and complete.	0	1	2	3	4	5	6
	» Content has depth and complexity of thought.	0	1	2	3	4	5	6
	» Content is organized.	0	1	2	3	4	5	6
PRESENTATION								
REPRESENTATION	» The model makes the viewers see the purpose (whether realistic and/or symbolical).	0	1	2	3	4	5	6
CONSTRUCTION	» The model clearly exhibits knowledge of a scale and uses it appropriately. If a realistic representation, the scale is measurable. If a symbolic representation, the model may or may not follow a measurable scale and may communicate ideas by dramatically altering the scale or only scaling objects relative to one another.	0	1	2	3	4	5	6
	» The model is constructed with detail. Materials enhance the meaning of the model.	0	1	2	3	4	5	6
LABELS	» Labels are clear and pertinent. They match the key. They are free from usage, punctuation, capitalization, and spelling errors. Sources, when used, are thoroughly cited.	0	1	2	3	4	5	6
CREATIVITY								
	» Originality is expressed in relation to the content.	0	1	2	3	4	5	6
	» Originality is expressed in relation to the presentation.	0	1	2	3	4	5	6
REFLECTION								
CONTENT	» Reflections include connections to previous learning and questions raised for future learning.	0	1	2	3	4	5	6
PRODUCT	» Reflections include improvements made over other times the product was created as well as suggestions for improvements when creating the same product in a future learning experience.	0	1	2	3	4	5	6
LEARNING	» Reflections include analysis of self as a learner, including effort, work habits, and thought processes.	0	1	2	3	4	5	6

Comments:

____

____

____

Meaning of Performance Scale:

6—PROFESSIONAL LEVEL: level expected from a professional in the content area
5—ADVANCED LEVEL: level exceeds expectations of the standard
4—PROFICIENT LEVEL: level expected for meeting the standard
3—PROGRESSING LEVEL: level demonstrates movement toward the standard
2—NOVICE LEVEL: level demonstrates initial awareness and knowledge of standard
1—NONPERFORMING LEVEL: level indicates no effort made to meet standard
0—NONPARTICIPATING LEVEL: level indicates nothing turned in

MODEL TIER 3—DAP TOOL

CONTENT								
	» Content is accurate and thorough in detail.	0	1	2	3	4	5	6
	» Product shows complex understanding and manipulation of content.	0	1	2	3	4	5	6
	» Product shows deep probing of content.	0	1	2	3	4	5	6
	» Organization is best suited to the product.	0	1	2	3	4	5	6
PRESENTATION								
REPRESENTATION	» The model employs a new idea in the representation whether that representation is real or symbolic.	0	1	2	3	4	5	6
CONSTRUCTION	» The construction as to the detail and materials is unique to highlight the model's purpose. More than one piece of sensory information is incorporated into the construction.	0	1	2	3	4	5	6
LABELS	» Labels effectively direct the purpose of the model. They are error free, with correct usage, punctuation, capitalization, and spelling used. All sources are cited correctly with the citation placed appropriately.	0	1	2	3	4	5	6
CREATIVITY								
	» Innovation is evident in relation to the content.	0	1	2	3	4	5	6
	» Innovation is evident in relation to the presentation.	0	1	2	3	4	5	6
REFLECTION								
CONTENT	» Reflections analyze and evaluate connections to previous learning and project insightful future connections.	0	1	2	3	4	5	6
PRODUCT	» Reflections analyze and evaluate the product components in light of past and future creations of the same product.	0	1	2	3	4	5	6
LEARNING	» Reflections include analysis of self as a learner and project how changes to the process would increase capacity as a learner.	0	1	2	3	4	5	6

Comments:

____

____

____

Meaning of Performance Scale:

6—PROFESSIONAL LEVEL: level expected from a professional in the content area
5—ADVANCED LEVEL: level exceeds expectations of the standard
4—PROFICIENT LEVEL: level expected for meeting the standard
3—PROGRESSING LEVEL: level demonstrates movement toward the standard
2—NOVICE LEVEL: level demonstrates initial awareness and knowledge of standard
1—NONPERFORMING LEVEL: level indicates no effort made to meet standard
0—NONPARTICIPATING LEVEL: level indicates nothing turned in

PAMPHLET TIER 1—DAP TOOL

CONTENT								
	» Is the content correct?	0	1	2	3	4	5	6
	» Has the content been thought about in a way that goes beyond a surface understanding?	0	1	2	3	4	5	6
	» Is the content put together in such a way that people understand it?	0	1	2	3	4	5	6
PRESENTATION								
TEXT	» Is the title clear? Does the text explain the topic? Does the text get across the purpose (e.g., informative, persuasive, etc.)? Are there sufficient details to develop the topic?	0	1	2	3	4	5	6
GRAPHICS	» Are the graphics (e.g., illustrations, photos, etc.) important to the topic? Are the graphics and text balanced?	0	1	2	3	4	5	6
LAYOUT	» Do the pamphlet folds increase reader understanding? Is the pamphlet pleasing to the eye?	0	1	2	3	4	5	6
CORRECTNESS	» Is the pamphlet mostly free from usage, punctuation, capitalization, and spelling errors? If sources are used, are they cited correctly?	0	1	2	3	4	5	6
CREATIVITY								
	» Is the content seen in a new way?	0	1	2	3	4	5	6
	» Is the presentation done in a new way?	0	1	2	3	4	5	6
REFLECTION								
CONTENT	» What connections can you make between what you have learned by completing this project and previous learning?	0	1	2	3	4	5	6
PRODUCT	» In what ways could you improve your product when completing this product with a different assignment?	0	1	2	3	4	5	6
LEARNING	» How did the amount of effort affect your learning about the content and creating the product?	0	1	2	3	4	5	6

Comments:

____

____

____

Meaning of Performance Scale:

6—PROFESSIONAL LEVEL: level expected from a professional in the content area

5—ADVANCED LEVEL: level exceeds expectations of the standard

4—PROFICIENT LEVEL: level expected for meeting the standard

3—PROGRESSING LEVEL: level demonstrates movement toward the standard

2—NOVICE LEVEL: level demonstrates initial awareness and knowledge of standard

1—NONPERFORMING LEVEL: level indicates no effort made to meet standard

0—NONPARTICIPATING LEVEL: level indicates nothing turned in

PAMPHLET TIER 2—DAP TOOL

CONTENT								
	» Content is accurate and complete.	0	1	2	3	4	5	6
	» Content has depth and complexity of thought.	0	1	2	3	4	5	6
	» Content is organized.	0	1	2	3	4	5	6
PRESENTATION								
TEXT	» Title enhances the pamphlet. Text highlights most important concepts in topic and detailed. The purpose is evident.	0	1	2	3	4	5	6
GRAPHICS	» Graphics (e.g., illustrations, photos, etc.) add information to the topic.	0	1	2	3	4	5	6
LAYOUT	» Layout design is organized and attractive. Multifold design showcases graphics and text. It is pleasing to the eye.	0	1	2	3	4	5	6
CORRECTNESS	» The pamphlet is free from usage, punctuation, capitalization, and spelling errors. Sources, when used, are thoroughly cited.	0	1	2	3	4	5	6
CREATIVITY								
	» Originality is expressed in relation to the content.	0	1	2	3	4	5	6
	» Originality is expressed in relation to the presentation.	0	1	2	3	4	5	6
REFLECTION								
CONTENT	» Reflections include connections to previous learning and questions raised for future learning.	0	1	2	3	4	5	6
PRODUCT	» Reflections include improvements made over other times the product was created as well as suggestions for improvements when creating the same product in a future learning experience.	0	1	2	3	4	5	6
LEARNING	» Reflections include analysis of self as a learner, including effort, work habits, and thought processes.	0	1	2	3	4	5	6

Comments:

____

____

____

Meaning of Performance Scale:
6—PROFESSIONAL LEVEL: level expected from a professional in the content area
5—ADVANCED LEVEL: level exceeds expectations of the standard
4—PROFICIENT LEVEL: level expected for meeting the standard
3—PROGRESSING LEVEL: level demonstrates movement toward the standard
2—NOVICE LEVEL: level demonstrates initial awareness and knowledge of standard
1—NONPERFORMING LEVEL: level indicates no effort made to meet standard
0—NONPARTICIPATING LEVEL: level indicates nothing turned in

PAMPHLET TIER 3—DAP TOOL

CONTENT								
	» Content is accurate and thorough in detail.	0	1	2	3	4	5	6
	» Product shows complex understanding and manipulation of content.	0	1	2	3	4	5	6
	» Product shows deep probing of content.	0	1	2	3	4	5	6
	» Organization is best suited to the product.	0	1	2	3	4	5	6
PRESENTATION								
TEXT	» Title and text reflect purpose. Text highlights most important concepts in clear, concise manner with critical details that develop the purpose.	0	1	2	3	4	5	6
GRAPHICS	» Graphics (e.g., illustrations, photos, etc.) enhance meaning.	0	1	2	3	4	5	6
LAYOUT	» Thoughtful manipulation of color, layout, and font reflects purpose. Multifold design enhances readability and meaning. It engages the reader.	0	1	2	3	4	5	6
CORRECTNESS	» The pamphlet is error free, with correct usage, punctuation, capitalization, and spelling used. All sources are cited correctly with the citation placed appropriately.	0	1	2	3	4	5	6
CREATIVITY								
	» Innovation is evident in relation to the content.	0	1	2	3	4	5	6
	» Innovation is evident in relation to the presentation.	0	1	2	3	4	5	6
REFLECTION								
CONTENT	» Reflections analyze and evaluate connections to previous learning and project insightful future connections.	0	1	2	3	4	5	6
PRODUCT	» Reflections analyze and evaluate the product components in light of past and future creations of the same product.	0	1	2	3	4	5	6
LEARNING	» Reflections include analysis of self as a learner and project how changes to the process would increase capacity as a learner.	0	1	2	3	4	5	6

Comments:

____

____

____

Meaning of Performance Scale:
6—PROFESSIONAL LEVEL: level expected from a professional in the content area
5—ADVANCED LEVEL: level exceeds expectations of the standard
4—PROFICIENT LEVEL: level expected for meeting the standard
3—PROGRESSING LEVEL: level demonstrates movement toward the standard
2—NOVICE LEVEL: level demonstrates initial awareness and knowledge of standard
1—NONPERFORMING LEVEL: level indicates no effort made to meet standard
0—NONPARTICIPATING LEVEL: level indicates nothing turned in

POWERPOINT TIER 1—DAP TOOL

CONTENT								
	» Is the content correct?	0	1	2	3	4	5	6
	» Has the content been thought about in a way that goes beyond a surface understanding?	0	1	2	3	4	5	6
	» Is the content put together in such a way that people understand it?	0	1	2	3	4	5	6
PRESENTATION								
TEXT	» Is the title clear? Does the text explain the topic without too much information on any one slide? Are headings and bulleted lists used well?	0	1	2	3	4	5	6
GRAPHICS	» Are the graphics (e.g., illustrations, photos, videos, multimedia, etc.) important to the topic? Can videos be played in full screen? Is there a careful mixture of text and graphics? Are graphics proportional? Is white space used well?	0	1	2	3	4	5	6
SLIDES	» Do the slides make sense following one another in both how they look and in what they mean? Does the slideshow appeal to the audience? Does it have smooth transitions without sound? If music is used, is it played across all slides if appropriate? Are presenter notes available?	0	1	2	3	4	5	6
DELIVERY	» *Verbal:* Is the PowerPoint developed for the expected audience and purpose through its word choice, sentence structure, and tone? Is the voice clear? Is the delivery smooth? Are the strengths of the PowerPoint utilized for an effective presentation?	0	1	2	3	4	5	6
	» *Nonverbal:* Is eye contact maintained? Are appropriate facial expressions and gestures incorporated? Is the speaker poised and comfortable? Are the strengths of the PowerPoint utilized for an effective presentation?	0	1	2	3	4	5	6
CORRECTNESS	» Is the PowerPoint mostly free from usage, punctuation, capitalization, and spelling errors? If sources are used, are they cited correctly?	0	1	2	3	4	5	6
CREATIVITY								
	» Is the content seen in a new way?	0	1	2	3	4	5	6
	» Is the presentation done in a new way?	0	1	2	3	4	5	6
REFLECTION								
CONTENT	» What connections can you make between what you have learned by completing this project and previous learning?	0	1	2	3	4	5	6
PRODUCT	» In what ways could you improve your product when completing this product with a different assignment?	0	1	2	3	4	5	6
LEARNING	» How did the amount of effort affect your learning about the content and creating the product?	0	1	2	3	4	5	6

Comments:

____

____

____

Meaning of Performance Scale:
6—PROFESSIONAL LEVEL: level expected from a professional in the content area
5—ADVANCED LEVEL: level exceeds expectations of the standard
4—PROFICIENT LEVEL: level expected for meeting the standard
3—PROGRESSING LEVEL: level demonstrates movement toward the standard
2—NOVICE LEVEL: level demonstrates initial awareness and knowledge of standard
1—NONPERFORMING LEVEL: level indicates no effort made to meet standard
0—NONPARTICIPATING LEVEL: level indicates nothing turned in

POWERPOINT TIER 2—DAP TOOL

CONTENT								
	» Content is accurate and complete.	0	1	2	3	4	5	6
	» Content has depth and complexity of thought.	0	1	2	3	4	5	6
	» Content is organized.	0	1	2	3	4	5	6
PRESENTATION								
TEXT	» Title enhances the PowerPoint. Text highlights most important concepts in topic in clearly organized slides. Text is limited to key ideas. Headings and bulleted lists enhance the PowerPoint.	0	1	2	3	4	5	6
GRAPHICS	» Graphics (e.g., illustrations, photos, videos, multimedia, etc.) add information to the topic and are proportional. Videos are shown in full screen. Layout design is organized and attractive. White space is used well.	0	1	2	3	4	5	6
SLIDES	» Slides maintain continuity in form and purpose. Slides have smooth transitions. Slideshow keeps audience's attention through graphics, text, and special effects, not sound effects. Presenter notes are available.	0	1	2	3	4	5	6
DELIVERY	» *Verbal:* The purposeful use of varied syntax and precise diction aids in audience understanding. Tone is consistent with purpose. Speaker's voice is strong and clear with appropriate intonations and pronunciations. Speaker exhibits confidence yet stirs interest in the audience. The PowerPoint strengths are intentionally developed for an effective presentation.	0	1	2	3	4	5	6
	» *Nonverbal:* Eye contact, facial expressions, and other forms of nonverbal communication aid in audience understanding, gain their trust, and further the purpose. The PowerPoint strengths are intentionally developed for an effective presentation.	0	1	2	3	4	5	6
CORRECTNESS	» The PowerPoint is free from usage, punctuation, capitalization, and spelling errors. Sources, when used, are thoroughly cited.	0	1	2	3	4	5	6
CREATIVITY								
	» Originality is expressed in relation to the content.	0	1	2	3	4	5	6
	» Originality is expressed in relation to the presentation.	0	1	2	3	4	5	6
REFLECTION								
CONTENT	» Reflections include connections to previous learning and questions raised for future learning.	0	1	2	3	4	5	6
PRODUCT	» Reflections include improvements made over other times the product was created as well as suggestions for improvements when creating the same product in a future learning experience.	0	1	2	3	4	5	6
LEARNING	» Reflections include analysis of self as a learner, including effort, work habits, and thought processes.	0	1	2	3	4	5	6

Comments:

____

____

____

Meaning of Performance Scale:
6—PROFESSIONAL LEVEL: level expected from a professional in the content area
5—ADVANCED LEVEL: level exceeds expectations of the standard
4—PROFICIENT LEVEL: level expected for meeting the standard
3—PROGRESSING LEVEL: level demonstrates movement toward the standard
2—NOVICE LEVEL: level demonstrates initial awareness and knowledge of standard
1—NONPERFORMING LEVEL: level indicates no effort made to meet standard
0—NONPARTICIPATING LEVEL: level indicates nothing turned in

POWERPOINT TIER 3—DAP TOOL

CONTENT								
	» Content is accurate and thorough in detail.	0	1	2	3	4	5	6
	» Product shows complex understanding and manipulation of content.	0	1	2	3	4	5	6
	» Product shows deep probing of content.	0	1	2	3	4	5	6
	» Organization is best suited to the product.	0	1	2	3	4	5	6
PRESENTATION								
TEXT	» Title reflects purpose. Text highlights most important concepts in clear, concise manner with careful thought given to amount and type of information on each slide.	0	1	2	3	4	5	6
GRAPHICS	» Proportional graphics (e.g., illustrations, photos, videos, multimedia, etc.) enhance meaning. Videos, if used, are in full screen to enhance slideshow. Thoughtful manipulation of color, layout, and font reflects purpose. Use of white space enhances slideshow.	0	1	2	3	4	5	6
SLIDES	» The continuity of the slides (i.e., font, color, background, movement, sound, and special effects) enhances the meaning. Slideshow engages the audience through its graphics, text, appearance, movement, sounds, and special effects. Music, if used, enhances the slideshow, playing across each slide. Presenter notes are well utilized.	0	1	2	3	4	5	6
DELIVERY	» *Verbal:* The intentional use of varied syntax and powerful diction enhances audience understanding. Effective rhetorical devices emphasize main ideas. Speaker's voice is strong, clear, and effective. Speaker exudes passion for the topic while being in total control of the presentation and audience. The nuances of the PowerPoint are maximized to engage the audience.	0	1	2	3	4	5	6
	» *Nonverbal:* Purposeful eye contact, facial expressions, and other forms of nonverbal communication enhance audience understanding and emphasize the purpose. The nuances of the PowerPoint are maximized to engage the audience.	0	1	2	3	4	5	6
CORRECTNESS	» The PowerPoint is error free, with correct usage, punctuation, capitalization, and spelling used. All sources are cited correctly with the citation placed appropriately.	0	1	2	3	4	5	6
CREATIVITY								
	» Innovation is evident in relation to the content.	0	1	2	3	4	5	6
	» Innovation is evident in relation to the presentation.	0	1	2	3	4	5	6
REFLECTION								
CONTENT	» Reflections analyze and evaluate connections to previous learning and project insightful future connections.	0	1	2	3	4	5	6
PRODUCT	» Reflections analyze and evaluate the product components in light of past and future creations of the same product.	0	1	2	3	4	5	6
LEARNING	» Reflections include analysis of self as a learner and project how changes to the process would increase capacity as a learner.	0	1	2	3	4	5	6

Comments:

____

____

____

Meaning of Performance Scale:
6—PROFESSIONAL LEVEL: level expected from a professional in the content area
5—ADVANCED LEVEL: level exceeds expectations of the standard
4—PROFICIENT LEVEL: level expected for meeting the standard
3—PROGRESSING LEVEL: level demonstrates movement toward the standard
2—NOVICE LEVEL: level demonstrates initial awareness and knowledge of standard
1—NONPERFORMING LEVEL: level indicates no effort made to meet standard
0—NONPARTICIPATING LEVEL: level indicates nothing turned in

SPEECH (ORAL) TIER 1—DAP TOOL

CONTENT								
	» Is the content correct?	0	1	2	3	4	5	6
	» Has the content been thought about in a way that goes beyond a surface understanding?	0	1	2	3	4	5	6
	» Is the content put together in such a way that people understand it?	0	1	2	3	4	5	6
PRESENTATION								
STRUCTURE	» Is an effective attention-getting device used? Is the main idea clear from the beginning? Is the speech logical in its organization, naturally flowing from one major idea to another? Does it come to an effective close?	0	1	2	3	4	5	6
ELABORATION AND SUPPORT	» Does all information relate to the main idea? Are ideas fully explained and supported? Is there a balance of general ideas with specific details? If quotations or other references are used, are they used carefully and appropriately?	0	1	2	3	4	5	6
DELIVERY	» Is eye contact made? Are appropriate facial expressions and gestures incorporated? Is the speaker's voice clear? Is the speaker poised and comfortable? Are notes used so that they do not distract the audience?	0	1	2	3	4	5	6
STYLE	» Is the speech developed for the expected audience and purpose? Are appropriate words used? Are the sentences varied in structure? Is a suitable tone used? Is figurative language used in an effective way? Is the grammar appropriate?	0	1	2	3	4	5	6
CREATIVITY								
	» Is the content seen in a new way?	0	1	2	3	4	5	6
	» Is the presentation done in a new way?	0	1	2	3	4	5	6
REFLECTION								
CONTENT	» What connections can you make between what you have learned by completing this project and previous learning?	0	1	2	3	4	5	6
PRODUCT	» In what ways could you improve your product when completing this product with a different assignment?	0	1	2	3	4	5	6
LEARNING	» How did the amount of effort affect your learning about the content and creating the product?	0	1	2	3	4	5	6

Comments:

____

____

____

Meaning of Performance Scale:
6—PROFESSIONAL LEVEL: level expected from a professional in the content area
5—ADVANCED LEVEL: level exceeds expectations of the standard
4—PROFICIENT LEVEL: level expected for meeting the standard
3—PROGRESSING LEVEL: level demonstrates movement toward the standard
2—NOVICE LEVEL: level demonstrates initial awareness and knowledge of standard
1—NONPERFORMING LEVEL: level indicates no effort made to meet standard
0—NONPARTICIPATING LEVEL: level indicates nothing turned in

SPEECH (ORAL) TIER 2—DAP TOOL

CONTENT								
	» Content is accurate and complete.	0	1	2	3	4	5	6
	» Content has depth and complexity of thought.	0	1	2	3	4	5	6
	» Content is organized.	0	1	2	3	4	5	6
PRESENTATION								
STRUCTURE	» The attention-getting device clearly gains audience interest. The main idea is clear and well developed. Smooth transitions between main points link to the purpose and any narrative threads. The speech is very logical in its organization. The conclusion, pulling together all aspects, comes to a strong closure.	0	1	2	3	4	5	6
ELABORATION AND SUPPORT	» Each idea is fully developed and relates to the purpose. A strong balance of general ideas and specific details creates a fluid discussion. Quotations or other references, if used, elaborate on or support the main points and are smoothly incorporated.	0	1	2	3	4	5	6
DELIVERY	» Eye contact, facial expressions, and other forms of nonverbal communication aid in audience understanding and further the purpose. Speaker's voice is strong and clear with appropriate intonations. Speaker exhibits calm yet stirs interest in the audience. Notes are used minimally if at all.	0	1	2	3	4	5	6
STYLE	» The purposeful use of varied syntax and precise diction aids in the audience understanding. Tone is consistent with purpose. Voice clearly stems from diction, syntax, and figurative language. Ethos is strongly realized in the audience. Grammar and usage are appropriate.	0	1	2	3	4	5	6
CREATIVITY								
	» Originality is expressed in relation to the content.	0	1	2	3	4	5	6
	» Originality is expressed in relation to the presentation.	0	1	2	3	4	5	6
REFLECTION								
CONTENT	» Reflections include connections to previous learning and questions raised for future learning.	0	1	2	3	4	5	6
PRODUCT	» Reflections include improvements made over other times the product was created as well as suggestions for improvements when creating the same product in a future learning experience.	0	1	2	3	4	5	6
LEARNING	» Reflections include analysis of self as a learner, including effort, work habits, and thought processes.	0	1	2	3	4	5	6

Comments:

Meaning of Performance Scale:
6—PROFESSIONAL LEVEL: level expected from a professional in the content area
5—ADVANCED LEVEL: level exceeds expectations of the standard
4—PROFICIENT LEVEL: level expected for meeting the standard
3—PROGRESSING LEVEL: level demonstrates movement toward the standard
2—NOVICE LEVEL: level demonstrates initial awareness and knowledge of standard
1—NONPERFORMING LEVEL: level indicates no effort made to meet standard
0—NONPARTICIPATING LEVEL: level indicates nothing turned in

SPEECH (ORAL) TIER 3—DAP TOOL

CONTENT								
	» Content is accurate and thorough in detail.	0	1	2	3	4	5	6
	» Product shows complex understanding and manipulation of content.	0	1	2	3	4	5	6
	» Product shows deep probing of content.	0	1	2	3	4	5	6
	» Organization is best suited to the product.	0	1	2	3	4	5	6
PRESENTATION								
STRUCTURE	» The attention-getting device cleverly and uniquely gains audience interest and provides a thoughtful transition to the thesis. The original and creative thesis guides the entire speech with a coherent narrative thread. Sophisticated transitions subtly link all aspects. Secondary arguments fully develop key concepts or ideas critical to the purpose. The speech is ideally organized. Conclusion emphasizes pertinent information. The significance of the conclusion is clear.	0	1	2	3	4	5	6
ELABORATION AND SUPPORT	» Each idea is thoroughly substantiated through pertinent detail or analyzed support from a variety of sources. Pertinent quotations and other references fully elaborate on or support the idea; their inclusion is seamless. The speech anticipates audience's possible misunderstandings and handles complex ideas clearly.	0	1	2	3	4	5	6
DELIVERY	» Purposeful eye contact, facial expressions, and other forms of nonverbal communication enhance audience understanding and emphasize the purpose. Speaker's voice is strong, clear, and effective. Speaker exudes passion for the topic while being in total control of the presentation and audience. No notes are used. Ideal usage and grammar are used.	0	1	2	3	4	5	6
STYLE	» The purposeful use of varied syntax and diction enhances audience's understanding. Tone clearly stems from diction, syntax, and figurative language. Effective rhetorical devices emphasize thesis.	0	1	2	3	4	5	6
CREATIVITY								
	» Innovation is evident in relation to the content.	0	1	2	3	4	5	6
	» Innovation is evident in relation to the presentation.	0	1	2	3	4	5	6
REFLECTION								
CONTENT	» Reflections analyze and evaluate connections to previous learning and project insightful future connections.	0	1	2	3	4	5	6
PRODUCT	» Reflections analyze and evaluate the product components in light of past and future creations of the same product.	0	1	2	3	4	5	6
LEARNING	» Reflections include analysis of self as a learner and project how changes to the process would increase capacity as a learner.	0	1	2	3	4	5	6

Comments:

____

____

____

Meaning of Performance Scale:
6—PROFESSIONAL LEVEL: level expected from a professional in the content area
5—ADVANCED LEVEL: level exceeds expectations of the standard
4—PROFICIENT LEVEL: level expected for meeting the standard
3—PROGRESSING LEVEL: level demonstrates movement toward the standard
2—NOVICE LEVEL: level demonstrates initial awareness and knowledge of standard
1—NONPERFORMING LEVEL: level indicates no effort made to meet standard
0—NONPARTICIPATING LEVEL: level indicates nothing turned in

TECHNICAL REPORT TIER 1—DAP TOOL

CONTENT								
	» Is the content correct?	0	1	2	3	4	5	6
	» Has the content been thought about in a way that goes beyond a surface understanding?	0	1	2	3	4	5	6
	» Is the content put together in such a way that people understand it?	0	1	2	3	4	5	6
PRESENTATION								
FORM	» Does the title describe the main idea? Is the topic clearly stated early in the paper? Do strong transitions lead from one section to another? Does each section have one main idea? Does it come to a close and link back to the topic?	0	1	2	3	4	5	6
DETAIL	» Is there enough detail to support the points? Does all information relate to the main idea? Are the ideas explained and supported? Are all figures and graphs explained?	0	1	2	3	4	5	6
STYLE	» Is it written for the expected audience? Are the words clear and concise? Has slang been avoided and all jargon been explained? Are the sentences straightforward and clear? Is it written in active voice and third person? Are tables, charts, and graphs used to organize data when appropriate?	0	1	2	3	4	5	6
LAYOUT	» Do headings help the audience understand the upcoming sections? Are important diagrams, charts, illustrations, or tables included and explained? Are units included with all data? Is the layout consistent as to font, bullets, underlining, and so forth?	0	1	2	3	4	5	6
CORRECTNESS	» Is the technical report mostly free from usage, punctuation, capitalization, and spelling errors? If sources are used, are they cited correctly?	0	1	2	3	4	5	6
CREATIVITY								
	» Is the content seen in a new way?	0	1	2	3	4	5	6
	» Is the presentation done in a new way?	0	1	2	3	4	5	6
REFLECTION								
CONTENT	» What connections can you make between what you have learned by completing this project and previous learning?	0	1	2	3	4	5	6
PRODUCT	» In what ways could you improve your product when completing this product with a different assignment?	0	1	2	3	4	5	6
LEARNING	» How did the amount of effort affect your learning about the content and creating the product?	0	1	2	3	4	5	6

Comments:

Meaning of Performance Scale:
6—PROFESSIONAL LEVEL: level expected from a professional in the content area
5—ADVANCED LEVEL: level exceeds expectations of the standard
4—PROFICIENT LEVEL: level expected for meeting the standard
3—PROGRESSING LEVEL: level demonstrates movement toward the standard
2—NOVICE LEVEL: level demonstrates initial awareness and knowledge of standard
1—NONPERFORMING LEVEL: level indicates no effort made to meet standard
0—NONPARTICIPATING LEVEL: level indicates nothing turned in

TECHNICAL REPORT TIER 2—DAP TOOL

CONTENT								
	» Content is accurate and complete.	0	1	2	3	4	5	6
	» Content has depth and complexity of thought.	0	1	2	3	4	5	6
	» Content is organized.	0	1	2	3	4	5	6
PRESENTATION								
FORM	» Title enhances the writing. The thesis of the writing is clear and immediate. Transitions between sections link to the purpose. Each section develops an idea critical to the purpose. The conclusion pulls together all aspects of the writing and clearly links to the thesis.	0	1	2	3	4	5	6
DETAIL	» Each idea is fully developed and relates back to the purpose of the writing. Possible reader questions are addressed. The writing clearly relates to the figures, graphs, and/or illustrations presented. Graphs are used to illustrate trends in data.	0	1	2	3	4	5	6
STYLE	» The straightforward, clear syntax aids in audience understanding. Precise and economical word choice appeals to audience and supports purpose. Ambiguity is avoided. Tone is consistent to purpose. Abstract ideas are carefully explained. Active voice and third person are used.	0	1	2	3	4	5	6
LAYOUT	» The layout clarifies the meaning through appropriate headings and labeling that specifically prepare the reader for the upcoming content. Illustrations, diagrams, charts, graphs, and/or tables simplify the explanation of complex ideas and are well placed. The layout is consistent as to font, bullets, underlining, and so forth, so that the document presents a unified, coherent impression to the reader.	0	1	2	3	4	5	6
CORRECTNESS	» The technical report is free from usage, punctuation, capitalization, and spelling errors. Sources, when used, are thoroughly cited.	0	1	2	3	4	5	6
CREATIVITY								
	» Originality is expressed in relation to the content.	0	1	2	3	4	5	6
	» Originality is expressed in relation to the presentation.	0	1	2	3	4	5	6
REFLECTION								
CONTENT	» Reflections include connections to previous learning and questions raised for future learning.	0	1	2	3	4	5	6
PRODUCT	» Reflections include improvements made over other times the product was created as well as suggestions for improvements when creating the same product in a future learning experience.	0	1	2	3	4	5	6
LEARNING	» Reflections include analysis of self as a learner, including effort, work habits, and thought processes.	0	1	2	3	4	5	6

Comments:

____

____

____

Meaning of Performance Scale:
6—PROFESSIONAL LEVEL: level expected from a professional in the content area
5—ADVANCED LEVEL: level exceeds expectations of the standard
4—PROFICIENT LEVEL: level expected for meeting the standard
3—PROGRESSING LEVEL: level demonstrates movement toward the standard
2—NOVICE LEVEL: level demonstrates initial awareness and knowledge of standard
1—NONPERFORMING LEVEL: level indicates no effort made to meet standard
0—NONPARTICIPATING LEVEL: level indicates nothing turned in

TECHNICAL REPORT TIER 3—DAP TOOL

CONTENT								
	» Content is accurate and thorough in detail.	0	1	2	3	4	5	6
	» Product shows complex understanding and manipulation of content.	0	1	2	3	4	5	6
	» Product shows deep probing of content.	0	1	2	3	4	5	6
	» Organization is best suited to the product.	0	1	2	3	4	5	6
PRESENTATION								
FORM	» Title reflects purpose. The thesis is immediately clear, and the writing is focused. Transitions subtly link all aspects together. Sections fully develop key concepts or ideas critical to the purpose. Conclusion refers back to the purpose of the document and summarizes pertinent information. The significance of the conclusion is explained.	0	1	2	3	4	5	6
DETAIL	» Each idea is thoroughly substantiated through pertinent detail and/or analyzed support. Writing anticipates readers' possible misunderstandings and handles complex ideas clearly. Strong, elaborate support substantiates points. Only pertinent information is included. The reader is clearly directed to figures and graphs for validation of ideas within the text. Explanations specify how variables were handled.	0	1	2	3	4	5	6
STYLE	» The straightforward syntax clearly enhances purpose. Diction is precise and economical to avoid ambiguity. Tone consistently maintains audience attention. Concrete images clarify abstract ideas. Active voice and third person are used skillfully.	0	1	2	3	4	5	6
LAYOUT	» Purposeful manipulation of layout enhances understanding through carefully selected headings. The format is highly consistent as to font, bullets, underlining, and so forth, so that a professional, unified impression is presented to the reader. Illustrations, diagrams, charts, graphs and/or tables develop and/or explain complex ideas fully. Placement enhances understanding.	0	1	2	3	4	5	6
CORRECTNESS	» The technical report is error free, with correct usage, punctuation, capitalization, and spelling used. All sources are cited correctly with the citation placed appropriately.	0	1	2	3	4	5	6
CREATIVITY								
	» Innovation is evident in relation to the content.	0	1	2	3	4	5	6
	» Innovation is evident in relation to the presentation.	0	1	2	3	4	5	6
REFLECTION								
CONTENT	» Reflections analyze and evaluate connections to previous learning and project insightful future connections.	0	1	2	3	4	5	6
PRODUCT	» Reflections analyze and evaluate the product components in light of past and future creations of the same product.	0	1	2	3	4	5	6
LEARNING	» Reflections include analysis of self as a learner and project how changes to the process would increase capacity as a learner.	0	1	2	3	4	5	6

Comments:

Meaning of Performance Scale:
6—PROFESSIONAL LEVEL: level expected from a professional in the content area
5—ADVANCED LEVEL: level exceeds expectations of the standard
4—PROFICIENT LEVEL: level expected for meeting the standard
3—PROGRESSING LEVEL: level demonstrates movement toward the standard
2—NOVICE LEVEL: level demonstrates initial awareness and knowledge of standard
1—NONPERFORMING LEVEL: level indicates no effort made to meet standard
0—NONPARTICIPATING LEVEL: level indicates nothing turned in

STUDENT REFLECTION: TIER 1

Directions: Please answer the following questions fully.

***Content:* What connections can you make between what you have learned by completing this project and previous learning?**

____
____
____
____
____
____
____

***Product:* In what ways could you improve your product when completing this product with a different assignment?**

____
____
____
____
____
____
____

***Learning:* How did the amount of effort affect your learning about the content and creating the product?**

____
____
____
____
____
____
____

STUDENT REFLECTION: TIER 2

Directions: Please reflect on the content, product itself, and yourself as a learner.

***Content:* Reflections include connections to previous learning and questions raised for future learning.**
How do the concepts and content relate to previous things you have studied? What connections can you make to other content areas or issues in the real world? What questions has this content raised for you? What aspect of the content do you want to learn more about?

____

____

____

____

____

***Product:* Reflections include improvements made over other times the product was created as well as suggestions for improvements when creating the same product in a future learning experience.**
If you have ever created this product before, how does this one compare? How is it better? How is it worse? What improvements could you make next time to have an even better product? Why is that important?

____

____

____

____

____

***Learning:* Reflection includes analysis of self as a learner, including effort, work habits, and thought processes.**
What have you realized about yourself as a learner? How much effort did you put into learning the content and developing the product? How could that be improved? Describe your work habits that were successful and those that were not. Describe your thought processes as you learned the content and created the product.

____

____

____

____

____

STUDENT REFLECTION: TIER 3

Directions: Please reflect on the content, the product itself, and yourself as a learner.

***Content:* Reflections analyze and evaluate connections to previous learning and project insightful future connections.**
How do the concepts and content relate to previous things you have studied? What connections can you make to other content areas or issues in the real world? What questions has this content raised for you? Is there some aspect of the content you want to learn more about?

____

____

____

____

____

***Product:* Reflections analyze and evaluate the product components in light of past and future creations of the same product.**
If you have ever created this product before, how does this one compare? How is it better? How is it worse? What improvements could you make next time to have an even better product? Why is that important?

____

____

____

____

____

***Learning:* Reflections include analysis of self as a learner and project how changes to the process would increase capacity as a learner.**
What have you realized about yourself as a learner? How much effort did you put into learning the content and developing the product? How could that be improved? Describe your work habits that were successful and those that were not. Describe your thought processes as you learned the content and created the product.

____

____

____

____

____

APPENDIX I

Study Guide

CH. 1–3

- The heading of Chapter 1 is "One-Size-Fits-All? You've Got to be Kidding!" What made an impact on you in Chapter 1? Do you remember teachers differentiating for your learning needs in school? (Be sure to reference page numbers.)
- The heading of Chapter 2 is "Multiple Ways to Define Academic Success: What Resonates with You?" What is your answer to this question? Cite examples from the book as well as any personal insights from your experience. (Remember to provide page numbers.)
- What steps do you need to take to create a classroom culture where students are comfortable with challenge and learning? One where different students are doing different things?
- What questions do you have over Chapters 1–3?

CH. 4–5

- The topic of Chapter 4 is preassessment. Which strategy have you not used? How and when will you implement that strategy in your classroom? What other preassessment strategies have you used?
- The authors repeatedly refer to "continuous progress," "intentional" decisions, and "extend their learning." In your opinion, why are the authors emphasizing these terms? (Don't forget to support your answer with page references.)
- What constitutes a tiered assignment? How have you implemented tiered assignments in your classroom? What issues and successes have you had?
- What questions do you have over Chapters 4–5?

CH. 6–8

- Chapter 6 explores tiering with Bloom's taxonomy. How have you used Bloom's to differentiate in your classroom? After reading the chapter, what might you do differently?

- Chapter 7 describes numerous ways to differentiate using Venn diagrams. Select a way to use a Venn diagram that you have not used but are willing to try. Describe how you will implement it into a future lesson or training.
- Think of several ways in which you might apply the Think-Tac-Toe strategy. Describe how you will apply this strategy in your classroom.
- What was an "A-Ha" moment or a reinforcement of your teaching style while reading this section? (Don't forget to give us the page number to reference.)
- What questions do you have over Chapters 6–8?

CH. 9–11

- What are key components in managing a differentiated classroom? How does or will this apply to your classroom setting? (Give reasons and page numbers.)
- Assessment is discussed throughout this book, including Chapter 10, "Taming the Assessment Beast." How will you alter assessment in your classroom based on your reading?
- What questions do you have over Chapters 9–11?

Note. Adapted from the book study guide created by Spring Branch ISD of the Houston Area Cooperative on the Gifted and Talented, 2011.

About the Authors

Julia Link Roberts, Mahurin Professor of Gifted Studies at Western Kentucky University (WKU), is Executive Director of the Carol Martin Gatton Academy of Mathematics and Science in Kentucky and The Center for Gifted Studies at WKU. Dr. Roberts is a member of the Executive Committee of the World Council for Gifted and Talented Children, president of The Association for the Gifted, Co-Chair of Advocacy and Legislation for the National Association for Gifted Children, and Legislative Chair of the Kentucky Association for Gifted Education. She has focused her writing on differentiation, gifted education, advocacy, and STEM schools; and is coauthor of seven books, several chapters, and numerous articles and columns. She received the 2011 Acorn Award as the outstanding professor at a Kentucky 4-year university, the first NAGC David Belin Advocacy Award, the 2012 NAGC Distinguished Service Award, and the 2011 William T. Nallia Award for innovative leadership from the Kentucky Association for School Administrators. Dr. Roberts enjoys working with children and young people, directing Saturday and summer programming, and traveling abroad with high school students.

Tracy Ford Inman has devoted her career to meeting the needs of young people, especially those who are gifted and talented. She has taught on both the high school and collegiate levels, as well as in summer programs for gifted and talented youth. This Who's Who Among American Educators teacher was a Kentucky Teacher of the Year semifinalist in 1992. Dr. Inman now serves as associate director of The Center for Gifted Studies at Western Kentucky University in Bowling Green, KY. She has presented on the state, national, and international levels; trained thousands of teachers in differentiation; published multiple articles, chapters, and books; and served as a writer and editor for the award-winning newsmagazine for The Center for Gifted Studies, *The Challenge*. She is currently president of the Kentucky Association for Gifted Education and serves as webmaster for The Association for Gifted, a division of the Council for Exceptional Children. At Western Kentucky University, she earned a bachelor's degree in English and graduated summa cum laude in 1986 as both an Ogden Scholar and a Scholar of Potter College. Her studies continued at Western with a certification in secondary education in 1988, a master's degree in education in 1992, an endorsement in gifted education in 2001, and an Ed.D. in 2011.